Click Start 6

Computer Science for Schools

2nd Edition

Anjna Virmani · Shalini Harisukh

CAMBRIDGE
UNIVERSITY PRESS

4843/24, 2nd Floor, Ansari Road, Daryaganj, Delhi - 110002

Cambridge University Press is part of the University of Cambridge.

It furthers the University's mission by disseminating knowledge in the pursuit of education, learning and research at the highest international levels of excellence.

www.cambridge.org
Information on this title: www.cambridge.org/9781107691780 Paperback
www.cambridge.org/9781107672079 Paperback with CD-ROM

© Cambridge University Press 2014

This publication is in copyright. Subject to statutory exception and to the provisions of relevant collective licensing agreements, no reproduction of any part may take place without the written permission of Cambridge University Press.

First published 2011
Second edition 2014
Reprinted 2014 (twice), 2016

Printed in India by Thomson Press India Ltd., New Delhi 110001

A catalogue record for this publication is available from the British Library

ISBN 978-1-107-69178-0 Paperback
ISBN 978-1-107-67207-9 Paperback with CD-ROM

Cambridge University Press has no responsibility for the persistence or accuracy of URLs for external or third-party internet websites referred to in this publication, and does not guarantee that any content on such websites is, or will remain, accurate or appropriate. Information regarding prices, travel timetables, and other factual information given in this work is correct at the time of first printing but Cambridge University Press does not guarantee the accuracy of such information thereafter.

NOTICE TO TEACHERS IN THE UK

It is illegal to reproduce any part of this work in material form (including photocopying and electronic storage) except under the following circumstances:
(i) where you are abiding by a licence granted to your school or institution by the Copyright Licensing Agency;
(ii) where no such licence exists, or where you wish to exceed the terms of a licence, and you have gained the written permission of Cambridge University Press;
(iii) where you are allowed to reproduce without permission under the provisions of Chapter 3 of the Copyright, Designs and Patents Act 1988, which covers, for example, the reproduction of short passages within certain types of educational anthology and reproduction for the purposes of setting examination questions.

NOTICE TO TEACHERS

The photocopy masters in this publication may be photocopied or distributed [electronically] free of charge for classroom use within the school or institution that purchased the publication. Worksheets and copies of them remain in the copyright of Cambridge University Press, and such copies may not be distributed or used in any way outside the purchasing institution.

Every effort has been made to trace the owners of copyright material included in this book. The publishers would be grateful for any omissions brought to their notice for acknowledgement in future editions of the book.

CONTENTS

	Overview	iv
	Preface	vi
1.	Know Your Computer	1
2.	Operating System	16
3.	Using Windows	27
4.	MS Word 2007 – Advanced Features	41
5.	MS Word 2007 – Using Mail Merge Features	59
6.	Advanced PowerPoint 2007	68
7.	More about MS Excel 2007	85
8.	Introduction to QBASIC	102
9.	QBASIC Statements	112
10.	QBASIC – Programming Statements I	122
11.	Introduction to Macromedia Flash	132
12.	Introduction to Email	147

Lesson Name	Contents	Objectives	Activities
1. Know Your Computer	• Early calculating devices • Evolution of computers • Classification of computers • Functional components of a computer • Categorisation of software	To familiarise students about the various generations of computers and to help them know about the computer memory	• To explore places where supercomputers and mainframes are used • To explore and to collect information about microprocessors • To make a list of the latest input and output devices available these days • To find out about various storage devices available in the market • To classify anti-virus software • To find out the software available in Open Office • To find out the characteristics of BASIC • Lab Work – Additional activities
2. Operating System	• Operating System • Booting • Functions of an Operating System • Types of Operating System • Operating System Interface • Importance of 'Shut Down'	To teach Operating System and booting a system	• To number the steps involved in booting a system in a sequence • To rewrite the jumbled words • Lab Work – Additional activities
3. Using Windows	• Advantages of Windows Operating System • Search option • Run option • On-Screen Keyboard • Control Panel	Learning about MS Windows as an Operating System	• To practise multitasking and use Search option • To open Paint using Run option • To create a pattern for the desktop background • To create a folder following specific instructions • Lab Work – Additional activities
4. MS Word 2007 – Advanced Features	• Headers and Footers • Footnotes and Endnotes • Drop Cap • Tab Stop • Using Show/Hide tool • Format Painter • Columns • Increase or decrease indentation • Thesaurus • Borders and Shading • Page Setup and Margins • Applying built-in styles	To make students learn about various advanced features of MS Word 2007	• To practise indentations in MS Word 2007 • To design a cover for the school magazine using the features of MS Word 2007 learnt in the chapter • Lab Work – Additional activities
5. MS Word 2007 – Using Mail Merge Features	• Mail Merge • Uses of Mail Merge • Creating the Main document • Creating a merged document	To enhance the knowledge of MS Word 2007 using Mail Merge	• To arrange the steps involved in using Mail Merge application in the correct sequence • Lab Work – Additional activities
6. Advanced PowerPoint 2007	• Creating a presentation using a template • Creating a presentation using themes • Photo Album • Slide Master • Custom Animation • Inserting charts and tables • Creating hyperlinks • Reusing slides	To learn the advanced features of MS PowerPoint 2007	• To create a presentation on the suggested concept based on the instructions given • To create a presentation with specific instructions • To import slides in the presentation prepared in an earlier activity. • Lab Work – Additional activities

Lesson Name	Contents	Objectives	Activities
7. More about MS Excel 2007	• Formatting numbers • Modifying data • Formatting data • Creating custom lists • Formulas and functions	To learn how to format data and to work with functions and formulae in MS Excel 2007	• To create MS Excel 2007 file, modify the data and use functions as per the instructions given. • Lab Work – Additional activities
8. Introduction to QBASIC	• QBASIC • Components of a QBASIC window • Writing and executing a program • How to open a program • How to save a program • How to exit QBASIC	To introduce students to the concept of QBASIC programming language	• To detect errors in the programs given • Lab Work – Additional activities
9. QBASIC Statements	• Character Set • Constants • Variables • PRINT statement • LET statement • INPUT statement • REM statement	To learn about various terms and basic statements used in QBASIC	• To find out whether string variables are valid or invalid • Lab Work – Additional activities
10. QBASIC – Programming Statements I	• IF… THEN • IF… THEN…ELSE • Using ELSEIF with IF…THEN statement	To learn about various looping statements in QBASIC	• To find the output of given statements and code • To write a program to find out whether the given input is accepted or rejected • Lab Work – Additional activities
11. Introduction to Macromedia Flash	• Starting Flash • Flash tools panel • Gradient effects • Important terms • Animation in Flash • Creating an animation • Symbols	Introducing students to the concept of Macromedia Flash	• To draw and color using tools in Macromedia Flash • To create an animation of a falling object • To create a logo in Flash and to add a symbol • To add more details to the animation of the falling object • Lab Work – Additional activities
12. Introduction to Email	• Uniform Resource Locator • Email • Advantages of email • Limitations of email • Creating and opening an email account • Composing an email • Signing out from an email account	To find out how emails work	• To create an email account and exchange mails • Lab Work – Additional activities

Click Start: Computer Science for Schools, Second Edition is the comprehensively updated version of the previous edition. The revised edition is primarily based on Windows 7 and Microsoft Office 2007 with updates from Windows 8 and Microsoft Office 2010.

Each level of the series has been designed keeping in mind the mental aptitude and learning ability of the learners as well as their interests. Efforts have been made to use examples from day-to-day life, which help the learners bridge the gap between the knowledge of the subject and the real world. The books are designed to offer a holistic approach and help in the overall development of the learners.

The special features of the book are:

- **Snap Recap** to recapitulate the concepts learnt earlier
- **Learning Objectives** to clearly define the aims and objectives of the chapter
- **Fact File** to enhance the knowledge of the students
- **Quick Key** and **Try This** to introduce shortcuts and alternative methodologies
- **Activities** interspersed within each chapter to promote application based learning
- **Exercises** to make tasks interactive and promote guided discussions
- **Glossary** and **Now You Know** to aid quick revision of the concepts learnt
- **Lab Work** to encourage learning by doing
- **Biographies** to inspire young learners
- **Teacher's Notes** provide creative suggestions to further strengthen learning
- **Teacher's Manual** to facilitate teaching

In addition to this, special icons, notes, shortcuts, troubleshooting tips, text related screen shots and illustrations have been used to support and strengthen the process of learning.

The Students' Books are available both with and without the CD-ROM.

The books, thus, will not only make learning fun but also help the learners achieve a certain level of expertise in this fast changing world of Computer Science.

Anjna Virmani

Shalini Harisukh

Know Your Computer

SNAP RECAP

1. Any raw data given to the computer using an input device is called input.
2. The raw data is manipulated by performing certain operations using the computer's processing device. This is called processing.
3. Output is the processed data given to the outside world using an output device.
4. Primary memory is also called internal memory. It is of two types: RAM and ROM.
5. Computer language is a set of commands or instructions that a computer understands.

LEARNING OBJECTIVES

You will learn about:
1. early calculating devices
2. evolution of computers
3. classification of computers
4. functional components of a computer
5. categorisation of software

Introduction

A computer is an electronic device which accepts data from the user, processes it and gives the desired output. It is a machine capable of performing calculations with the help of mechanical computing device. The evolution of computers started way back in the late 1930s. Computers at that time used binary language for its operations.

Early Calculating Devices

A few calculating devices used prior to the development of computers are discussed here.

Abacus

Abacus, the first calculating machine, was developed in China. It is used to count numbers and perform simple calculations such as addition and subtraction.

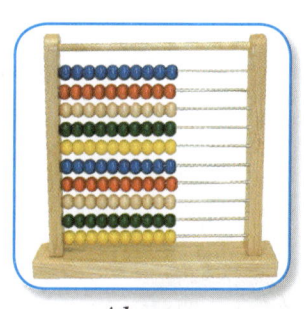

Abacus

Napier's Bones

Napier's Bones was developed by Sir John Napier in 1616. The device was used to perform calculations involving addition, subtraction, multiplication and division. It was named so as the numbers were carved on bones or strips of wood.

Napier's Bones

Pascaline

Pascaline, one of the first mechanical calculators, was invented by Blaise Pascal in 1641. Though it could perform only subtraction and addition, yet it became very popular.

Pascaline

Evolution of Computers

From everyday task to moving satellites in space, computers have revolutionised almost everything in our society. The development of computers has been classified into generations. Let us learn about them now.

First generation computers – Vacuum tube based computers

First generation computers

In the evolution of computers, the first generation was characterised by the use of vacuum tubes. The first generation computers were built to solve physics equations using electronic vacuum tubes as the switching components. These used **machine language**. *A machine language is a low-level programming language and is written using long strings of 0s and 1s for computing.* Machine language varies with the computer used.

The first generation computers were expensive and bulky. The vacuum tubes did not support multitasking. Programs written in machine language were cumbersome and difficult to remember.

FACT FILE

The UNIVAC and ENIAC computers are examples of first generation computing devices. The UNIVAC was the first commercial computer.

Second generation computers – Transistor based computers

In the 1960s, transistor based computers replaced vacuum tubes which marked the second generation of computers. Transistors made computers smaller and cheaper. They also made computers energy efficient, but the transistors were subjected to damage because of the emission of large amount of heat from the computer.

Second generation computers

Computers belonging to this generation used punched cards for input. They used **assembly language** *which is a low-level programming language. An assembly language is based on the english alphabet.* The instructions are written in the form of codes. Assembly language is machine dependent, and has to be written based on the configurations of the computer.

Third generation computers – Integrated Circuit based computers

The integrated circuit based computers marked the third generation of computers. Small transistors were placed on silicon chips, called semiconductors, which increased the speed and efficiency of computers.

Third generation computers

The third generation computers were based on **high-level languages**. *A high-level language uses the english alphabet and mathematical symbols.* It is easy to use and understand. It is not machine dependent. The programs written in high-level language are called **source programs**. For example, Fortran, COBOL, BASIC, C, C++, Java are a few examples of high-level languages.

Fourth generation computers – Microprocessor

Introduction of microprocessors was the hallmark of fourth generation computers. They facilitated automation of industrial process and office. Around 1970, this technology of placing thousands of integrated circuits onto a single silicon chip, that made up a microprocessor, was made available.

Microprocessor is compact and easy to maintain. It has a high processing speed. However, it has limitations on the size of data.

Microprocessor

Fifth generation computers – Artificial Intelligence

The development of fifth generation computers is underway. They are going to be based on the principles of artificial intelligence and natural language recognition. This technique will be used to design robots.

Developers are aiming at developing computers capable of organising themselves. So, the evolution of computers still continues.

Classification of Computers

On the basis of their size and speed, computers are generally classified as follows:

1. Microcomputer
2. Minicomputer
3. Mainframe computer
4. Supercomputer

Fifth generation computers

Microcomputer

Microcomputer, was earlier, a commonly used term for personal computers. A personal computer assemblage consists of CPU, computer memory (primary and secondary) and various input and output devices. Only one person can use it at a time. It is slow and has relatively less storage capacity as compared to a minicomputer or a mainframe computer. It is commonly used in classrooms, homes, banks, universities, etc.

There are various kinds of microcomputers available nowadays. Let us study about them here.

Desktop: It is a microcomputer designed to fit comfortably on top of a desk, typically with the monitor in front and the system unit on the side.

Laptop: It is a portable microcomputer. You can keep it on your lap. Nowadays, laptop computers are more commonly called **notebook** computers.

Tablet: It is a mobile computer. It offers the users a touchscreen environment that may or may not be accompanied by a stylus (a pointing device). They are available in a variety of sizes and have a built-in/virtual keyboard.

Smartphone: It is a mobile phone built on a mobile OS. It has enhanced features as compared to an ordinary mobile phone like compact digital cameras, GPS, web-browsers, Wi-Fi, broadband facility, etc.

Desktop

Laptop

Tablet

Smartphones

Minicomputer

A minicomputer is much larger than microcomputer and also much more expensive. It thus lies between microcomputers and mainframe computers and are often referred to as **midrange computers**. It possesses most of the features found on a mainframe computer, but on a limited scale. It can still have many terminals, but not as many as the mainframe. It can store a large amount of information, but again usually not as much as the mainframe. It uses an enhanced instruction set to facilitate scientific processing and commercial applications. Medium and small businesses and colleges typically use minicomputers.

Minicomputer

Mainframe computer

Mainframe computers are very large, often filling an entire room. They can store an enormous amount of information, and perform many tasks simultaneously. They can communicate with many users at the same time and are very expensive. Mainframe computers usually have several terminals connected to them. These terminals look like small computers but they are only devices that are used for sending and receiving information from the actual computer using wires. Terminals can be located either in the same room with the mainframe computer, or they can also be in different rooms, buildings, cities, etc. Large businesses, government agencies, banks and universities usually use mainframe computers. Big hospitals, airline reservation companies, and many other big companies prefer mainframe computers because of their capability of retrieving enormous data.

Mainframe computers

Supercomputer

Supercomputer is one of the many types of modern computing machines which are big, powerful and are capable of doing very speedy calculations. It is because of their high speed processing ability that supercomputer systems are used in animation graphics, weather forecasting, nuclear research work, petroleum research works, crypt analysis, molecular modelling and the likes.

The difference between the mainframes and supercomputers is that while mainframe machines are primarily used for a number of purposes, supercomputers are designed to serve a singular purpose.

Supercomputer

ACTIVITY

A. Find out the places where the supercomputers and the mainframe computers are used.

B. A microprocessor is a multipurpose, programmable device that takes input and provides output. Intel 4004 is the world's first commercially available microprocessor. It was the first complete CPU on one chip. Intel Corporation designed it.

Take the help of the Internet and find out more about microprocessors.

Functional Components of a Computer

The functional components of a computer are (Fig. 1.1):

1. Input devices
2. Central Processing Unit
3. Output devices

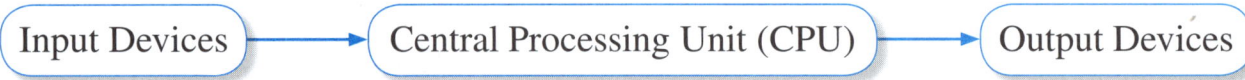

Fig. 1.1 *Functional components of a computer*

Note: The input and output devices attached to a computer are called computer peripherals.

Input devices

Data is accepted by a computer through the input devices attached to it. The standard input device is a keyboard. Examples of other input devices are Joystick, Mouse, Web camera, Magnetic Ink Character Recognition Reader, Optical Mark Recognition Reader, Optical Character Recognition, Light Pen, Touchscreen, Smart Card Reader, Digital Reader, etc.

You have already read about some of the commonly used input devices in earlier classes. You will learn about a few more here.

Bar code reader: It is used by a computer to scan and identify the product or item codes in the supermarkets, book stores, and many other places. The code for each item, be it the price code, item code, etc. is a unique combination of vertical bars and can be identified by a bar code reader.

Barcode

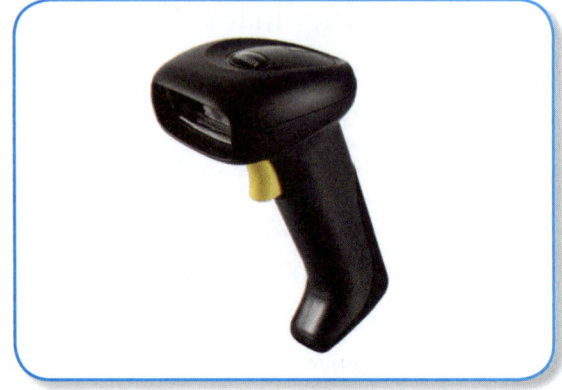

Bar code reader

FACT FILE

QR Codes (Quick Response Codes) are special barcodes that can be read using QR reading devices, mainly installed as an application on smartphones. These codes link the user directly to text, emails or websites.

Magnetic Ink Character Recognition (MICR) Reader: It reads the special characters printed using a special magnetic ink on cheques, etc. Cheque number, bank code and branch code are printed on cheques using magnetic ink, making them difficult to forge. The MICRs scan this information and are thus capable of sorting cheques.

Magnetic Ink Character Reader

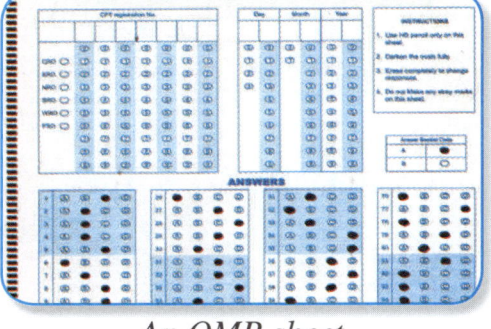
An OMR sheet

Optical Mark Recognition (OMR) Reader: It is used for recognising a pre-specified space on a paper that is marked by a pencil or pen. It is commonly used for marking the answers on examination sheets.

Central Processing Unit

The Central Processing Unit (CPU) is the control centre of a computer. It guides, directs and governs its performance. It is known as the brain of the computer. The CPU has three components which are responsible for different functions. These are discussed here.

Arithmetic Logic Unit (ALU): The ALU performs all the arithmetic and logical operations within a computer. This part provides the arithmetic and decision making capability to a computer.

FACT FILE

Every computer contains an internal clock that regulates the rate at which instructions are executed and synchronises all the different computer components. The CPU requires a fixed number of clock ticks (or clock cycles) to execute each instruction. The faster the clock ticks, the more instructions the CPU can execute per second. Clock speeds are expressed in megahertz (MHz) or gigahertz (GHz).

Control Unit (CU): The CU controls and guides the interpretation, flow and manipulation of all data and information. The CU sends control signals until the required operations are done properly by the ALU and memory.

Another important function of CU is program execution, that is, carrying out all the instructions stored in the program. The control unit even controls the flow of data from input devices to memory and from memory to output devices.

Memory Unit (MU): MU is that part of the computer where the data is stored and is accessible to CPU. The various measurement units of computer memory are given here.

1. *Bit:* A bit means a binary digit, that is, there are only two possibilities for each digit, either 0 or 1. A bit is an elementary unit of the memory.

   A number of bits together when combined in different ways are used for storing data in a computer.

2. *Byte:* A group of 8 bits is called a byte. One byte is the smallest unit which can represent a meaningful data item or a character in a computer. Memory is generally measured in terms of bytes.

3. *Nibble:* A group of 4 bits is called a nibble.

Note: The computer memory can also be expressed in other units and their interrelationship is given below:

1 byte	= 8 bits	1024 terabyte (TB)	= 1 petabyte (PB)
1024 bytes	= 1 kilobyte (KB)	1024 petabyte (PB)	= 1 exabyte (EB)
1024 kilobyte (KB)	= 1 megabyte (MB)	1024 exabyte (EB)	= 1 zettabyte (ZB)
1024 megabyte (MB)	= 1 gigabyte (GB)	1024 zettabyte (ZB)	= 1 yottabyte (YB)
1024 gigabyte (GB)	= 1 terabyte (TB)		

The computer memory is basically of two types: primary memory and secondary memory (Fig. 1.2).

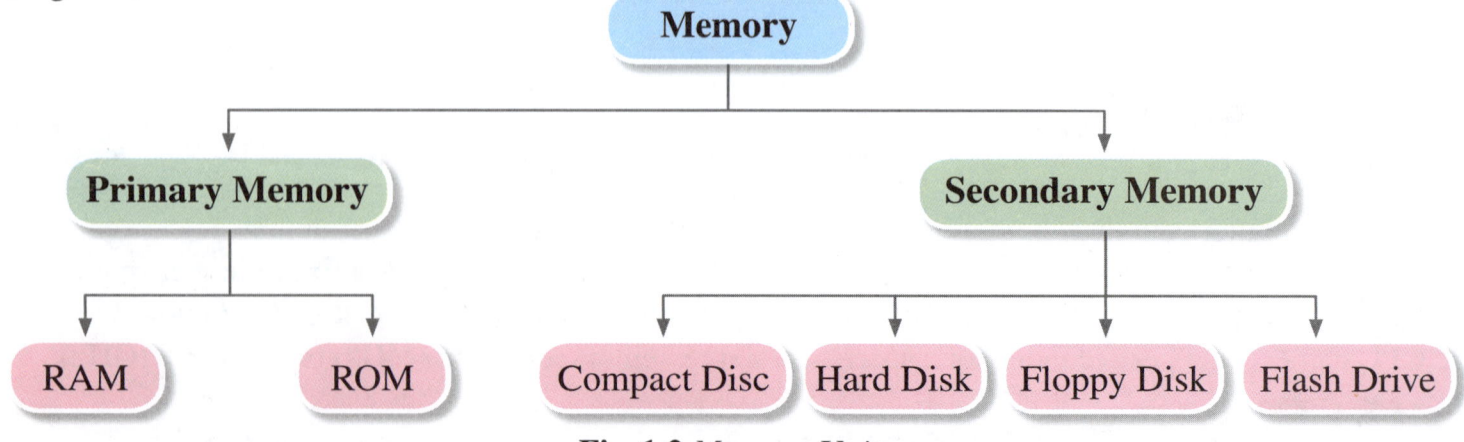

Fig. 1.2 *Memory Unit*

Primary memory

Primary memory is the basic requirement of a computer. It determines the size and number of software that a computer can store. Primary memory stores two types of programs: system software and application software. You will learn more about them later in this chapter.

Moreover, the primary memory limits the amount of data that a computer can process. CPU can use this memory directly while processing information. On the basis of volatility of storage of data, primary memory is classified into volatile (RAM) and non-volatile (ROM). See Table 1.1.

Table 1.1 *Difference between RAM and ROM*

RAM	ROM
1. RAM stands for Random Access Memory.	1. ROM stands for Read Only Memory.
2. It is a temporary memory.	2. It is a permanent memory.
3. It is volatile in nature, that is, the information stored in RAM is designed to clear when the computer is not on.	3. It is a non-volatile memory, that is, the information stored in ROM is not cleared when the computer is not on.
4. It is the main internal storage area that a computer uses to run programs and store data. It is also called read/write memory.	4. It is a built-in computer memory that can be read by a computer but cannot be modified. It is a memory unit that can only be read from.

Secondary memory

Secondary memory is also known as auxiliary memory. It is used for storing data or programs on a temporary or on a permanent basis. The secondary memory is available in the form of storage devices. For example, floppy disk, hard disk, compact disc, flash drive, etc.

The CPU cannot access secondary memory directly while processing information. The data is transferred to the primary memory when required. The computer uses its input and output devices to access data stored in the secondary memory.

Storage devices

FACT FILE

Cache memory can be used for increasing the capacity of the primary memory and to make the processing faster.

Output unit

Output devices are used for getting information from a computer. For example, Visual Display Unit (VDU) or monitor is an output device that displays the information on the screen. The information shown on a display device is called **soft copy**. You can also obtain information from a computer on a physical medium such as paper, transparency film, etc. with the help of a printer. Printed information is called **hard copy**.

Now, let us learn about a few more output devices.

Liquid Crystal Display (LCD) projector: Output from a computer can be also viewed on a large screen or flat surfaces other than the monitor using an LCD projector. It is used for showing PowerPoint presentations in many organisations.

Plotters: These are the output devices used for making high-quality graphics, charts, diagrams, maps, etc. Plotters use an ink jet or ink pens to create the desired output on paper.

LCD projector

There are different type of plotters available. The three basic types of plotters are discussed here.

1. *Inkjet plotter:* It sprays small droplets of ink onto a piece of paper thereby creating an image.
2. *Flatbed plotter:* The pen or the inkjet moves in horizontal and vertical directions over a fixed horizontal flat surface on which paper is mounted.
3. *Drum plotter:* It uses a drum revolver or roller to move the paper and the pen or the jets of the ink during the printing process. The paper is placed over the drum which is then rotated. The pen is moved along the horizontal or vertical direction to print the output.

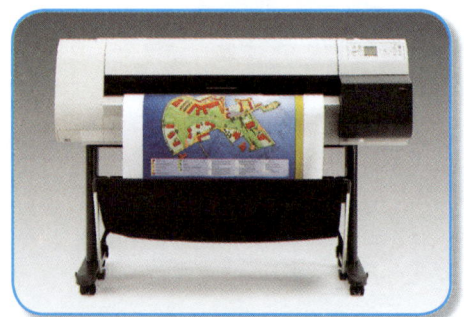

Inkjet plotter   *Flatbed plotter*   *Drum plotter*

ACTIVITY

A. Make a list of the latest input and output devices available in the market these days.
B. Have you heard about a flash drive? What is its use?
C. Make a list of storage devices available in the market.

FACT FILE

Computer works on the theory of GIGO (Garbage In Garbage Out). It means that wrong input will give wrong output.

Categorization of Software

Software is a set of programs that runs a computer system. Computer software is stored and executed with the help of computer hardware. Major categories of software that form part of a computer system are discussed here.

System software

System software is a program that manages and supports the computer resources and operations of a computer system while it executes various tasks such as processing of data and information, controlling the hardware components and allowing users to use the application software. In other words, system software is a bridge between computer system hardware and the application software. Operating System (OS) is an example of system software.

System software controls the internal computer operations. It can be further classified into four categories.

Operating System: An operating system is a software which acts as an interface between the user and the computer (that is, all computer resources). It is an important component that controls all other components of the computer system. Without an operating system, a computer is of no use. Some of the commonly used operating systems are Windows, DOS, UNIX, etc.

Compilers: It is a language translator that translates the high-level language program into machine language. It converts the entire program in one go and reports all the errors of the program along with their line numbers at the end. For example, C language has a compiler. The translated program is called the **object program** or **object code**.

Interpreter: This language processor converts high-level language program into machine language by converting and executing it line by line. If there is any error in any line, the interpreter reports it immediately and program execution cannot resume until it is rectified. However, it is a smaller program than a compiler. For example, BASIC has an interpreter as the translator.

Assembler: It is a language translator that converts a program written in assembly language into machine language.

Application software

Application software is a set of programs necessary to carry out operations for a specified application. These are the programs written by programmers to enable computers to perform a specific task. Various application software and their examples are given in Table 1.2.

Table 1.2 *Various Application Software and their examples*

Application Software	Example(s)
Word Processors	MS Word
Presentation tool	MS PowerPoint
Spreadsheet package	MS Excel, Lotus 123
Database Management System	MS Access, Sybase
Business software	Inventory Management, Payroll system, Financial Accounting, Hotel Management, etc.

Utility software

Utilities are those application programs that assist a computer by performing housekeeping functions like backing up disk or scanning/cleaning viruses or arranging information, etc. They ensure the smooth functioning of a computer.

Some important utilities are text editor used for creating and editing text files, backup utility that facilitates the backing-up of disks, compression utility that facilitates compression of files, disk defragmentation utility that attempts to minimise the fragmentation on the disk, and anti-virus software that ensures a virus-free environment.

FACT FILE

The open source application software provides the source code along with the .exe file so that users can do the changes in the code to suit their requirement. The substitute of MS Office is Open Office.

ACTIVITY

A. Under which category will you classify anti-virus software? Make a list of the commonly used anti-virus software.

B. Find out the different presentation, calculation and documentation software available in Open Office with the help of the Internet.

C. Find out whether BASIC language is a compiler or an interpreter. Give reason(s) for your answer.

GLOSSARY

Abacus: It is the first calculating machine that performed simple arithmetic calculations.

Application software: It is a set of programs necessary to carry out operations for a specified application.

Arithmetic Logic Unit (ALU): It performs all the arithmetic and logical operations within the computer.

Assembly language: It is a low-level programming language based on the english alphabet.

Assembler: It converts a program written in assembly language into machine language.

Bit: It means a binary digit.

Byte: It is a group of eight bits.

Compiler: It is a language translator that translates high-level language program into machine language.

Control Unit (CU): It controls and guides the interpretation, flow and manipulation of all data and information.

Desktop: It is a computer designed to fit comfortably on the top of a desk.

High-level language: It is a language that uses the english alphabet and mathematical symbol and on which the third generation of computers are based.

Interpreter: It is language processor which converts high-level language program into machine language by converting and executing it line by line.

Laptop: It is a portable computer that can be placed on your lap.

Machine language: It is a language written using long strings of 0s and 1s for computing.

Mainframe computer: It is a very large computer, often filling an entire room.

Memory Unit (MU): It is the part of a computer, accessible to CPU, where data is stored.

Microcomputer: It was a commonly used term for personal computers.

Minicomputer: It is much larger than a microcomputer, and is also much more expensive.

Napier's Bones: It was used for performing simple arithmetic calculations.

Nibble: It is a group of 4 bits.

Operating System: It is a software that acts as an interface between the user and the computer.

Pascaline: It was one of the first mechanical calculators to be developed.

Primary memory: It is the basic requirement of a computer.

Secondary memory: It is the memory used for storing data or programs on a temporary or on a permanent basis.

Smartphone: It is a mobile phone built on a mobile OS with enhanced features compared to an ordinary mobile phone.

Source program: It is a program written in a high-level language.

Supercomputer: It is a modern computing machine that is capable of giving very speedy calculations.

System software: It is the software that controls the internal computer operations.

Tablet: It is a mobile computer with a touchscreen and a built in virtual keyboard.

Utility software: It is a set of application programs that assist the computer by performing housekeeping functions.

NOW YOU KNOW

1. Some of the early calculating devices are Abacus, Napier's Bones and Pascaline.
2. First generation computers were characterised by the use of vacuum tubes. They used machine language.
3. Second generation computers were marked by the replacement of vacuum tubes with transistors. They used assembly language.
4. Third generation computers were marked by the use of integrated circuits. They were based on high-level languages.
5. Introduction of microprocessors was the hallmark of fourth generation computers.
6. The fifth generation computers are being developed. They are going to be based on the principles of artificial intelligence and natural language recognition.
7. Computers are commonly classified on the basis of their size and speed as microcomputer, minicomputer, mainframe computer and supercomputers.
8. Functional components of a computer are input devices, Central Processing Unit and output devices.
9. The CPU has three components which are responsible for different functions: ALU, CU and MU.

EXERCISE

A Fill in the blanks.

1. .... was used in the first generation of computers and was replaced by .... in the second generation.
2. Secondary memory is also known as ....
3. .... part of CPU is responsible for the calculation in computers.
4. .... and .... are the primary memory of the computer.
5. .... are those application programs that assist the computer by performing housekeeping functions.
6. In a .... plotter, the pen moves in horizontal and vertical direction whereas, in an .... plotter, small droplets of ink are sprayed on paper.

B **Give one word for the following statements.**

1. A portable microcomputer that is small enough to be kept on your lap.
2. Computers used in hospitals, air line reservation companies, and many big companies.
3. The physical components of the computer which you can touch and feel.
4. The speed at which a microprocessor executes instructions.
5. The volatile memory of the computer.

C **Classify the following as an input, output or a storage device.**

1. Light Pen
2. MICR
3. Plotters
4. Flash Drive
5. Scanner
6. Speaker
7. Microphone
8. Compact Disc
9. Bar code reader

D **Answer the following questions.**

1. Name the different generations of computers.
2. How are computers classified on the basis of their size and speed?
3. Explain the two types of memory available in computers.
4. Write a short note on secondary memory of computers.
5. What is a utility software? Give examples.

LAB WORK

Design your own computer system. Find a magazine or brochure with pictures of computers and related accessories. Cut out pictures of items that you would wish to include in your computer system and paste the pictures on a sheet of paper.

TEACHER'S NOTES

1. Conduct a discussion on evolution and uses of smartphones. Ask the students to make a list of various smartphones available in market these days.
2. Ask the students to make a short presentation on the various input, output and storage devices available in the market these days. Relevant pictures and genuine facts can be taken from the Internet.

2 Operating System

SNAP RECAP

1. An operating system is a system software which is necessary for the computer to work. It works like a manager which manages all tasks.
2. Windows is the most commonly used operating system.

LEARNING OBJECTIVES

You will learn about:

1. Operating System (OS)
2. booting
3. functions of an OS
4. Types of OS
5. operating system interface
6. importance of 'Shut Down'

Operating System (OS)

Computers cannot function on their own. They require programming instructions to work and manage the system. This job is done by an operating system. *An operating system is a system software. It may be regarded as the backbone of a computer, and is an intermediary between the user and the computer.* It performs the basic tasks of a computer. These are given below.

1. It recognises input from the keyboard.
2. It sends output to the display screen.
3. It keeps track of files and directories on the disk.
4. It controls the peripheral devices (input and output devices) such as printers.
5. It acts as an interface between the hardware of a computer and the user.

Some of the commonly used operating systems are Disk Operating System (DOS), MS Windows, Linux, Windows NT and Mac.

Icons of a few operating systems

FACT FILE

The technology upgradation that is different from its previous type is called a **version.** The various versions of Windows are Windows 95, Windows 98, Windows 2000, Windows ME, Windows NT, Windows XP, Windows Vista, Windows 7 and Window 8.

Booting

Booting is a process that starts the operating system when the user turns on a computer system. It is a self-starting process and is basically of two types:

1. *Warm boot:* It is pressing the Restart button while the computer is already on.
2. *Cold boot:* It is pressing the power switch when the computer is switched off.

Process of booting

When you switch on a computer, the operating system is loaded into RAM automatically.

It follows the sequence given below. These steps are part of booting process (Fig. 2.1).

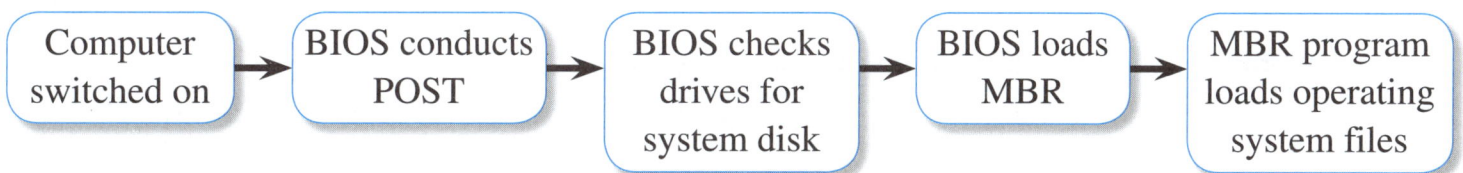

Fig. 2.1 *Flowchart showing the process of booting*

1. As soon as the computer is turned on, a software, namely, Balance Input-Output System (**BIOS**) is run. This software is built into a computer's ROM.

Note: BIOS starts the operating system and supports the transfer of information between hardware devices.

2. BIOS first conducts a Power-On Self Test (**POST**) to make sure all the components of the computer are in a working condition with a proper power supply.

3. The BIOS then looks for the special boot programs that will actually load the operating system from the hard disk.

4. A computer may have several disks or drives. The operating system is loaded in one of the disks. BIOS first looks for a floppy disk on Drive A. If there is no system disk in it (where the operating system is loaded), BIOS then looks for the system files at a specific place on your hard disk.

5. BIOS next looks at the first sector of the hard disk, and copies the information from it onto specific locations in RAM. This information is known as the **boot record** or **Master Boot Record (MBR).**

6. MBR program will now load the system files of an operating system into the RAM.
7. Once the system files are loaded, the OS is ready to take control of the system.
8. OS remains in the computer's memory till the power is on.

ACTIVITY

Number the steps in the correct order for booting a system.

- BIOS loads Master Boot Record program

- Operating system remains in memory till power is on

- BIOS conducts POST

- Computer switched on

- Master Boot Record program loads operating system files

- Operating system remains in memory till power is on

Functions of an Operating System

An operating system does the job of a system manager. It performs various important functions (Fig. 2.2) which are discussed here.

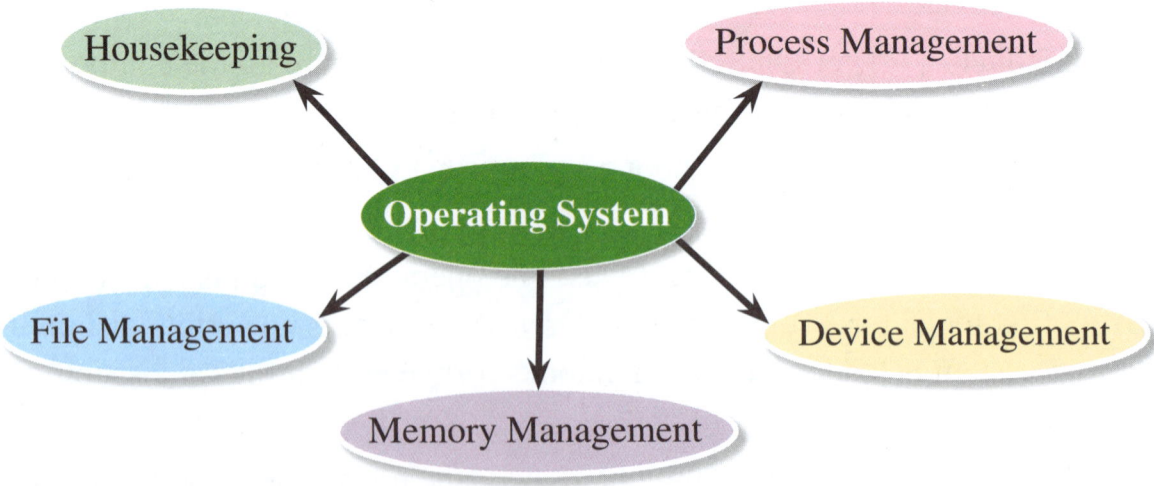

Fig. 2.2 *Various functions of an operating system*

Process management

An operating system controls and schedules the processes for execution by the CPU. It is responsible for allocating the CPU's time to each process. You may think of the process as an application, but that does not give the complete picture of how processes relate to the operating system and hardware. An application in MS Office, is indeed a process. However, it may cause several other background processes to begin, such as, virus checks, memory management, etc.

After a job is done or a process is completed, the CPU becomes idle. After that if there are other processes in queue (Fig. 2.3), then the time is allocated to each process of the CPU. This whole system is managed to ensure maximum output from the system.

Fig. 2.3 *CPU process queue*

Device management

Device management is an important function of an operating system. It coordinates and controls the various input and output devices attached to the system. When the system is ready to take input then the input device is made available to the user and when the processing job is over then the output is redirected to the output device.

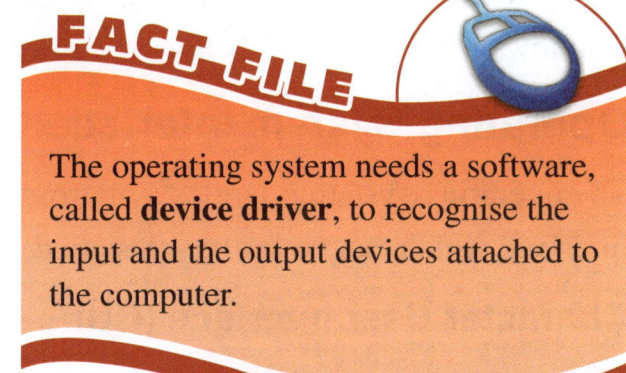

The operating system needs a software, called **device driver**, to recognise the input and the output devices attached to the computer.

Memory management

Whenever you start any application software, it gets loaded onto the system memory and when you open any file then a copy of that file is loaded onto the memory from the disk. This is done by an operating system. It allocates certain memory area to itself with the help of the booting process and sets aside the remaining area for various application programs.

File management

A lot of data is stored on the hard disk which in turn is formed of millions of tracks and sectors. At the time of storing data on the disk, it is not compulsory that it occupies the sectors in a sequence. It is the job of an operating system to read the file from different tracks and sectors when required, and also store it in the available space. Thus, an operating system manages the reading and writing of the file system. It also operates the user and application file access authorisations.

Housekeeping

Housekeeping includes all the services necessary to ensure smooth operation of the computer system, like security, protection, resource accounting, back up, etc.

Types of Operating System

Single-user operating system

As the name implies, single-user operating system is designed so that only one user can effectively work on a computer at a time. This is the type of operating system most people use on their desktops and laptops today. Windows 98, DOS and the Mac OS are a few examples of a single-user operating system.

Multi-user operating system

A multi-user operating system supports multiple users at the same time and/or different times. The operating system must make sure that the requirements of the different users are balanced, and that each of the programs they are using has sufficient and separate resources so that a problem with one user does not affect the entire community of users. For example, UNIX, Windows NT and Novell Netware, can support hundreds and thousands of networked users.

Operating System Interface

The operating system provides a platform on which the application program runs. It provides an interface which can be further classified.

Character User Interface (CUI)

In CUI, the operating system provides an environment where the user needs to type a command to perform a particular action. For example, Disk Operating System (DOS).

Graphical User Interface (GUI)

In GUI, the operating system provides a graphical environment where the mouse acts as a pointing device. The user can perform an action just by a mouse-click. For example, Windows operating system.

Importance of Shut Down

By now you are well aware that Windows remains in the computer memory till the power is on. After completing the work, these operating system files are sent back to the hard disk properly so that no damage is caused to these files. This process is known as **shut down** of an operating system.

If you switch off the computer without giving a proper shut down command then there are very high chances of losing the data and it may also damage the Windows operating system.

Follow these steps to shut down a computer properly:

1. Click on **Start** ⟹ **Shut down** option (Fig. 2.4).

2. For other options, click on the arrow right to **Shut down** option. It generally shows the following options (Fig. 2.5):

   - *Switch user:* It switches the user without closing the programs currently in use.
   - *Log off:* It closes all programs running on the computer, however the computer still runs.
   - *Lock:* It locks the computer and the work on programs running can be resumed on unlocking the computer.
   - *Restart:* If due to some error the computer needs to be shut down, then it can be restarted by using the **Restart** option. This option shuts down the Windows properly and then starts it again immediately.
   - *Sleep:* It puts the computer in a low-power state and saves the work being done so that it can be resumed from the point where it was left off.

Fig. 2.4 *Using Start menu to shut down*

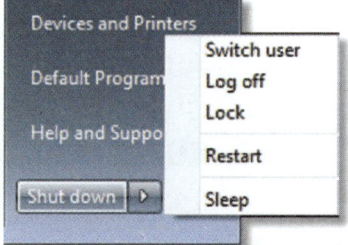

Fig. 2.5 *Shut down options*

FACT FILE

Like Sleep in desktops, Hibernation is a power-saving mode developed for laptops. It keeps the active documents and programs running on the hard disk and puts the computer in low-power state so that work can be resumed quickly. This allows the users to restore work even in case of power failure.

ACTIVITY

Rewrite the jumbled words.

LIFE _____   VERSER _____

CUP _____   TARTSRE _____

GLOSSARY

BIOS: It stands for Basic Input – Output System.

Booting: It is a process that starts the operating system when the user turns on a computer system.

Cold boot: It is the process of pressing on the power switch when the computer is shut down.

CUI: It stands for Character User Interface.

GUI: It stands for Graphical User Interface.

Master Boot Record: It is the information that BIOS copies onto the RAM.

Multi-user Operating System: It supports multiple users at the same time and/or different times.

Operating System: It is a system software that is an intermediary between the user and the computer.

POST: It stands for Power-On Self Test.

Single-user Operating System: It is a system where only one user can effectively work on a computer at a time.

Warm boot: It is the process of pressing the Restart button while the computer is already on.

NOW YOU KNOW

1. An operating system performs several basic functions.
2. When you switch on a computer, the operating system is loaded onto the RAM automatically in a specific sequence.
3. An operating system does the job of a system manager, and performs the following important functions: Process Management, Device Management, Memory Management, File Management and Housekeeping.
4. In Character User Interface, the operating system provides an environment where the user needs to type a command to perform a particular action. For example, Disk Operating System.
5. In Graphical User Interface, the operating system provides a graphical environment where the user can perform an action by just a mouse-click. For example, Windows operating system.
6. In Windows after completing the work, operating system files are sent back to the hard disk properly to prevent damage. This process is known as shut down of an operating system.

EXERCISE

A **Fill in the blanks.**

1. .... and .... are the two types of booting.
2. An operating system is a .... software.
3. When the system is switched on then the .... loads onto the RAM.
4. .... operating system is selected when one user needs to do one thing at a time.
5. An operating system works as a .... manager.

B **Match the following.**

1.	CUI	a.	Computer shuts down and starts immediately
2.	MBR	b.	CPU is managed efficiently
3.	Standby	c.	Stored information
4.	Restart	d.	Commands are written to perform an action
5.	Process management	e.	Computer is in low power state

C **Give differences between:**

1. Warm Boot and Cold Boot
2. CUI and GUI
3. Single-user operating system and Multi-user operating system
4. File management and Memory management

D **Answer the following questions.**

1. What is an operating system? What basic tasks does it perform?
2. Enlist the steps of booting.
3. Explain any three important functions of an operating system.
4. Explain the two operating system interface.
5. Why is it important to properly shut down your computer?

LAB WORK

A. The Disk Operating System (DOS) supports CUI. Find out some more details about DOS. You can take the help of your teacher or the Internet.

B. Create a flowchart in MS Word 2007 showing the booting process in computers.

Linux

Linux is a Unix-like computer operating system designed by Linus Torvalds. It was released on 5 October, 1991, when Torvalds was still a student at the University of Helsinki, Finland. Linux is free and an open source operating system software, that is it is free to use, modify and distribute both commercially and non-commercially. Anyone with licenses such as the GNU General Public License can modify and improve the program as per their own requirement. They can even release their improved version to the public. Because of this, Linux has grown from a small number of C files in 1991 to over 370 megabytes of source code in 2009. All this is because, in Linux, you have free access to the source code.

Linux is also multitasking, multi-user operating system which means that many people can run many different applications on one computer at the same time. This differs from MS-DOS, where only one person can use the system at a particular time. When many people are working, then each user is identified by the system through their unique **Login Id**, and **Password**. Debian, Red Hat Enterprise Linux, Mandriva, open SUSE and Arch Linux are popular Linux distributions. More than 90% of world's 500 fastest supercomputers including top 10 fastest supercomputers run on some variant of Linux.

Some key features of Linux are:

- **Multi-user operating system**

  Linux supports multiple users at one time. In these types of OS, there is a server and all the users are provided different terminals.

- **Free and open source**

  It means it is a free software which can easily be downloaded from the Internet and anybody can use and modify it as per their requirement.

- **Multitasking**

  Linux allows more than one program to run at a time. The user can create a word document and at the same time, can download files from the Internet and also get the printing done.

- **Multiplatform**

  Linux operating system can run on many different computer platforms.

- **Security**

  Linux is one of the most secure operating systems. File access permission systems prevent access by unwanted visitors or viruses. Every user needs their own user id and password.

- **Portable**

  A Linux kernel and application program can be installed on any kind of hardware platform.

- **Hierarchical File System**

  Linux provides a standard file structure in which files are arranged.

- **Shell**

  Linux provides a special interpreter program which is used to execute commands of the operating system.

Components of Linux

Linux system is divided into following major components/layers (see the figure below):

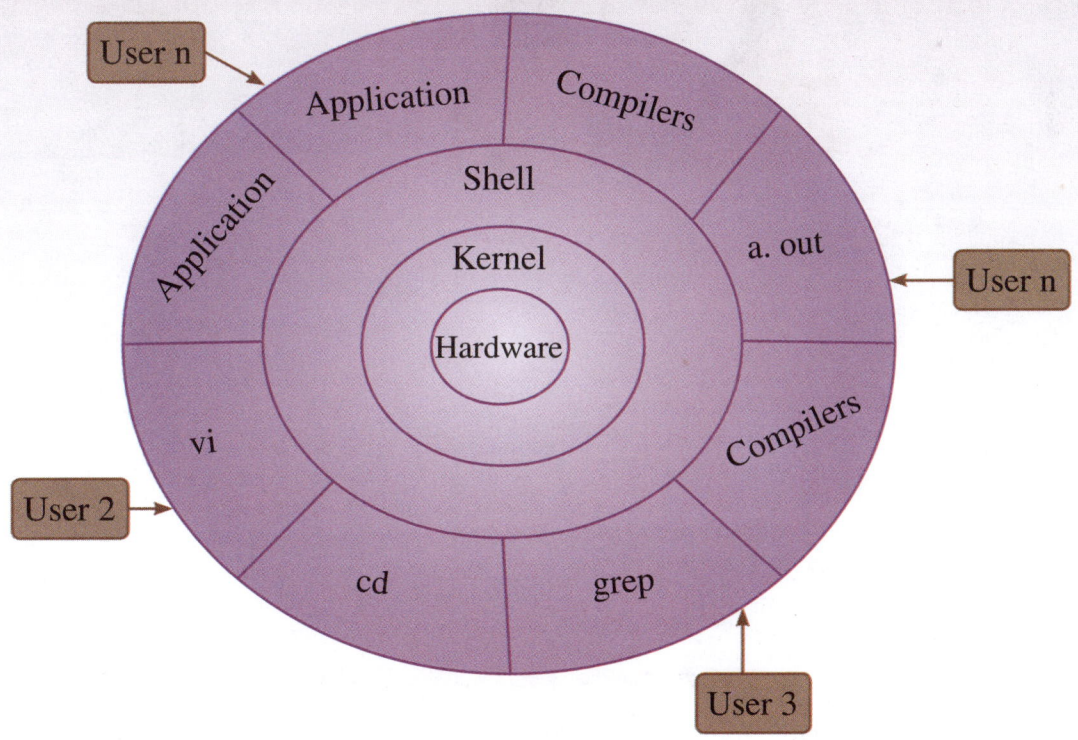

1. *Hardware:* It consists of all peripheral devices like RAM, CPU, etc.
2. *Kernel:* Kernel is the main part of the operating system. It performs the task of creating and maintaining the Linux environment. It acts as an interface between the hardware and the shell. It also controls the hardware, CPU, memory, hard disk, network card, etc. attached to the computer.
3. *Shell:* It is a program that acts as a command interpreter which is an interface between the user and the operating system. It interprets the commands entered by the user and passes them to the kernel. There are number of different Shells available like Bourne shell (sh), Kornshell (ksh), C Shell (csh). Each provides a slightly different interface between the user and the Linux operating system.
4. *Utilities and Application Programs:* These are the programs like Word Processors, Spreadsheets, Database Management Systems, etc. that are supported by Linux environment.

TEACHER'S NOTES

1. Engage the students in a discussion on the places where the multi-user system is used.
2. Ask the students to use the Internet to learn more about advantages of CUI and GUI.

3 Using Windows

SNAP RECAP

1. Windows is an operating system that makes your computer run.
2. Desktop background is the list of designs used for decorating the desktop.
3. Screen saver displays the moving images that start automatically when the computer is idle for a specified amount of time.
4. Windows comes with a number of standard applications referred to as Accessories.

LEARNING OBJECTIVES

You will learn about:
1. advantages of Windows operating system
2. searching for files and folders
3. using Run option
4. On-Screen Keyboard
5. Control Panel – display, mouse, regional settings

Introduction

An operating system acts as an intermediate between the user and the machine. It provides a software platform on which the application program runs. So, the choice of an operating system should be determined on the basis of an application requirement for your system.

MS Windows is becoming very popular these days and you shall find out the reasons for that below.

Advantages of Windows Operating System

Windows is an operating system which supports the Graphical User Interface environment. All commands can be executed easily and efficiently at a click of the mouse. Some of the advantages of Windows as an operating system are listed here.

1. *Graphical User Interface:* It is also known as GUI. It offers graphical icons and visual indicators based interface as compared to text based interfaces.
2. *Easy to use and learn:* Working with Windows is easy as it just requires a few mouse-clicks to do the work.
3. *Multitasking:* In Windows, you can work on multiple programs at the same time. Programs open in the form of a window, which can be easily controlled with the help of **Alt + Tab** key (Fig. 3.1). For example, you can create documents as well as listen to music on a computer at the same time.

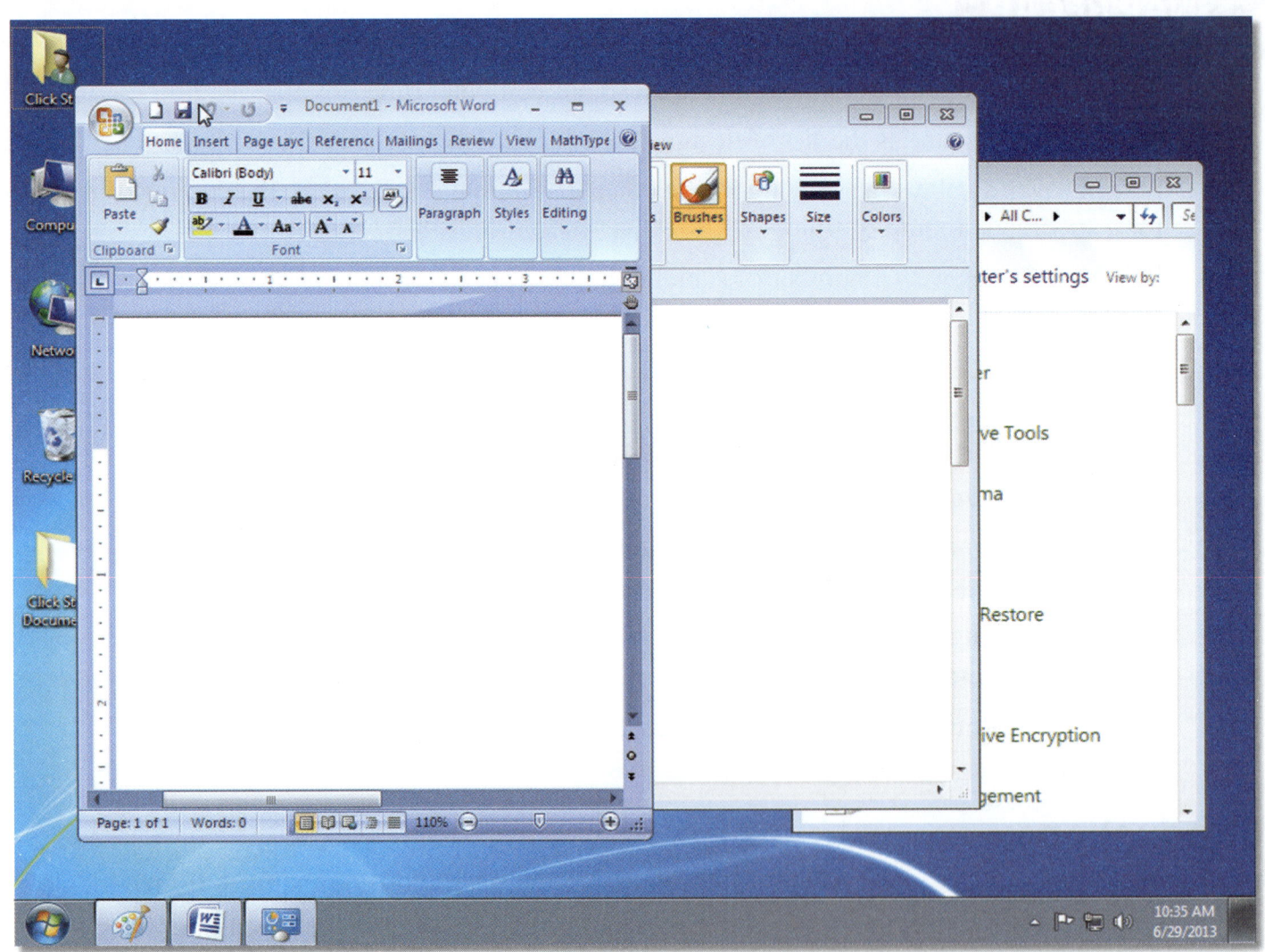

Fig. 3.1 *Multiple programs opened at the same time*

Search Option

Have you ever felt the need of searching for a file on your computer? Maybe you wrote a letter to someone, and wanted to see its content again. Maybe you saved a report on your computer and forgot its location. The Search option is one of the most convenient ways to find things on your computer. The exact location of the items does not matter as the search box will search your programs and all the folders, and will display the result.

Search option is present as a box in the Start menu. It is mainly used for searching files and folders stored on the computer disk, that is, it helps us to search for a document, an application, a computer on network or a user connected on the network. The search criteria can also contain a text or a phrase which is a part of the document.

Follow these steps to search for a file or folder:

1. Click on the **Start** button.
2. Type the file or folder name or keywords in the search box in the lower-left corner (Fig. 3.2).
3. While typing, the items matching your search text will appear on the **Start** menu. Click on the desired file to open it (Fig. 3.3).

To search for a file in a folder or library follow the steps given below.

1. Open the desired folder or library.

Fig. 3.2 *Selecting the Search option*   **Fig. 3.3** *Search results in the Start menu*

2. Type the file name or a word or a part of the word in the search box (Fig. 3.4).

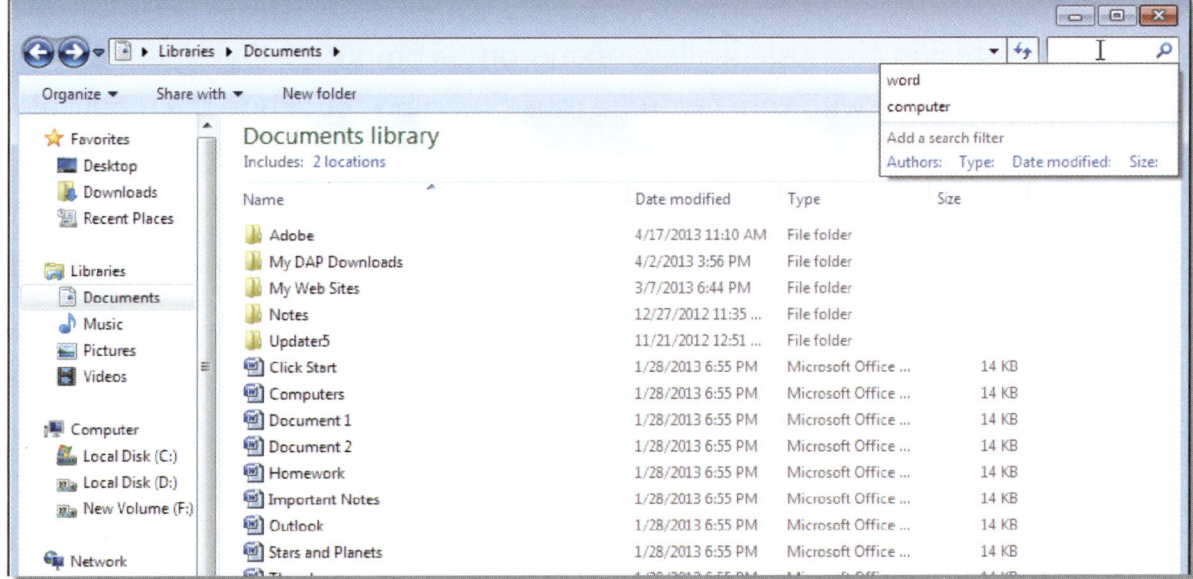

Fig. 3.4 *Searching for a file in a folder*

3. All the files containing the word or part of the word will be listed in the Search Results (Fig. 3.5). Click on the desired file.

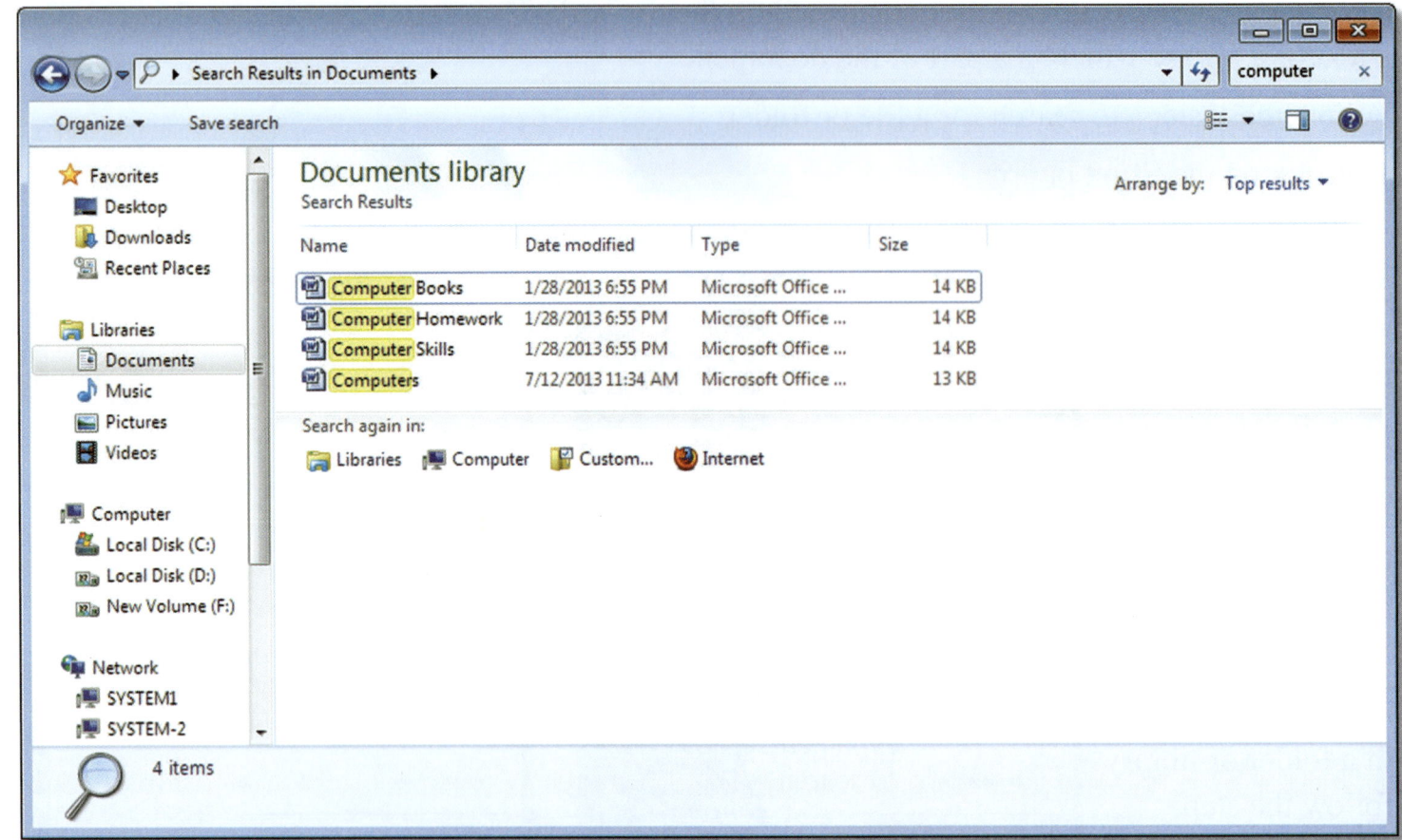

Fig. 3.5 *List of files containing the typed keyword*

ACTIVITY

Complete the following activity.

1. Do you like listening to music while working on a computer? If yes, you can open the Windows Media Player with your favourite music running. Minimise the media player and continue to do your work. Which feature of the Windows operating system lets you do these two tasks together?

2. Also, search for the Music folder using the Search option, to find the song you wish to listen to.

Run Option

The Run option from the Start button is used for executing a file or application directly. For example, the user can open the Notepad application by specifying **Notepad** in the **Run** dialog box.

Follow the steps given below:

1. Click on **Start** ⟹ **All Programs** ⟹ **Accessories** ⟹ **Run** option (Fig. 3.6).
2. The **Run** dialog box opens (Fig. 3.7).

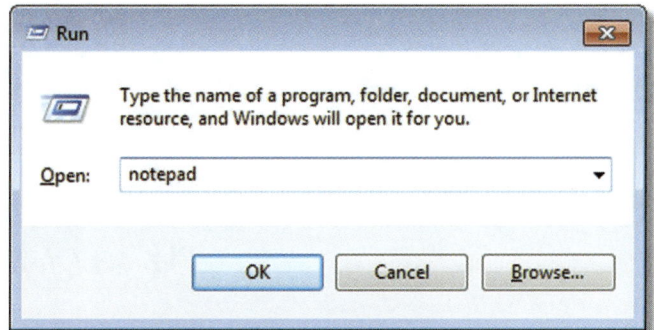

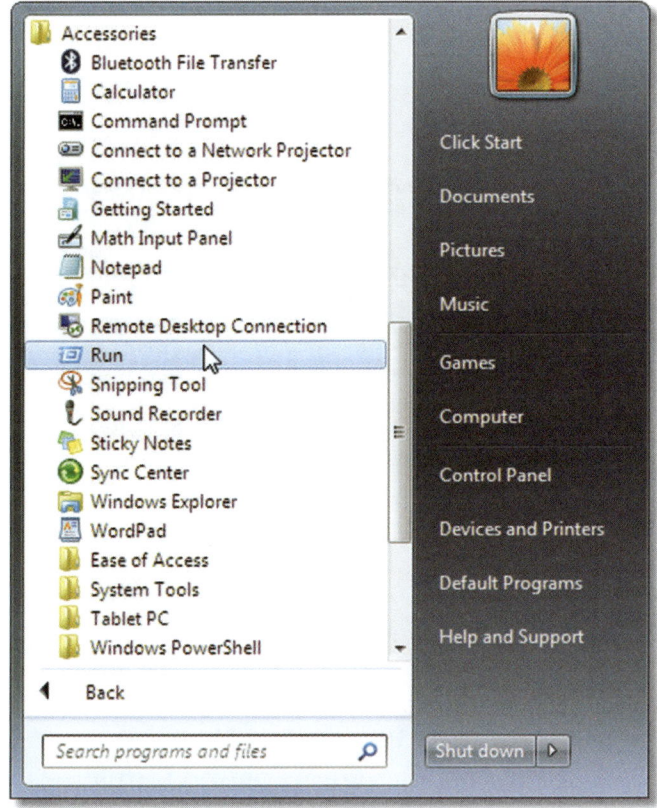

Fig. 3.7 *Run dialog box*

3. In **Run** dialog box, type the name of the file or program in **Open**: text box.
4. Click on **OK**.

Fig. 3.6 *Run option in Accessories folder*

5. If the exact location of the program or document is not known then click the **Browse...** button and select the program or document from the specified folder.

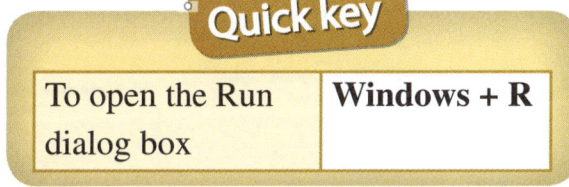

To open the Run dialog box	Windows + R

On-Screen Keyboard

An On-Screen Keyboard is an important utility program. It displays a **virtual keyboard** on the computer screen which allows the user to use the mouse pointer to type. On-Screen Keyboard can also help people who do not know how to type and for whom using mouse click is easier than using a keyboard.

Follow these steps to access On-Screen Keyboard:

1. Click on **Start** ⟹ **All Programs** ⟹ **Accessories** ⟹ **Ease of Access** ⟹ **On-Screen Keyboard** option (Fig. 3.8).

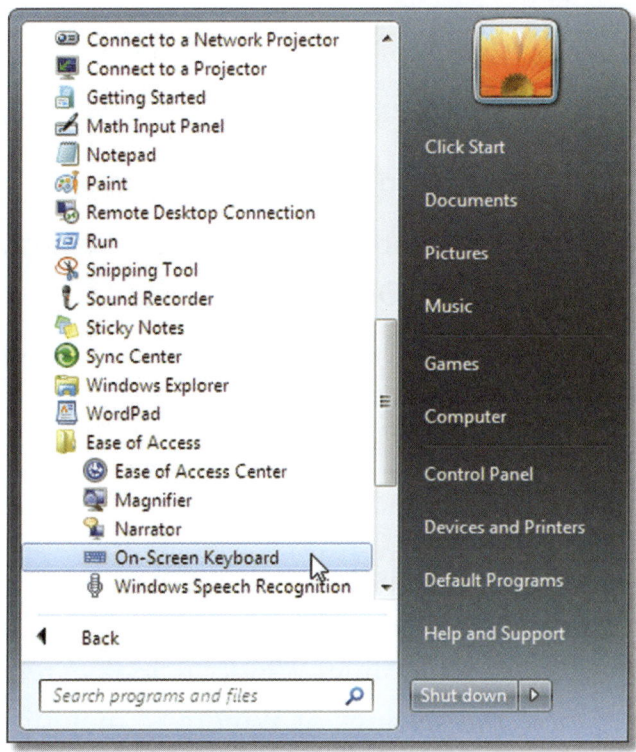

Fig. 3.8 *Selecting On-Screen Keyboard option*

2. A On-Screen Keyboard appears on the screen (Fig. 3.9).

Fig. 3.9 *On-Screen Keyboard*

Open the **Run** dialog box and type **osk**. Click OK. The On-Screen keyboard will appear on the screen.

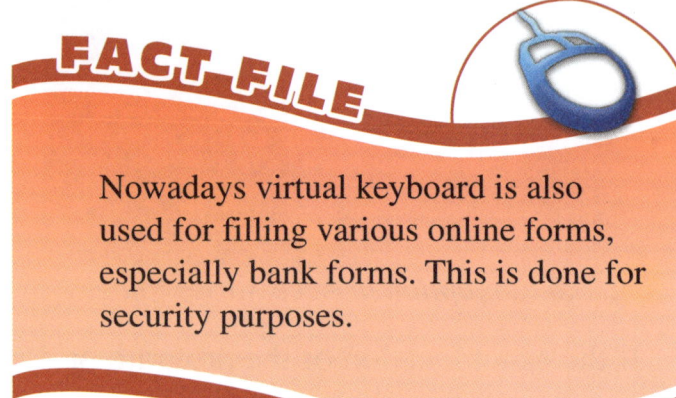

Nowadays virtual keyboard is also used for filling various online forms, especially bank forms. This is done for security purposes.

ACTIVITY

A. Complete the following activity based on the instructions given below.

1. Open Paint using Search option.
2. Create any pattern for the desktop background, and write one sentence on it using the On-Screen Keyboard.
3. Save the file with the name 'MyDesktop.bmp'.
4. Close the file.

Control Panel

You can use Control Panel to change settings for Windows. These settings control nearly everything about how Windows looks and works. You can use Control Panel to make changes to the look and settings of Windows, including the color of your desktop, windows, hardware and software setup and configuration, Network, Internet, etc. (Fig. 3.10).

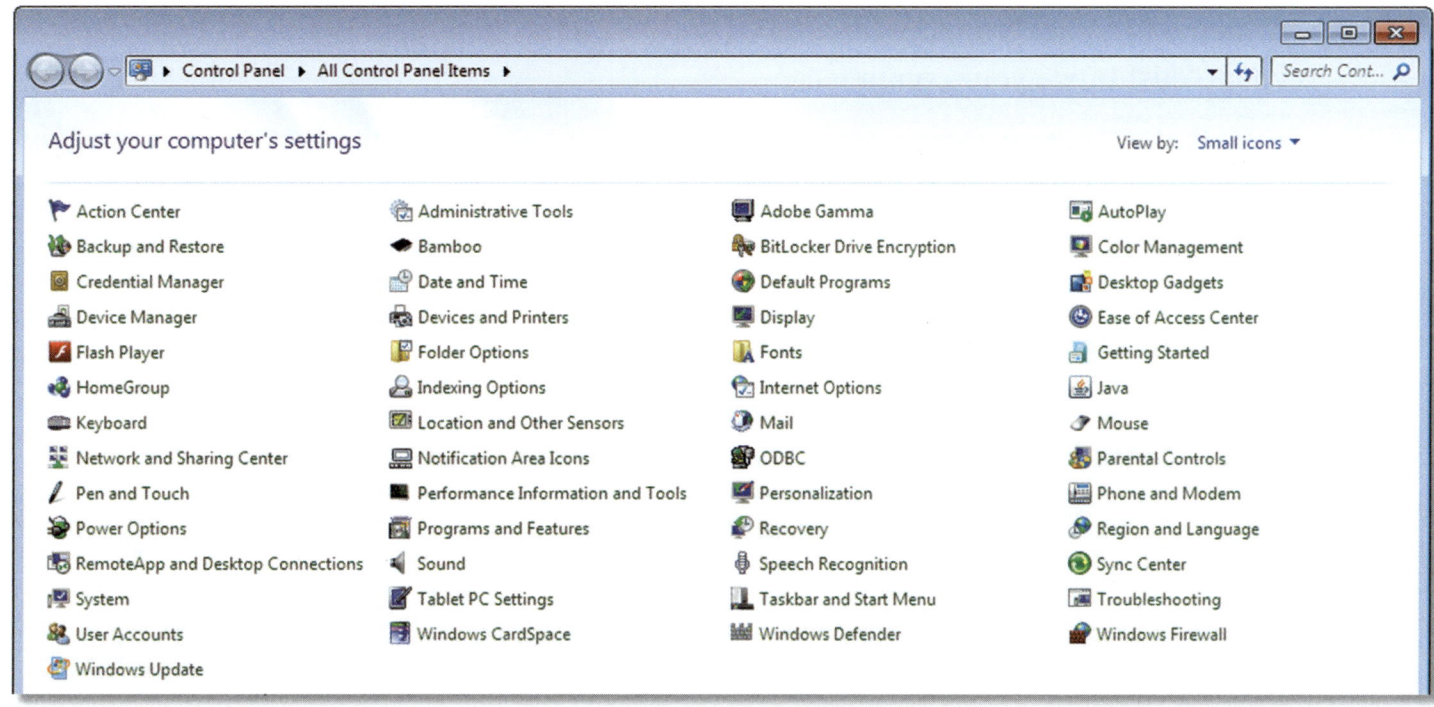

Fig. 3.10 *Control Panel window*

 **Note:** The name of an application may vary with the version of an operating system. For example, in Windows XP, you see **Display** as the option whereas in Windows 7 it is **Personalization**.

Personalization icon

In Windows 7, Personalization icon of Control Panel is used for changing the appearance of the desktop such as background, screen saver, colors, and sounds.

Follow these steps to change, say the theme of a desktop:

1. Click on **Start** ⟹ **Control Panel**.

2. In the **Control Panel** window, select the **Personalization** icon.

3. The **Personalization** window opens (Fig. 3.11).

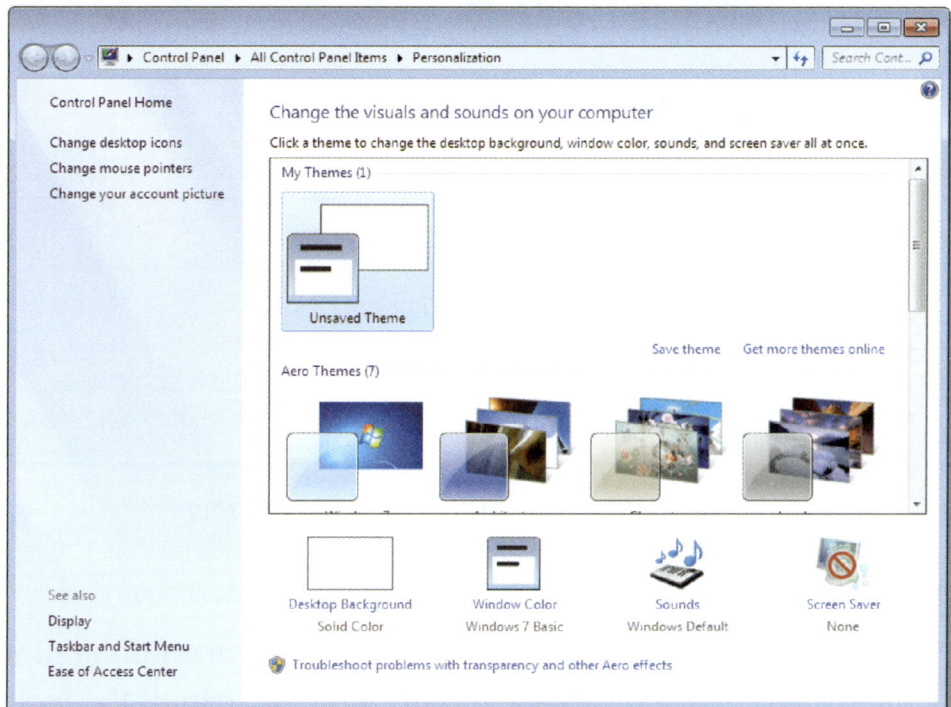

Fig. 3.11 *Personalization window*

 **Note:** A theme is a background with a set of sounds, icons and other elements that helps you to customise your computer.

4. Click on the theme of your choice from the categories given. The computer will request you to wait for some time showing the **Please Wait** box and the selected theme will be applied.

5. You can further enhance your theme effects using options like selecting specific pictures from that category, **Picture position:, Change picture every:**, **Shuffle** checkbox (when active) in the **Desktop Background** window (Fig. 3.12).

6. You can also change the color of your window and add sound effects using the **Window Color** and add **Sounds** options respectively in the **Personalization** window.

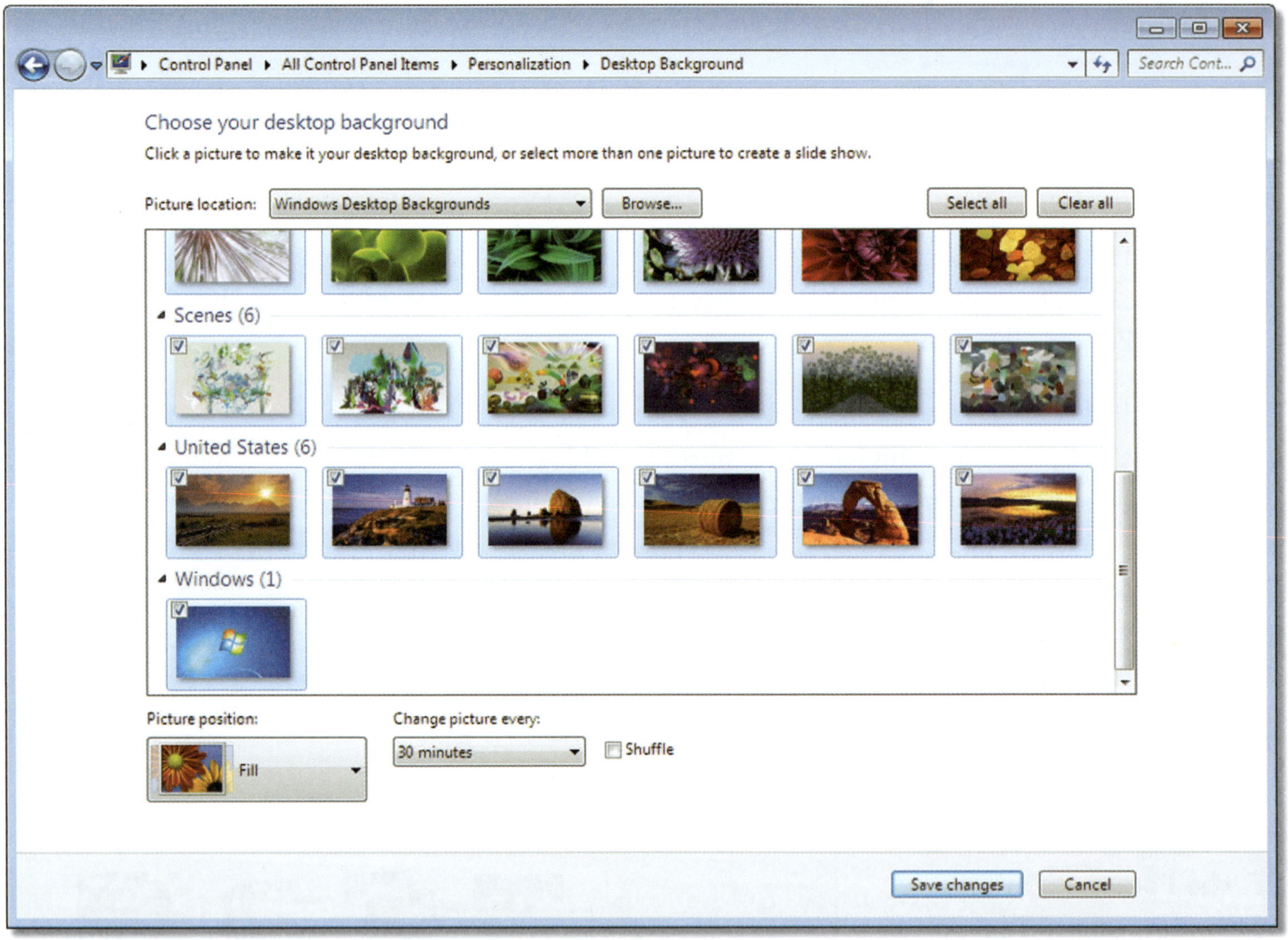

Fig. 3.12 *Selecting themes on a desktop*

Mouse icon

You can change the mouse settings such as button configuration, double-click speed, mouse pointer shape, motion speed and trails with the help of the mouse icon.

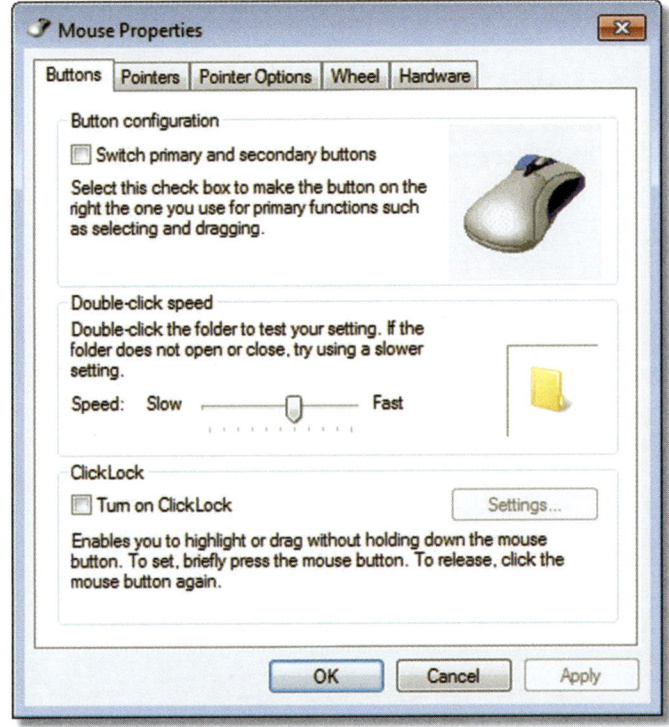

Fig. 3.13 *Using Mouse Properties window*

Follow these steps to change mouse settings for button configuration:

1. Click on **Start** ⟹ **Control Panel**.
2. In the **Control Panel** window, click on the **Mouse** icon.
3. The **Mouse Properties** window opens (Fig. 3.13).
4. Click on the **Buttons** tab.
5. In the **Button configuration** section, the default use of the mouse is set for the right-handed people, that is, left button for click and double-click and right button for shortcut menus. But if you want to reverse the buttons then click on the **Switch primary and secondary buttons** checkbox.
6. You can also change the speed of double-click by dragging the pointer either to right or left in the **Double-click speed** section.
7. Click on the **Turn on ClickLock** option in **ClickLock** section, if you want to drag the mouse without holding down the mouse button.
8. Click on **Apply**. Click on **OK**.

Follow these steps to change the mouse pointer shape:

1. Click on **Start** ⟹ **Control Panel** ⟹ **Mouse** icon.
2. Click on the **Pointers** tab (Fig. 3.14).
3. Select the desired option from the predefined set of mouse pointers available in the **Scheme** drop-down list.
4. Based on the category selected, a list of mouse pointers will be displayed in the **Customize:** section.
5. If you want a pointer shadow then click on the **Enable pointer shadow** checkbox.
6. Click on **Apply**. Click on **OK**.

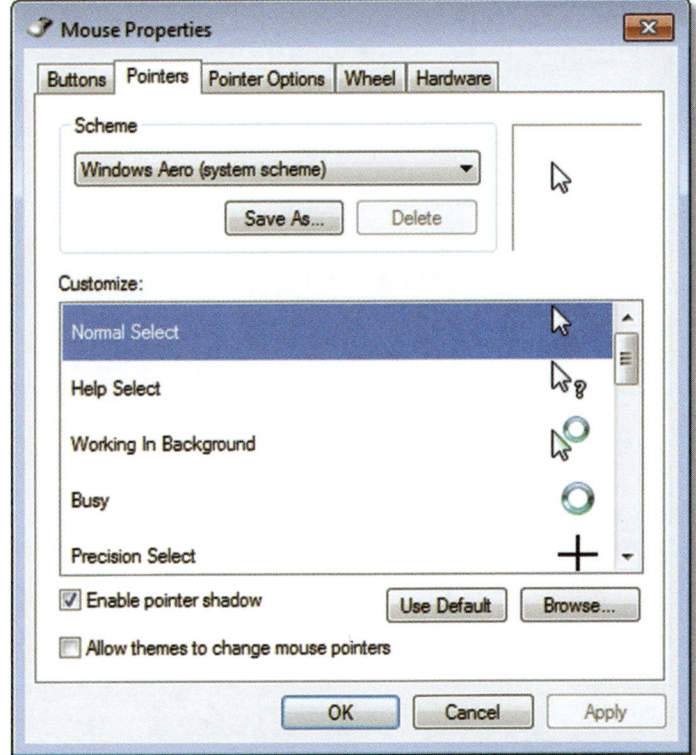

Fig. 3.14 *Using Pointer tab of Mouse Properties*

Follow these steps to change Pointer Options of the mouse:

1. Click on **Start** ⟹ **Control Panel** ⟹ **Mouse** icon.
2. Click on the **Pointer Options** tab (Fig. 3.15).
3. Select the desired pointer-speed by dragging the pointer either to the left to slow down or to the right to move fast in the **Motion** section.
4. If you want the mouse pointer to point to the default button in a dialog box then click to tick the **Automatically move pointer to the default button in a dialog box** checkbox in the **Snap To** section.
5. Select the **Display pointer trails** checkbox in the **Visibility** section if you want the pointer to trail the mouse on the screen.
6. If you want the mouse pointer not to be visible when you type, then click to tick the **Hide pointer while typing** checkbox.
7. Click on **Apply**. Click on **OK**.

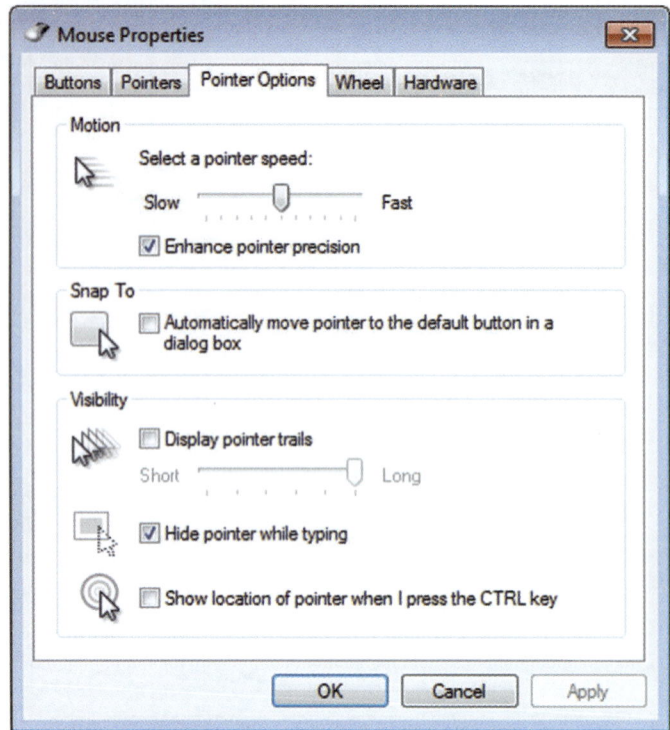

Fig. 3.15 *Using Pointer Options tab of Mouse Properties*

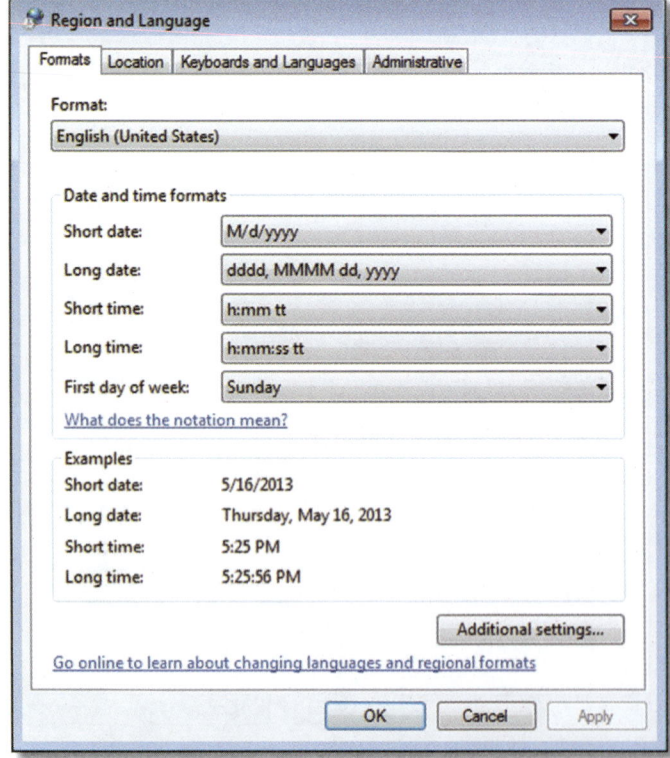

Fig. 3.16 *Region and Language dialog box*

Region and Language icon

Region and Language icon is used for changing the settings of the display of languages, numbers, time and date.

Follow the steps given below:

1. Click on **Start** ⟹ **Control Panel**.
2. In **Control Panel** window, click on the **Regional and Language** icon.
3. The **Region and Language** dialog box opens (Fig. 3.16).
4. The date and time formats can be changed from the respective drop-down lists in the **Date and time formats** section.
5. Click on **Apply**. Click on **OK**.

ACTIVITY

Complete the following activity.

1. Open the Personalization window using the Control Panel.
2. Use the file 'MyDesktop.bmp' created earlier in Paint as the Desktop Background.
3. Change the mouse settings by increasing the double-click speed, apply the mouse trail and change the shape of the mouse pointer.
4. Change time in 24 hours format.

GLOSSARY

Desktop background: It is an image used as a background on a computer screen.

Graphical User Interface: It offers graphical icons and visual indicators based interface.

Multitasking: It is the ability to do more than one thing at a time.

Theme: It is a background with a set of sound, icons and other elements that helps you in customising your computer.

Virtual keyboard: It is a utility program that displays an On-Screen Keyboard allowing the usage of mouse pointer to type.

NOW YOU KNOW

1. Operating system acts as an intermediate between the user and the machine. It provides a software platform on which application programs run. So, the choice of an operating system should be determined on the basis of an application requirement for the system.
2. Windows is an operating system which supports the Graphical User Interface environment. All commands can be executed easily and efficiently with a mouse-click.
3. Search box is located in the Start menu. It is mainly used for searching files and folders stored on computer disk, that is, it helps to search for a document, an application and even a computer on network.
4. The Run option located in the Start button is used for executing a file or application directly. The user can open Notepad by specifying Notepad in the Run dialog box.
5. Control Panel is a part of Microsoft Windows operating system. It allows the user to display and make changes to various basic settings of the computer system.

6. Personalization icon located in the Control Panel is used for changing the appearance of the desktop such as background, screen saver, colors and sounds.

7. Mouse icon in the Control Panel is used for changing the mouse settings such as button configuration, double-click speed, mouse pointer shape and motion speed and trails.

8. Region and Language icon of Control Panel is used for changing the settings of the display of languages, numbers, time and date.

EXERCISE

A Fill in the blanks.

1. ………………… is an operating system that supports the Graphical User Interface.

2. An ………………………… is a utility program that displays a virtual keyboard on the computer screen and allows the user to type using the mouse pointer.

3. ………………… icon in the Control Panel is used for changing the mouse settings such as button configuration, double-click speed.

4. ………………… icon of Control Panel is used for changing the settings of the display of languages, numbers, time and date.

5. The ……………… option from the Start button is used for executing a file or application directly.

B State whether the following sentences are True or False.

1. You can open Notepad using Run option.

2. An On-Screen Keyboard is not an important utility program.

3. Personalization settings save the file from unwanted damage.

4. Search option is located in the Start menu.

5. Run option is located on the desktop.

C **Give one word for the following:**

1. The option used in the Start menu to execute a file or an application directly.
2. A virtual keyboard.
3. The icon used for setting a Screen saver in the Control Panel.
4. Locating the files and folders stored on a computer disk.
5. Changing the date and time settings in the Control Panel.

D **Answer the following questions.**

1. Give any three advantages of using Windows as an operating system.
2. Why do you use Run option in the Start menu?
3. What is the use of search box in the Start menu?
4. How to open the On-Screen Keyboard?
5. What is the Control Panel? What all changes can you do using the various options in the Control Panel?

LAB WORK

Complete the following activity based on the instructions given.

1. Find out the icons present on your desktop and make a list of them in your notebook.
2. Try to open those icons and see what all you can do using them.
3. Make some changes on your desktop and the mouse settings of your computer.
4. Before leaving the lab reset the settings to default.

SEYMOUR CRAY

Seymour Cray was born on 28 September, 1925 in Chippewa Falls, Wisconsin. He worked extensively on computer technologies ranging from vacuum tubes and magnetic amplifiers to transistors. He designed the first fully transistorised computers. He also created the first supercomputer, named, Cray-1 in 1976. His Cray-1 computer established a new standard in supercomputing.

Windows 8 Updates

Sky Drive

Sky drive is a free integrated cloud service provided by Microsoft. With the help of SkyDrive we can save, sync and access all our files, photos and documents across different devices like desktop, laptop, tablet and mobile devices. Earlier it was called Windows Live SkyDrive but an updated version of it was released with Windows 8 and it was renamed SkyDrive.

 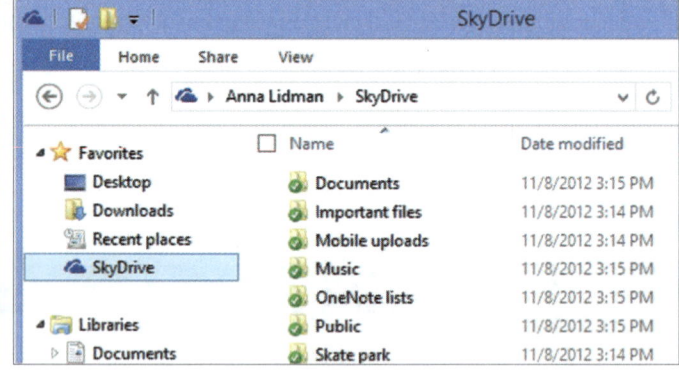

Share

In Windows 8, we can share files, photos or webpages with people we know without leaving the application we are using. To Share, use the Share charm: ⊞ + H.

TEACHER'S NOTES

1. Ask the students to prepare a short document on typing without using the keyboard.
2. Explore the various other options of the Control Panel with the students.

4 MS Word 2007 – Advanced Features

SNAP RECAP

1. Formatting is the process of applying font style, colors, etc. to a text or a paragraph.
2. A font name refers to the shape of characters.
3. The size of the text is called the font size and is measured in points.
4. The way in which a character is emphasised is called its font style.
5. The text alignment refers to the text layout with respect to document margins.

LEARNING OBJECTIVES

You will learn about:

1. headers and footers
2. footnotes and endnotes
3. drop cap
4. tab stop
5. using Show/Hide tool
6. Format Painter
7. columns
8. how to increase and decrease indentation
9. Thesaurus
10. borders and shading
11. page setup and margins
12. applying built-in styles

Introduction

You have already studied about some of the features of MS Word 2007 and the different formatting tips.

MS Word 2007 also provides certain additional features that make your work easy and well-structured. You can add page numbers, headers and footers, and can also look up a word in the Thesaurus to find similar words.

Headers and Footers

A header or footer is text or graphics such as a page number, the date or a company logo that is usually printed at the top or bottom margin of each page in a document. They give identification to a page while accessing the document.

A header is the text that appears at the top margin of every page while footer is the text that appears at the bottom margin of every page.

How to insert header and footer

Follow these steps to insert a header and a footer in a MS Word 2007 document:

1. Click on **Insert** tab ⟶ **Header & Footer** group (Fig. 4.1).

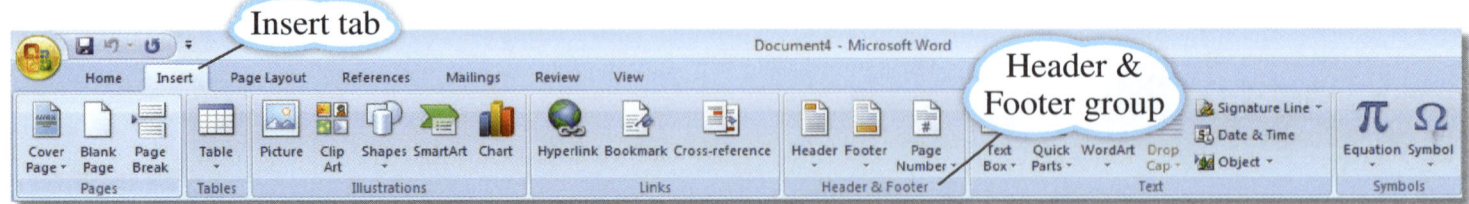

Fig. 4.1 *Using Insert tab to add headers and footers*

2. Click on the **Header** drop-down list and select the style of your choice (Fig. 4.2).

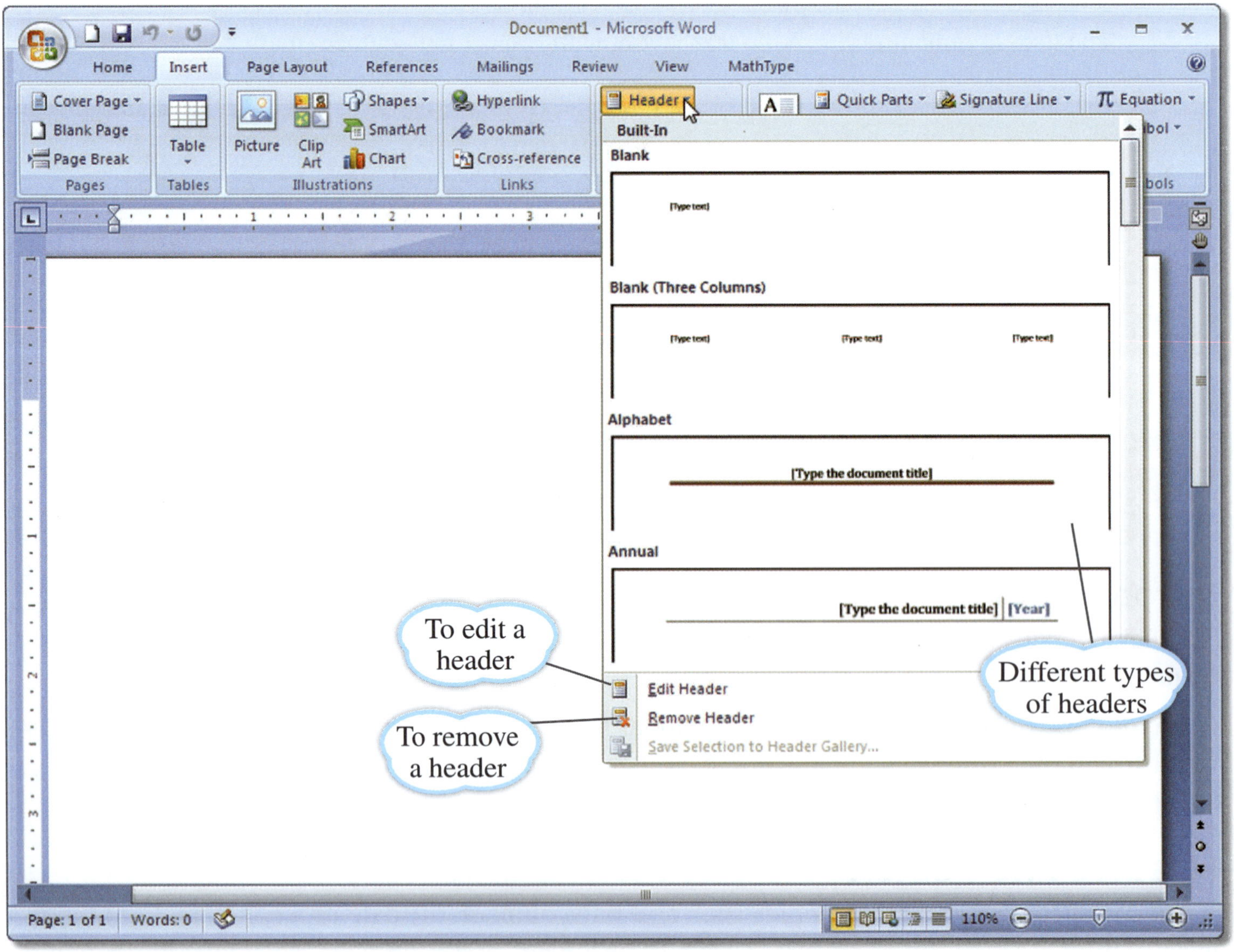

Fig. 4.2 *Header drop-down list*

TRY THIS!

You can also move between the header and footer areas by clicking on **Go to Header** and **Go to Footer** options, respectively, in the **Navigation** group of the **Design** tab.

3. The header area is displayed as a dotted line. The cursor appears in the header region (Fig. 4.3).

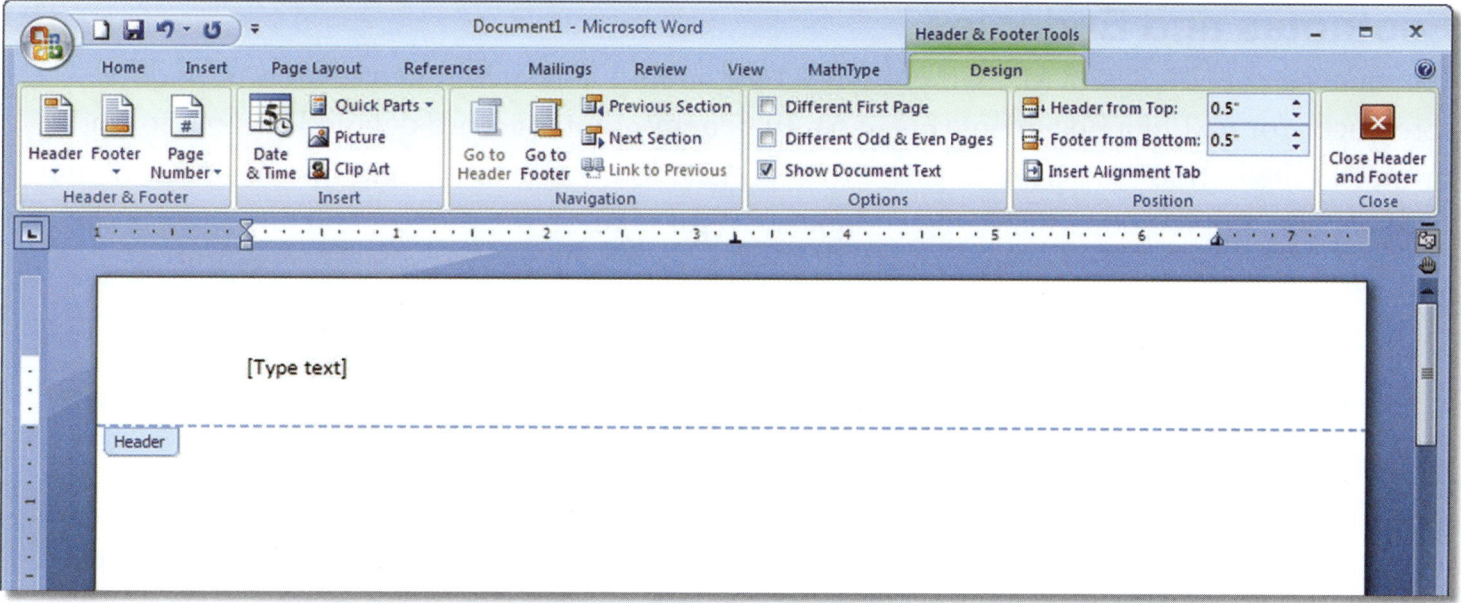

Fig. 4.3 *Inserting Header*

4. A new tab, **Design** will open when the cursor is in the header area (Fig. 4.4).

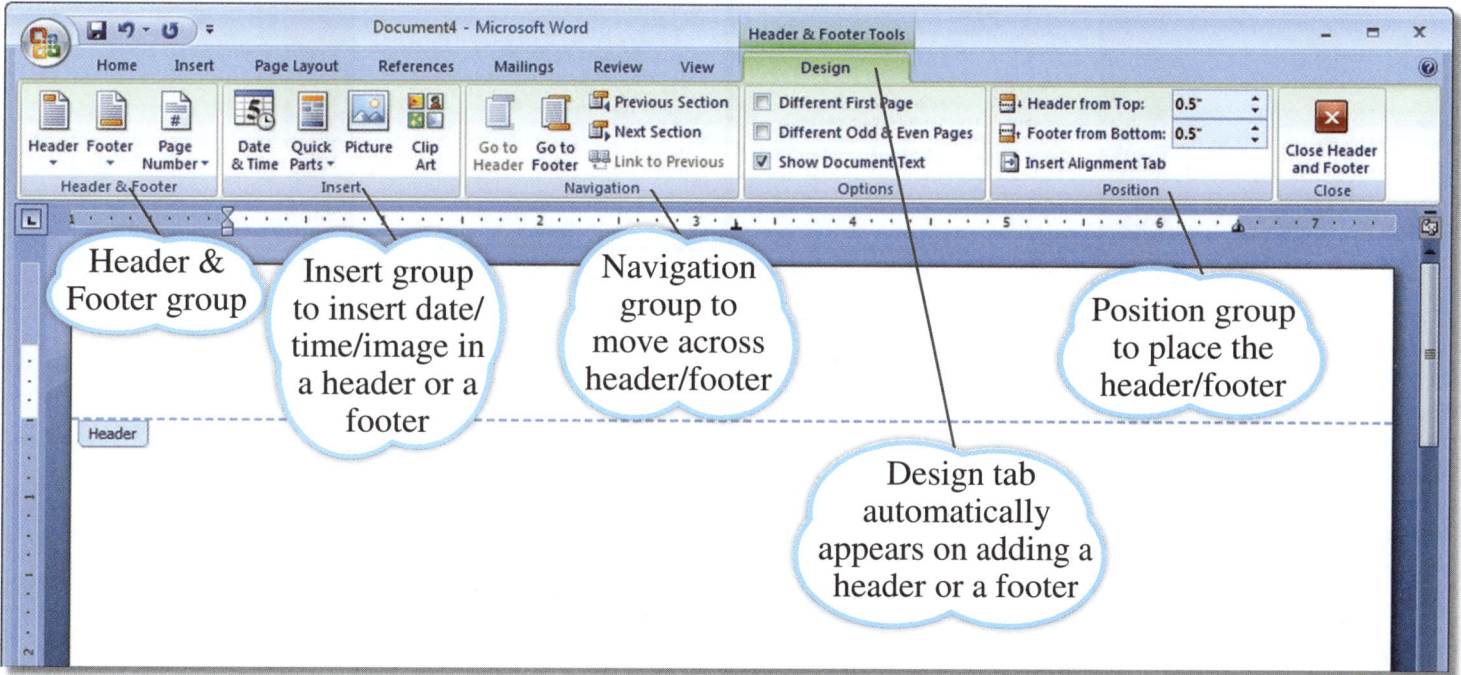

Fig. 4.4 *Options in Design tab for headers and footers*

5. You can enter the desired text in header area. You can also change the alignment and the position of the header.

6. Click on the **Footer** drop-down list in the **Insert** tab, to insert a footer. Now, the cursor will blink in the footer area of the document.

7. Select a style from the **Page Number** drop-down in the **Header & Footer** group of the **Insert tab** to insert page numbers in the document.

8. Click on **Close Header & Footer** option in the **Close** group of the **Design** tab.

Footnotes and Endnotes

Footnotes and endnotes in MS Word are used for adding notes, comments, or to provide references for text in a document (Fig. 4.5). In general, footnotes are detailed comments and printed at the bottom of a page to give extra information about something that has been written on that page. On the other hand, the endnotes are for citation of sources, and are given at the end of the document.

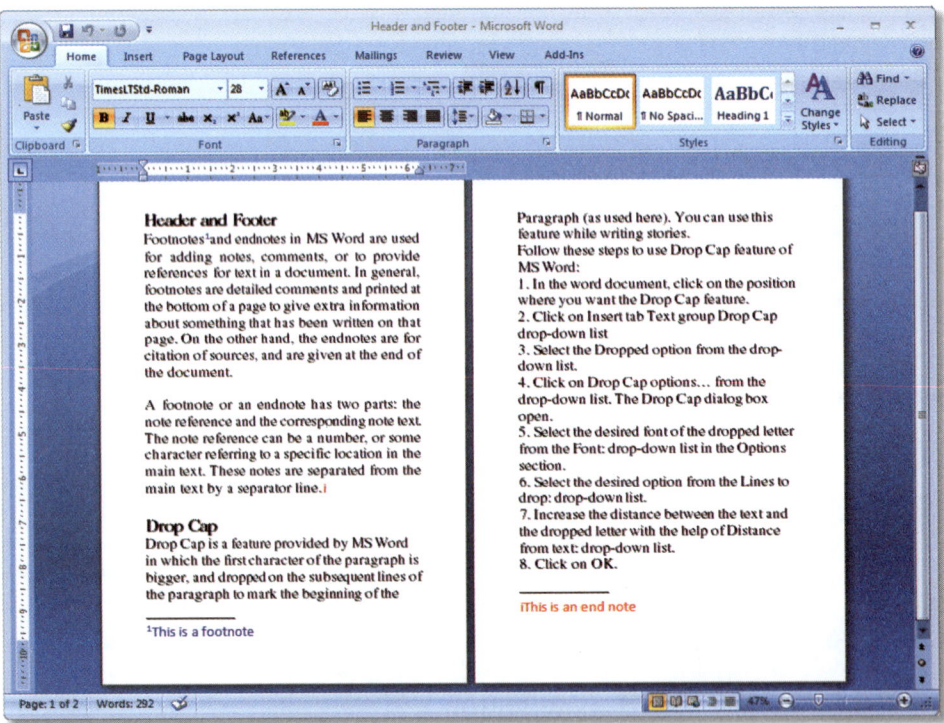

Fig. 4.5 *Footnote and Endnote*

A footnote or an endnote has two parts: the *note reference* and the corresponding *note text*. The note reference can be a number, or some character referring to a specific location in the main text. These notes are separated from the main text by a separator line.

Inserting a footnote or an endnote

A few steps are followed to insert a footnote or an endnote:

1. In your MS Word 2007 document, click on the position where you want a reference for the note to be added.

2. Click on **References** tab ⟹ **Footnotes** group ⟹ **Insert Footnote** option. A footnote will be added (Fig. 4.6).

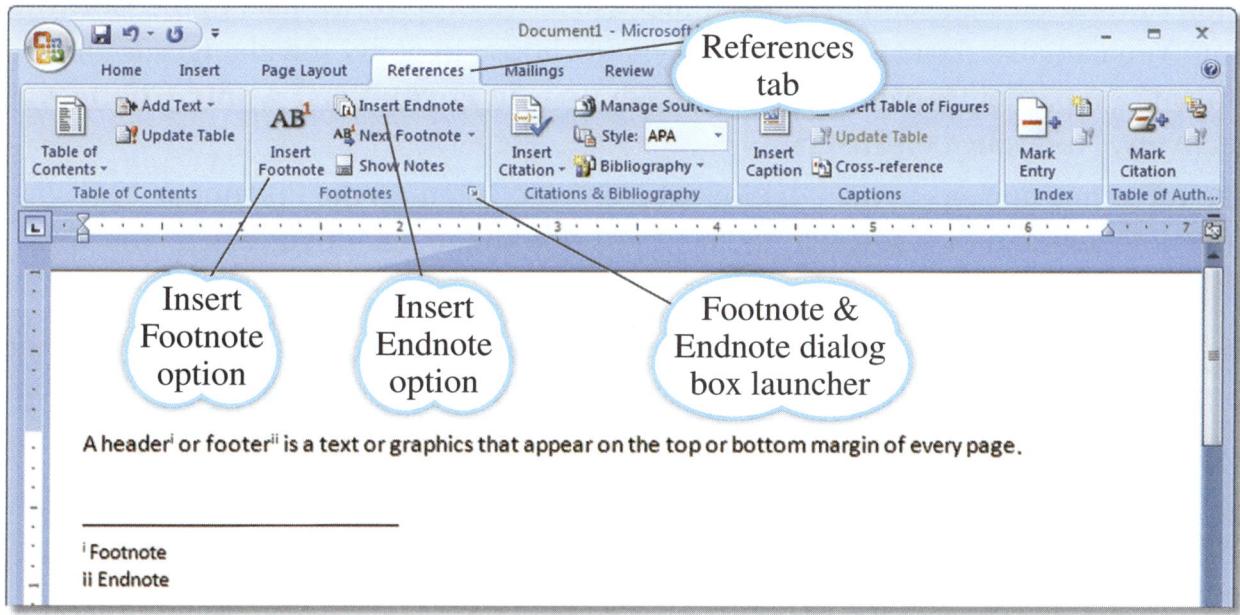

Fig. 4.6 *Inserting a note*

3. Click on the **Footnote & Endnote** dialog box launcher in the **Footnotes** group of the **Insert** tab to open the **Footnote and Endnote** dialog box (Fig. 4.7).

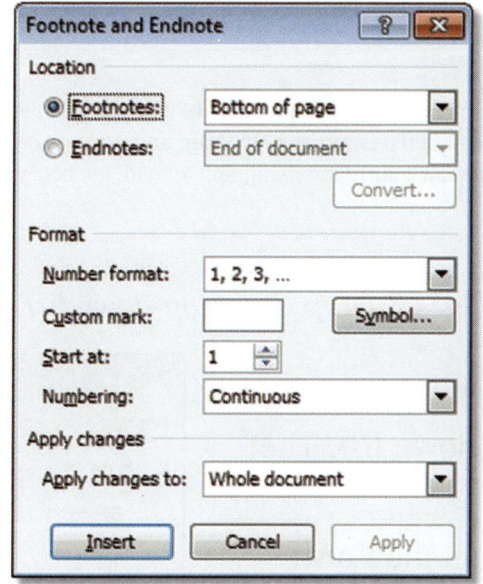 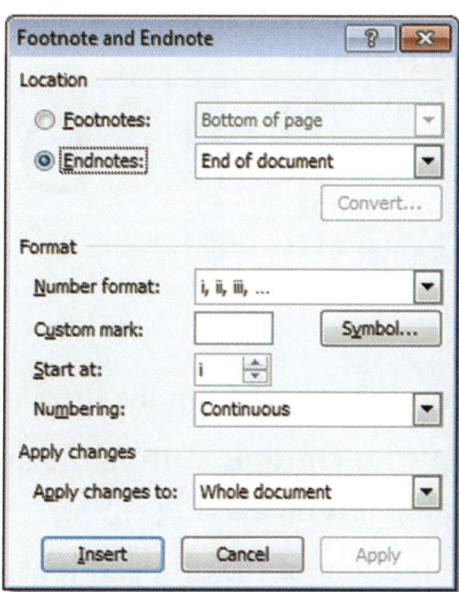

Fig. 4.7 *Footnote and Endnote dialog box*

FACT FILE

By default, the footnotes are numbered as 1, 2, 3 … and the endnotes as i, ii, iii … .

4. To create a footnote, click on the **Footnotes:** option and for the endnote click on the **Endnotes:** option in the **Location** section. It can even be formatted. You can select the location of footnotes and endnotes from the respective drop-down lists in the **Location** section. You can also format the numbering and choose to apply the changes to the whole document or a particular part of it using the options in **Format** and **Apply Changes** sections, respectively. Now, click on **Insert**.

5. A note reference appears at the position where you clicked on the document. You can now add the note text and then scroll to the next position in the document where you want to insert a footnote or an endnote.

 MS Word 2007 automatically applies the correct number format when additional footnotes or endnotes are inserted in a document.

Drop Cap

Drop Cap is a feature provided by MS Word in which the first character of the paragraph is bigger, and dropped on the subsequent lines of the paragraph to mark the beginning of the paragraph (as used here). You can use this feature while writing stories.

Follow these steps to use Drop Cap feature of MS Word 2007:

1. In the Word 2007 document, click on the position where you want to add the Drop Cap feature.

2. Click on **Insert** tab ⟹ **Text** group ⟹ **Drop Cap** drop-down list (Fig. 4.8).

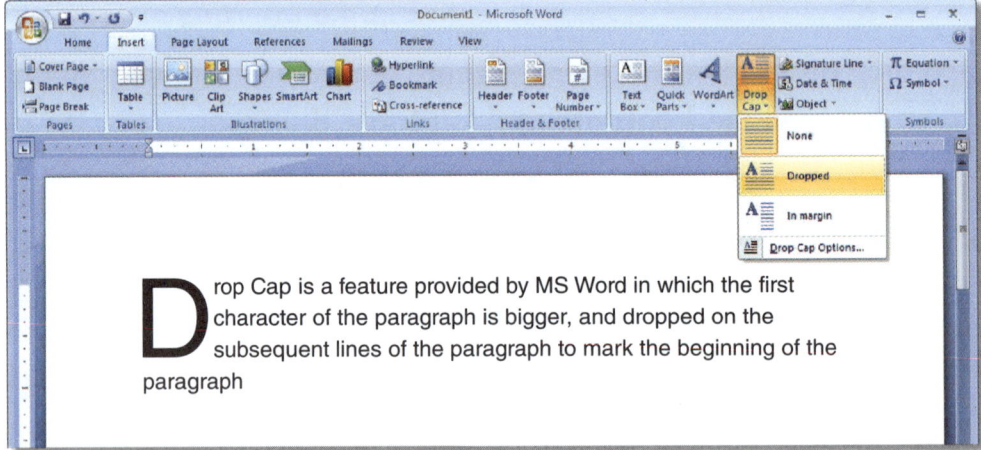

Fig. 4.8 *Drop Cap drop-down list*

3. Select the **Dropped** option from the drop-down list.

4. Click on **Drop Cap Options…** from the drop-down list. The **Drop Cap** dialog box opens (Fig. 4.9).

5. Select the desired font of the dropped letter from the **Font:** drop-down list in the **Options** section.

6. Select the desired option from the **Lines to drop:** list.

7. Increase the distance between the text and the dropped letter with the help of **Distance from text:** list.

8. Click on **OK**.

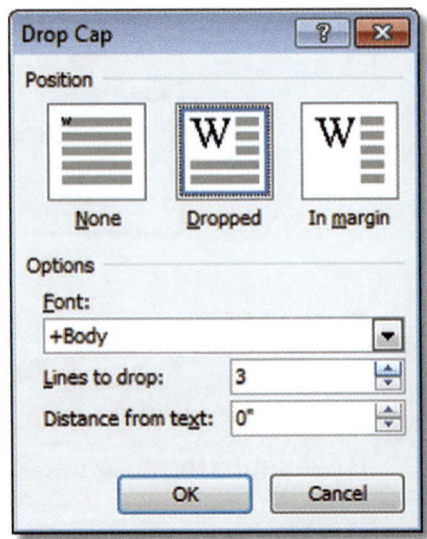

Fig. 4.9 *Drop Cap dialog box*

FACT FILE

You can use the Drop Cap feature only with the first character of a word and not the entire word.

Tab Stop

Tab Stop refers to a preset text position. The Tab Stop feature in MS Word enables the user to change the default distance covered by the Tab key for the preparation of a columnar data in MS Word.

Note: Press the **Tab** key to move the cursor half an inch forward in a MS Word document.

Inserting Tab Stop

Tab Stop can be inserted at any position on the ruler within the margins. When a Tab Stop is set, MS Word automatically removes the default Tab Stops to the left.

There are several types of Tabs that are available in MS Word 2007. A few are discussed here.

Left Tab: With this kind of Tab Stop, text or numbers are left-aligned in the column.

Right Tab: With this kind of Tab Stop, text or numbers are right-aligned in the column.

Center Tab: With this kind of Tab Stop, text or numbers are center-aligned in the column.

Decimal Tab: With this kind of Tab Stop, fractional figures are aligned in such a way that all the decimal points are vertically aligned.

Deleting Tab Stop

Select each tab and drag it towards the document to delete tab stops.

Let us create a list of friends (Fig. 4.10) to understand this concept.

To create this list, a few steps need to be followed. These are:

1. Select the **Left Tab** from the Tab Selector, placed on the left side of the ruler.

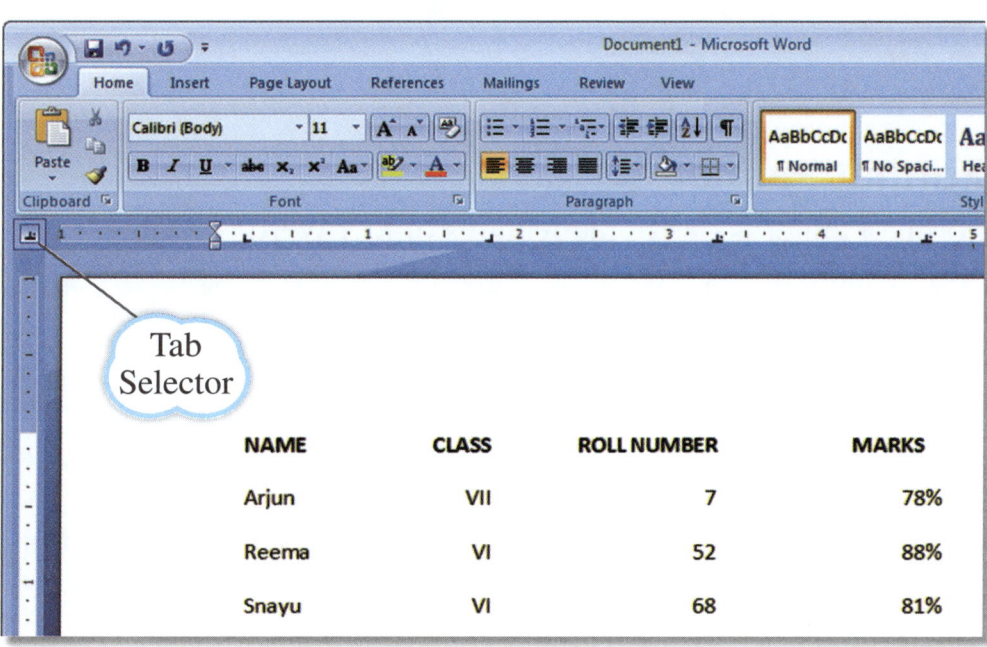

Fig. 4.10 *Inserting Tab Stop*

2. Click at the desired position on the **Horizontal Ruler** to define the location of the **Left Tab**. Type **NAME**.
3. Now, select the **Right Tab** from the Tab Selector.
4. Click at the desired position on the **Horizontal Ruler** to define the location of the **Right Tab**. Bring the cursor to **NAME** and press the **Tab** key, write **CLASS**.
5. Select the **Center Tab** from the Tab Selector.
6. Click at the desired position on the **Horizontal Ruler** to define the location of the **Center Tab**. Bring the cursor to **CLASS** and press the **Tab** key, write **ROLL NUMBER**.
7. Now, select the **Decimal Tab** from the Tab Selector.
8. Click at the desired position on the **Horizontal Ruler** to define the location of the **Decimal Tab**. Bring the cursor to **ROLL NUMBER** and press the **Tab** key, write **MARKS**.
9. Move to the new line and type the values for each column.
10. Move to the next column using **Tab** key.
11. Once the list is completed, delete Tab Stop.

Using Show/Hide Tool ¶

There are some non-printing characters that are used for displaying the formatting of a word document. They only appear on the screen and not in the printout. In order to display Word's non-printing characters, click on the **Show/Hide** ¶ option in the **Paragraph** group of the **Home** tab.

The following are some of the symbols representing the usage of the keyboard key at that location in the document. These are displayed when the Show/Hide button is ON.

Symbols	¶	.	→
Keys	Enter key	Space Bar	Tab key

Format Painter

Format Painter is one of the features of MS Word 2007 which allows the user to copy the format from one place to another.

Follow these steps to copy the format:

1. Place the cursor on the paragraph text that contains the formatting to be copied.
2. Click on **Home** tab ⇒ **Clipboard** group ⇒ **Format Painter** option.
3. The mouse pointer changes to 🖌I.
4. Now select the paragraph text on which the format is to be copied.

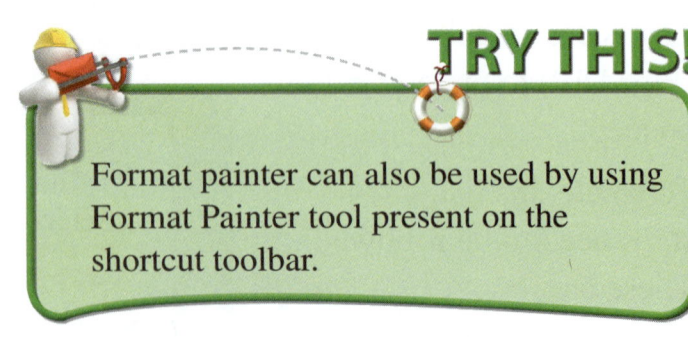

TRY THIS!
Format painter can also be used by using Format Painter tool present on the shortcut toolbar.

Note: Double-click on the **Format Painter** option to apply formatting at multiple places.

Columns

MS Word allows the user to display the data in the form of vertical columns in the same way as it appears in a newspaper. Already created document can also be converted into columns.

How to make columns in MS Word 2007

1. Select **Page Layout** tab ⟹ **Page Setup** group ⟹ **Columns** drop-down list (Fig. 4.11) and select the column style of your choice.

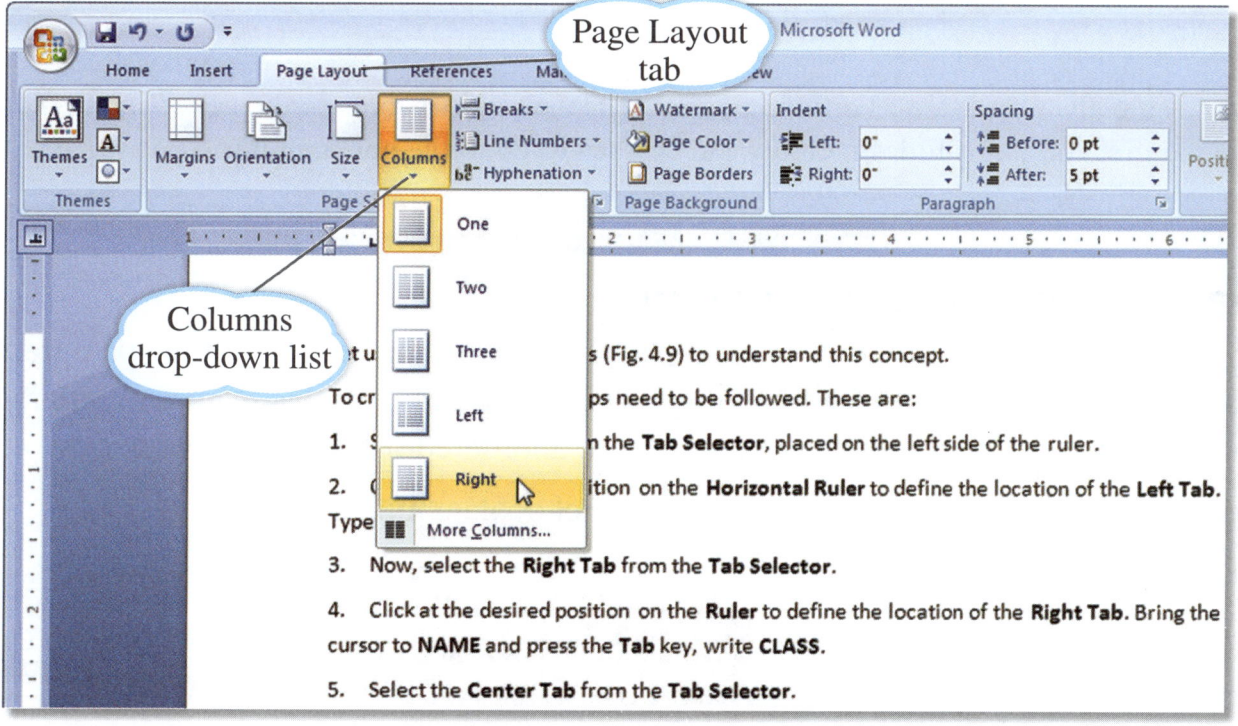

Fig. 4.11 *Inserting columns*

2. For choosing more column styles select, **More Columns…** option. The **Columns** dialog box opens (Fig. 4.12).

3. In the **Presets** section, select the desired number of columns, say, 'Three' with the help of **Number of columns:** list.

4. To give equal width between the three columns created, click to tick the **Equal column width** checkbox in the **Width and spacing** section.

5. If **Equal column width** checkbox is not selected, then select the desired width and spacing between the columns from **Col#:**, **Width:** and **Spacing:** lists.

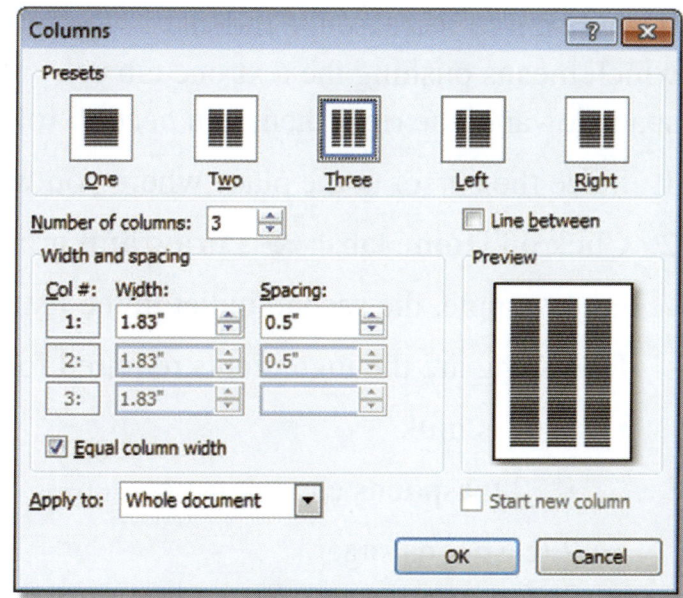

Fig. 4.12 *Creating Columns*

6. In **Apply to:** drop-down list, select **This point forward** option to apply this effect in the document from current position onwards or else select **Whole document**.
7. If **Line between** option checkbox is selected then a line will be visible between the columns in the document.
8. Click on **OK**.

FACT FILE

Columns are always treated as different pages. The cursor will come to the next column only when the first column is full. Enter key can be used to go to the next column.

Increase or Decrease Indentation

Hanging indent is the way of representing a paragraph when the first line of the paragraph is more towards the left side than the following ones. You usually use this feature in ordered or unordered lists in documents. For example, see the unordered list given below.

Following are the ingredients required for making chocolate milkshake:

- 1 glass milk
- 2 teaspoons chocolate powder
- 2 teaspoons sugar
- Blender

FACT FILE

There are 9 levels of indentation in MS Word. This means you can decrease or increase the indents of the paragraph to 9 levels.

How to increase indent

If you want to increase the indent, which means pushing the text one tab space towards the right then, you need to follow these steps:

1. Place the cursor at the place where you wish to increase indentation.
2. Click on **Home** tab ⟹ **Paragraph** group ⟹ **Increase Indent** option .

   For example, the second bullet in the list given below shows increased indentation.

   Following are the ingredients required for making chocolate milkshake:

   - 1 glass milk
     - 2 teaspoons chocolate powder
   - 2 teaspoons sugar
   - Blender

How to decrease indent

If you want to decrease the indent, which means pushing the text one tab space towards the left, then you need to follow these steps.

1. Place the cursor over the place where you wish to decrease indentation.
2. Click on **Home** tab ⟹ **Paragraph** group ⟹ **Decrease Indent** option.

Thesaurus

Microsoft Office has some features that help you to look up for meanings/synonyms (words with similar meaning) for a given word. One of these features is Thesaurus. The basic function of Thesaurus is to look up synonyms for a particular word. It is just like a dictionary, and can be used for replacing a word with one of its synonyms.

Follow these steps to use the Thesaurus in MS Word 2007:

1. Select the word for which you want an alternative word.
2. Click on the **Review** tab ⟹ **Proofing** group ⟹ **Thesaurus** option (Fig. 4.13).

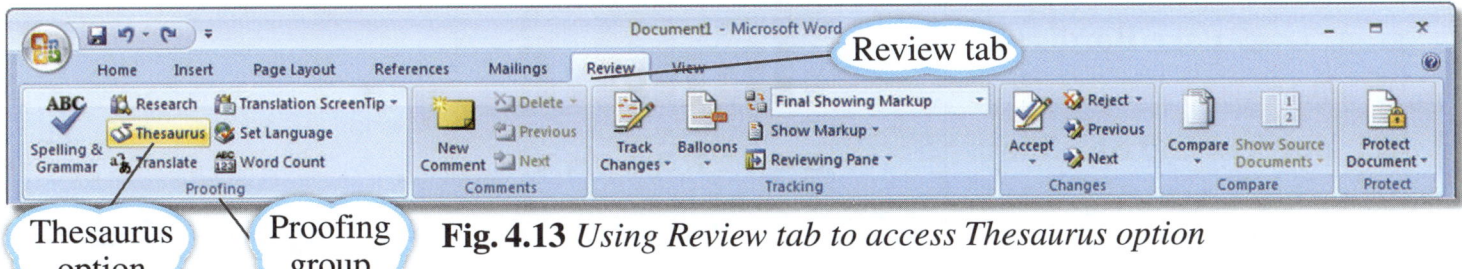

Fig. 4.13 *Using Review tab to access Thesaurus option*

3. The **Research** task pane appears (Fig. 4.14).
4. The **Search for:** field displays the word you have selected and for which you want another word. It also contains the drop-down list of all reference books. Here, **Thesaurus: English (United Kingdom)** is selected.
5. Below it, a list of the suggested synonyms appears. To use one of the words, point to it, click the down arrow key. Click **Insert** or **Copy** from the drop-down list.

ACTIVITY

Create the following list in a Word 2007 document.

1. Computer Science
2. Social Science
   o Civics
   o Geography
   o History
3. Computer Science
   o Social Science
   o Civics
   o Geography
4. History

Fig. 4.14 *Research task pane*

Borders and Shading

MS Word allows users to add borders and apply shading options to a page and the selected text. A border is a line or a pattern surrounding the page or a cell in the margin area. You can set the text apart from the rest of the document by adding borders and shading.

Applying shading

The steps to apply shading to a page in MS Word 2007 are given here:

1. Select the paragraph(s) where you wish to apply shading.
2. Click on **Page Layout** tab ⟹ **Page Background** group ⟹ **Page Borders** option.
3. The **Borders and Shading** dialog box opens (Fig. 4.15). Click on the **Shading** tab.
4. Select the color of your choice in the **Fill** section.

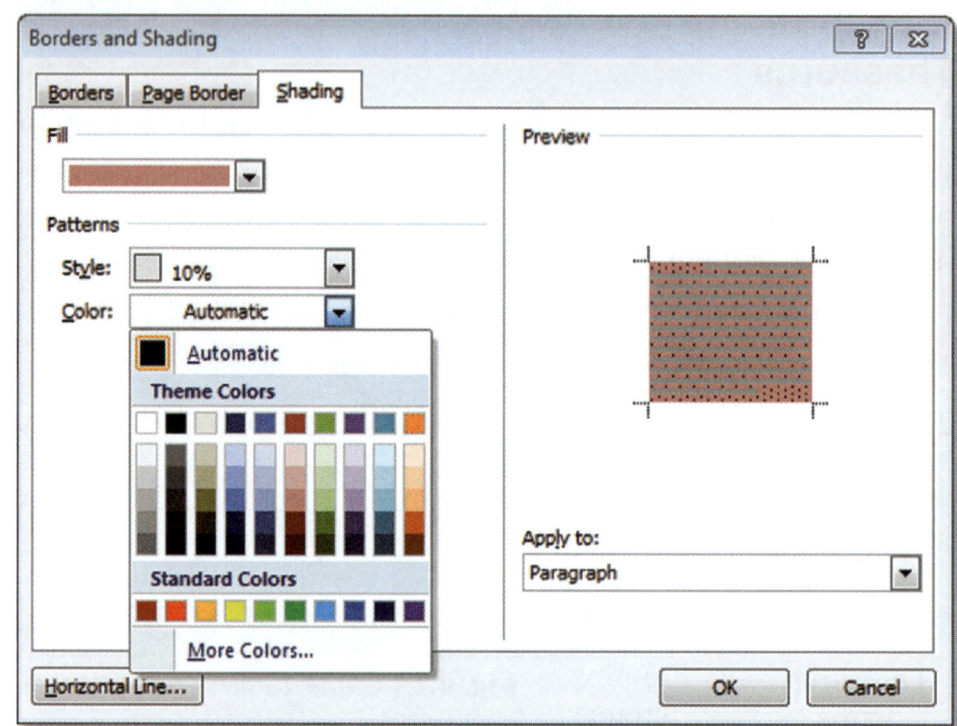

Fig. 4.15 *Borders and Shading dialog box*

5. Select appropriate options from the **Style:** and **Color:** drop-down lists in the **Patterns** section.
6. Select the desired option from the **Apply to:** drop-down list in **Preview** section.
7. Click on **OK**.

Removing shading

The steps to remove shading from a page in MS Word 2007 are given here:

1. Select the paragraph from where the shading has to be removed.
2. Click on **Page Layout** tab ⟹ **Page Background** group ⟹ **Page Borders** option.
3. The **Borders and Shading** dialog box appears.
4. Click on the **Shading** tab.
5. In the **Fill** section, click on **No Color** option from the drop-down list.
6. In the **Patterns** section, select **Clear** option from the **Style:** drop-down list.
7. Click **OK**.

Page Setup and Margins

Page margins are the blank spaces near the edges of the page. Texts and graphics are normally confined or set over the printable area inside the margins. However, some items can be positioned on the margins. For example, headers, footers, and page numbers.

You generally work using the default Page Margins but you can alter them using the following steps:

1. Click on **Page Layout** tab ⟹ **Page Setup** group ⟹ **Page Setup** dialog box launcher.
2. The **Page Setup** dialog box appears (Fig. 4.16). It has three tabs: **Margins**, **Paper** and **Layout**.
3. Select the **Margins** tab.

Fig. 4.16 *Page Setup dialog box*

4. In the **Margins** tab, in the **Margins** section, select the desired option from:
   - **Top:, Bottom:, Left:** and **Right:** lists to increase or decrease sizes of the four margins.
   - **Gutter:** list to add extra space to the side or top margin of a document you plan to bind. A gutter margin ensures that text does not hide due to binding (Fig. 4.17).

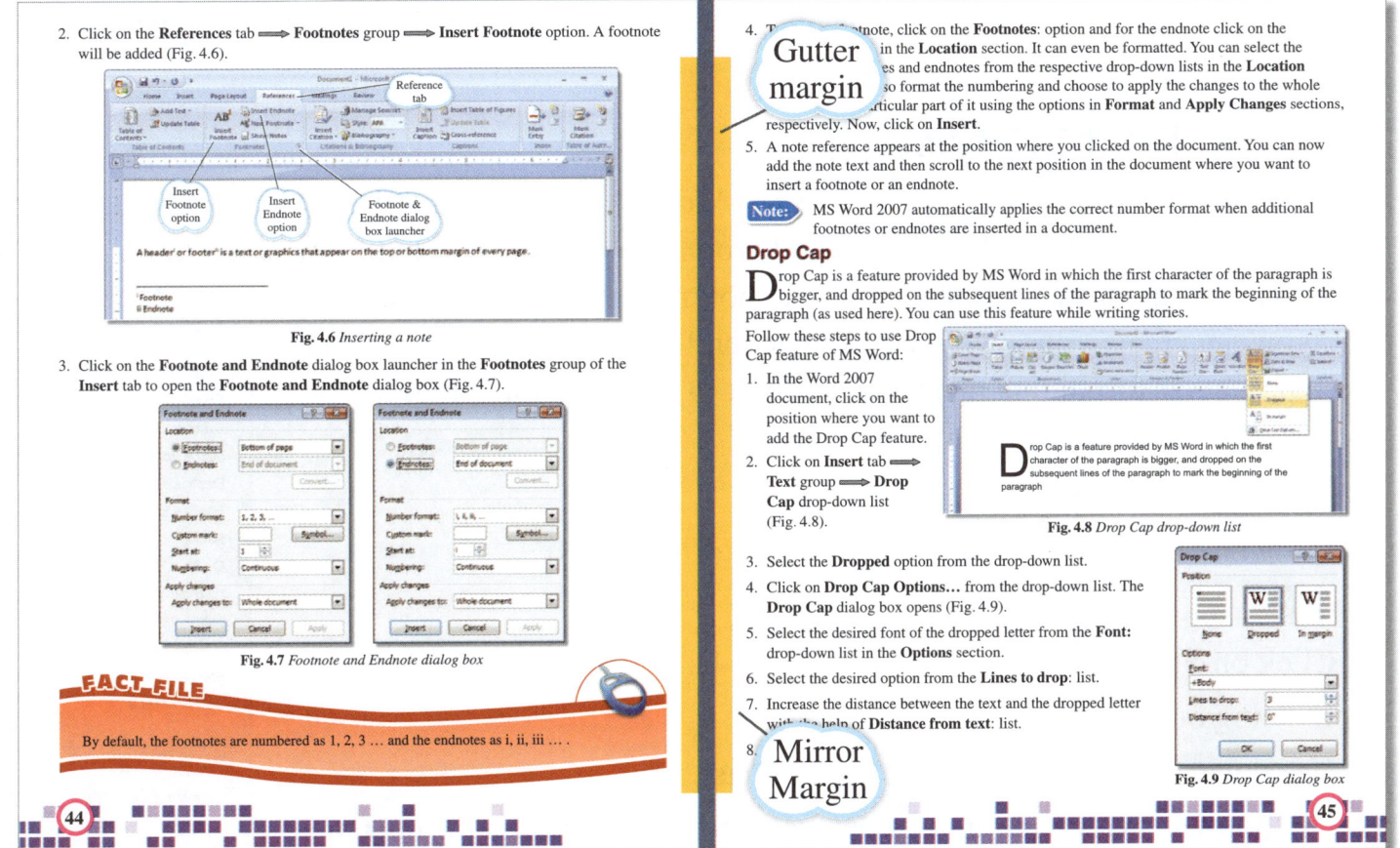

Fig. 4.17 *Book fold View*

5. In the **Orientation** section, select:
   - **Portrait** option to print the document vertically.
   - **Landscape** option to print the document horizontally.
6. In the **Pages** section, select the appropriate option from **Multiple pages:** drop-down list:
   - **Normal** option for getting the normal document.
   - **Mirror margins** option for setting the facing pages in a document such as books, magazines, etc.
   - **2 pages per sheet** option for printing two pages on one sheet.
   - **Book fold** option for creating booklets with the specific number of pages.
7. In the **Preview** section, select either of the options from **Apply to**: drop-down list:
   - The **Whole document** option
   - **This Point forward** option
   - **This section** option
8. Click on **Default…** button to reset the default values for the Page Margin. When you click on this button then you will get the **Microsoft Office Word** dialog box (Fig. 4.18). Click on **Yes** to apply the default settings.
9. Click on **OK** for applying these changes in the current document.

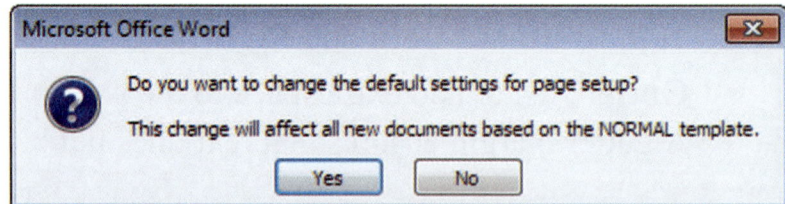

Fig. 4.18 *Microsoft Office Word dialog box*

Applying Built-in Styles

Styles are used for formatting the text in MS Word. A **style** is a set of formatting instructions. In MS Word 2007, you have a number of built-in formatting styles. If the available styles do not match your requirements then you can create your own style. The general idea is to modify a style to suit a particular formatting need, and apply it to the text or a paragraph.

Follow these steps to apply built-in style:

1. Select the text or paragraph.
2. Click on **Home** tab ⟹ **Styles** group ⟹ **Styles** list.

   Click on **Styles** dialog box launcher (Fig. 4.19).

From here you can:

- Use down arrow key to choose from the list.
- Use **Show Preview** checkbox to see the effect of the style on the document.
- Use **Clear All** option to remove all styles from the document.

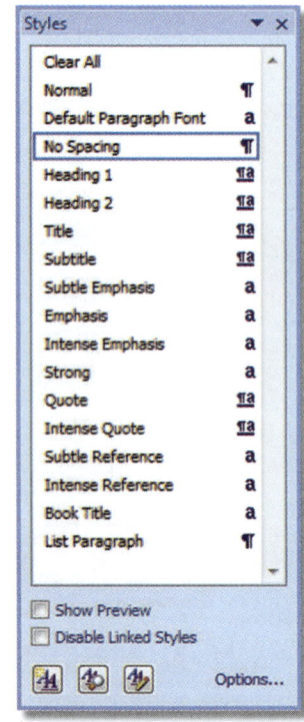

Fig. 4.19 *Styles Pane*

Quick key

Apply Heading 1	**Alt + Ctrl + 1**	Normal Style	**Ctrl + Shift + N**
Apply Heading 2	**Alt + Ctrl + 2**	Paste Format	**Ctrl + Shift + V**
Apply Heading 3	**Alt + Ctrl + 3**	Thesaurus	**Shift + F7**
Apply List Bullet	**Ctrl + Shift + L**	Insert Footnote	**Ctrl + Alt + F**
Cancel	**Esc**	Show/Hide option	**Ctrl + Shift + ***
Hanging Indent	**Ctrl + T**	Insert Endnote	**Ctrl + Alt + D**
Copy Format	**Ctrl + Shift + C**	Styles	**Alt + Ctrl + Shift + S**

ACTIVITY

Design a cover for your school magazine. You may make use of the features of MS Word 2007 learnt in this chapter to do so. The cover page design should have the following.

1. An interesting layout
2. Attractive page borders
3. Title of the magazine
4. Name of the school and class at the bottom of the page (Footer)
5. Month and year must be highlighted at the top right side (Header)
6. Implement the gutter margin on the left position

Apply in-built styles of MS Word 2007 wherever possible.

GLOSSARY

Drop Cap: It is a feature in which the first character of the paragraph is bigger and dropped on the subsequent lines of the paragraph.

Endnote: It is a citation of sources which are given at the end of a document.

Footer: It is the text that appears at the bottom margin of every page.

Footnotes: It is a comment printed at the bottom of a page which gives extra information about something that has been written on that page.

Hanging Indent: It is when the first line of the paragraph is more towards the left side than the following ones.

Header: It is the text that appears at the top margin of every page.

Mirror margins: It is for setting the facing pages in a document such as books.

Page margins: It is the blank space near the edges of the page.

Style: It is a set of formatting instructions.

Tab Stop: It refers to a preset text position.

Theasurus: Its basic function is to look up synonyms for a particular word.

NOW YOU KNOW

1. Page numbers are helpful in documents that have more than one page.
2. The non-printing characters are visible on the screen using Show/Hide tool.
3. Format Painter allows the user to copy the formatting from one place to another.
4. MS Word allows the user to display the data in the form of vertical columns.
5. You can increase and decrease indent using the corresponding options.
6. MS Word allows the user to apply borders and shading effects to a page and selected text.
7. Styles are used for formatting text in MS Word and it also offers a number of built-in formatting styles.

EXERCISE

A   Fill in the blanks.

1. ………………………………… section is used for placing the text that appears in the beginning of every page.
2. ………………………………… represents the first line hanging over the rest of the lines.
3. ………………………………… option copies the format from one place to another.
4. ………………………………… refers to a preset text position.
5. The ………………………………… is for looking up synonyms for a particular word.

B **State whether the following sentences are True or False.**

1. You cannot alter the default setting of page margins.

2. Only pages can be formatted with borders in MS Word 2007.

3. Shading can be applied using Borders and Shading dialog box.

4. You can also give your own styles besides using built-in styles.

5. Drop Cap feature is not of any use in MS Word 2007.

C **Match the following:**

1.	Mirror margins	a.	It can be applied to a text or a paragraph.
2.	Hanging Indents	b.	The fractional figures are aligned.
3.	Decimal Tab Stop	c.	The text is right aligned.
4.	Right Tab Stop	d.	It is used for making books and magazines.
5.	Shading	e.	The first line is a little more towards the left than the following lines.

D **Answer the following questions.**

1. What is the purpose of a Tab key? How can you change its default shift? **HOTS**

2. Name the different margins available in Page Setup dialog box.

3. Why do you use page numbers in a document?

4. Where do you add a footnote and an endnote?

5. How can you insert page numbers in a MS Word 2007 document?

LAB WORK

A. Create a comprehensive travel brochure for a travel destination of your choice. Make it four columned in the Landscape orientation of MS Word 2007 document. This brochure should include information on:

1. the location
2. how to reach there
3. the recreational activities available
4. travel recommendations
5. different kinds of travel packages offered.

B. Make a report on your favourite singer. The report should include:

1. a title page
2. table of contents
3. biography of the singer
4. a list of his/her famous songs
5. a list of awards won by the singer
6. a gallery page showcasing his/her photographs, etc.

MS Office 2010 Updates

- In **MS Word 2010**, before you share any document, you can use the **Document Inspector** to ensure that the document you are sharing does not contain any hidden content or personal information. The **Document Inspector** can find and remove information in headers and footers, comments, hidden text, etc.

- Go to the **File** tab and click on **Check for Issues** option in the **Prepare** section. A submenu opens up. Select **Inspect Document** option and the **Document Inspector** opens up. Select the content you want to inspect and click on the **Inspect** button on lower-right corner of the box.

TEACHER'S NOTES

1. Analyse the different features of a newspaper article like indent, columns, borders, etc. Ask the students to write an article on the topic of their choice and use the different advanced features of MS Word 2007. They can also add footnotes and endnotes.

2. Share with the students an unedited procedure for preparing a cup of tea. Ask the students to edit it in MS Word 2007 based on the features they learned.

5 MS Word 2007 – Using Mail Merge Features

LEARNING OBJECTIVES

You will learn about:
1. Mail Merge
2. uses of Mail Merge
3. creating the Main document
4. creating a merge document

Mail Merge

Mail Merge is an important and a very useful feature of MS Word. Mail Merge means merging two files or documents. If you have to send a common letter or an invitation to several recipients, then mail merge is a good option. In Mail Merge, you need a data source (to have variable data) file and a word document (to have common data) to form a third file, that is, the merged data which can be used for mailing purpose. Mail Merge is commonly used to create personalised form letters. For example, a birthday party invitation card can be created and then merged with the addresses in the address book to create multiple invitations without typing each of them individually. It is important to understand the following terms before you learn how to create a merged document.

Main document

Main document is the document which has a common data like a letter or an invitation card that needs to be created in multiple numbers. It will be merged with the data file. This document can be the active document or can be created later on.

Address book/Data source

Address book is the tabular data arranged in the form of rows and columns. It is also known as a data source. It is merged with the main document.

Form letters

The final letter/invitation, etc. will be obtained after the data source file and the main document have been merged. The new document formed is also known as a **merged document**.

Uses of Mail Merge

By using mail merge, you can create:

A set of labels or envelopes: Here the destination address varies but the address of the sender is the same.

A set of form letters, email messages or faxes: The basic content is the same in all the letters, messages or faxes along with the same sender address, but each contains different personal details of the receivers.

A set of numbered coupons: The coupons are identical except that each contains a unique number.

Creating the Main Document

You can use the Mail Merge option on a blank document or on one that you have already created.

Here, by using Mail Merge on a blank document you will learn to create letters. You can also create email messages, envelopes, labels and directory.

Follow the steps given below to merge the documents for creating letters.

1. Open a new MS Word 2007 document. Click on the **Mailings** tab.
2. In the **Start Mail Merge** group, click on the **Start Mail Merge** drop-down list (Fig. 5.1).

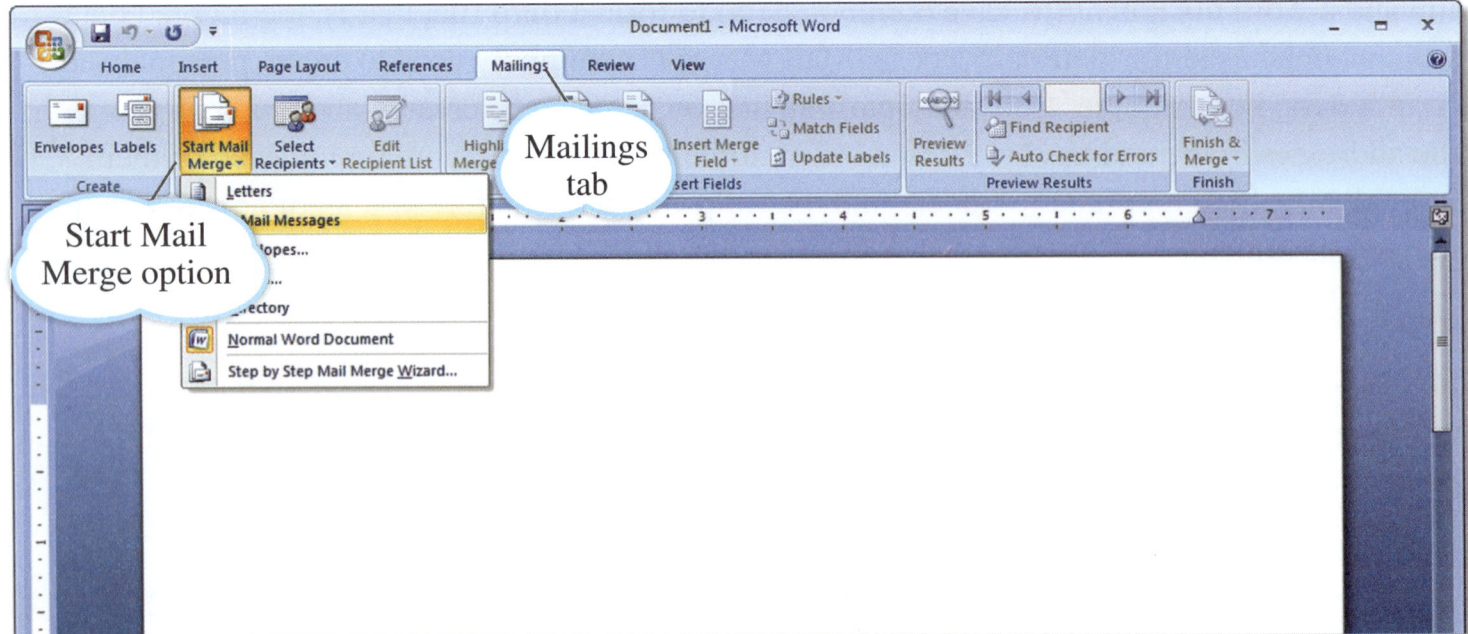

Fig. 5.1 *Opening Mail Merge in MS Word 2007*

3. Select **Step by Step Mail Merge Wizard…** option from the drop-down list.
4. **Mail Merge** task pane will appear on the right side of the screen (Fig. 5.2). Select the **Letters** option from the given list.

Note: Letters are also the default selection for document type in MS Word 2007.

5. At the bottom of the task pane, click **Next: Starting document** under the **Step 1 of 6** section (Fig. 5.3).
6. Select **Use the current document** option as the starting document (Fig. 5.4). Use this selection in order to proceed with the blank document.

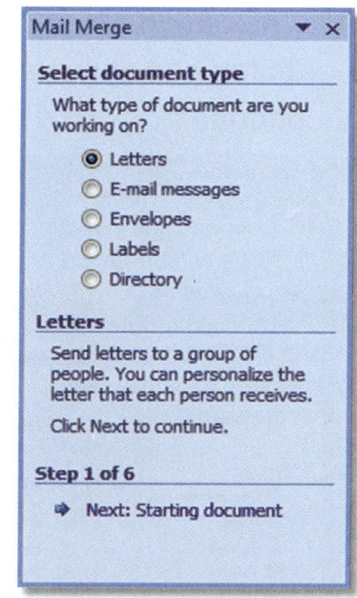

Fig. 5.2 *Selecting document type*

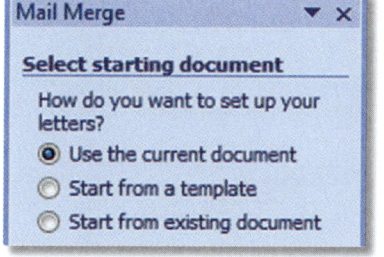

Fig. 5.3 *Step 1 of 6 section of the task pane*

Fig. 5.4 *Selecting starting document*

Note:
- **Use the current document:** It is used where a new letter or an already opened letter is to be used.
- **Start from a template:** It is used when a ready-to-use mail merge template is to be used.
- **Start from existing document:** It is used when an existing document is used and changes are made to it.

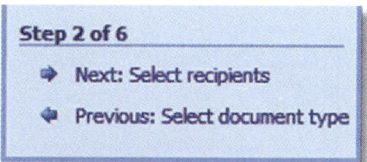

7. In the **Step 2 of 6** section in the task pane, click **Next: Select recipients** (Fig. 5.5).

Fig. 5.5 *Step 2 of 6 of the Task Pane*

Note: As you proceed through the Mail Merge steps in the task pane, you can go back and forth at any time you desire using the **Previous:** option in **Step** section of the task pane. This makes mail merge logical and handy.

Selecting your merged file

1. Once you have followed the above steps, select the list of recipients from the **Select recipients** section for merging them with your mail (Fig. 5.6). Here, you will **Use an existing list** that has been created using MS Excel 2007 spreadsheet. You can also use Outlook mail contacts, tables in MS Word 2007 or several other sources.

Fig. 5.6 *Selecting recipients*

2. Click the **Browse…** option in the **Use an existing list** section. The **Select Data Source** dialog box appears (Fig. 5.7). Select the database file and its type, and click on the **Open** button.

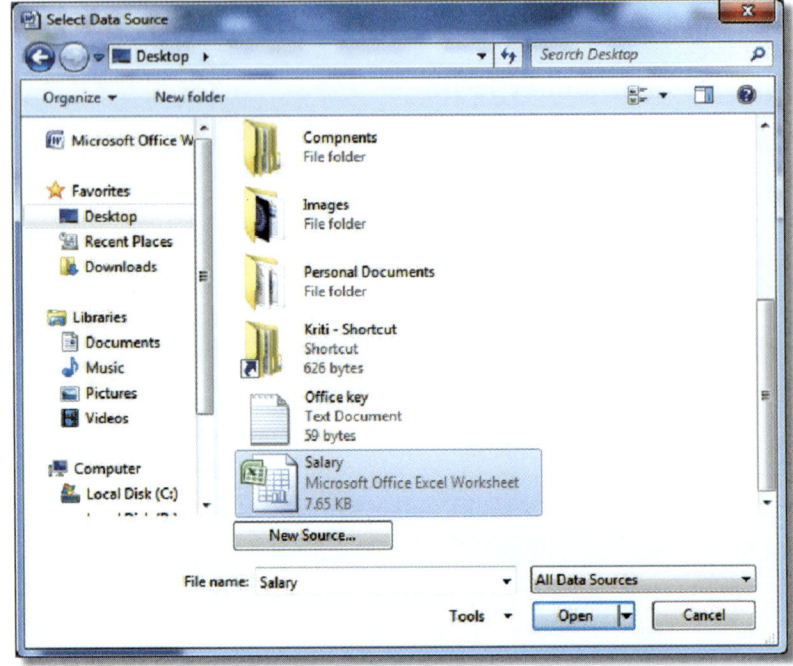

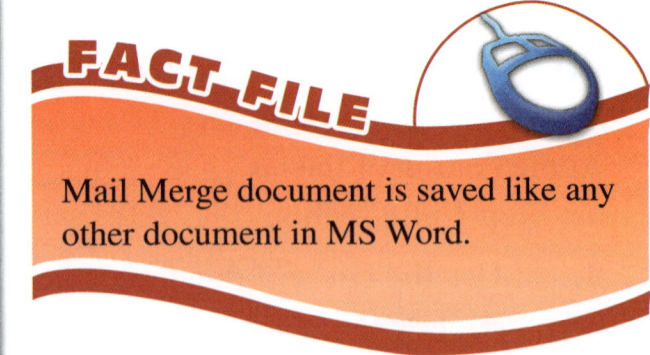

Mail Merge document is saved like any other document in MS Word.

Fig. 5.7 *Select Data Source dialog box*

3. Once the data source is selected, the **Mail Merge Recipients** dialog box appears (Fig. 5.8). Click to select the required data from the table and click on **OK**.

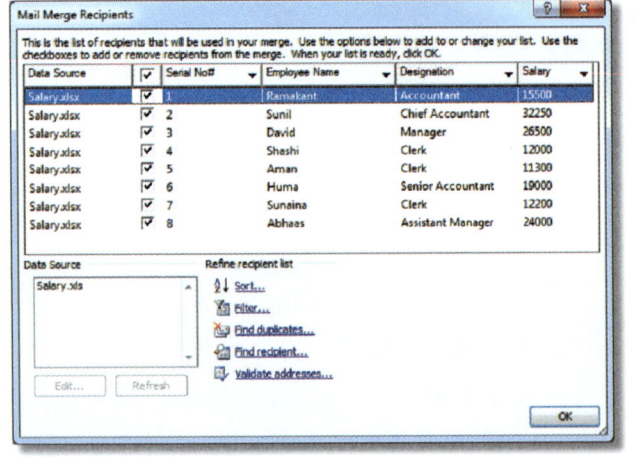

Fig. 5.8 *Mail Merge Recipients dialog box*

4. In the section **Use an existing list**, you will notice that the **Browse…** selection has been replaced with different options (Fig. 5.9). The task pane now indicates the MS Excel 2007 database (or any other source) you selected and allows you to edit the list which appeared when you made this selection.

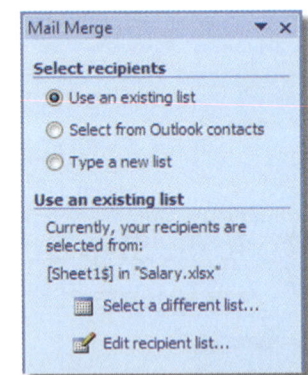

Fig. 5.9 *Use an existing list section*

Creating the Merged Document

Having selected your data source, you are now ready to create your Mail Merge document.

1. Look at the **Step 3 of 6** section of the task pane and click **Next: Write your letter** (Fig. 5.10).

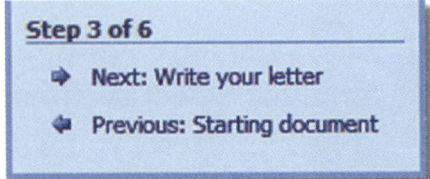

Fig. 5.10 *Step 3 of 6 section of the Task Pane*

2. You will now be taken to the **Write your letter** section (Fig. 5.11). Write the main contents of your letter in the empty document of MS Word 2007.

Fig. 5.11 *Writing your letter*

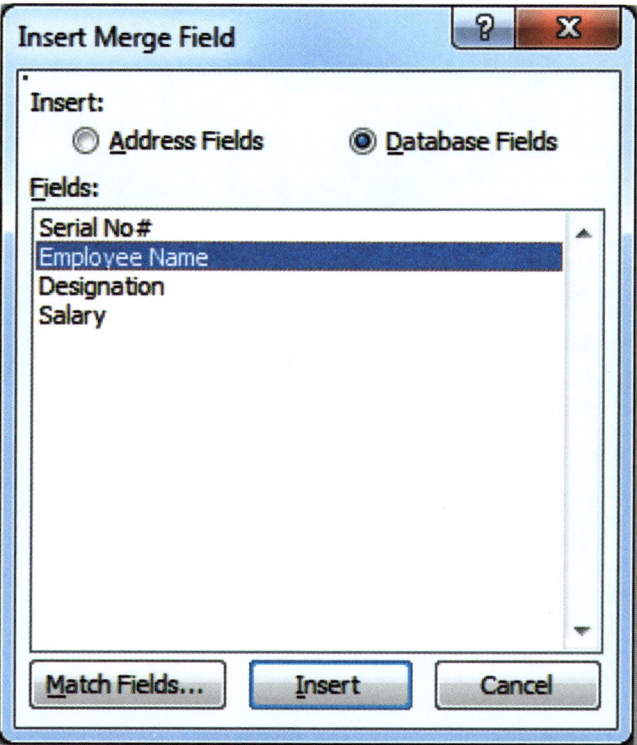

Fig. 5.12 *Insert Merge Field option box*

3. Click on the MS Word 2007 document and place the cursor where you want the first name to appear.

4. In the task pane click on the **More items...** option. **Insert Merge Field** dialog box will appear (Fig. 5.12).

5. Click on the desired field that should appear in the letter. Select **Insert** and then click on **Close**.

This is how the data source or the address book is merged with the main document and the data from the address book will now appear in the merged file.

Previewing your documents

To preview the merged documents follow the steps given here:

1. Click the **Next: Preview your letters** option in the **Step 4 of 6** section of the task pane (Fig. 5.13).

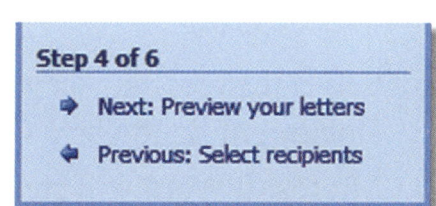

Fig. 5.13 *Step 4 of 6 section of the task pane*

2. You can now browse your address and greetings by clicking the arrow on the right and left of **Recipient:** under the **Preview your letters** section (Fig. 5.14).

 **Note:** As you browse through your documents, if you see the one you wish to remove, you can click the **Exclude this recipient** button in the **Make changes** section.

3. Click on **Next: Complete the merge** option in the **Step 5 of 6** section of the task pane.

4. Task pane now shows the **Complete the merge** section (Fig. 5.15).

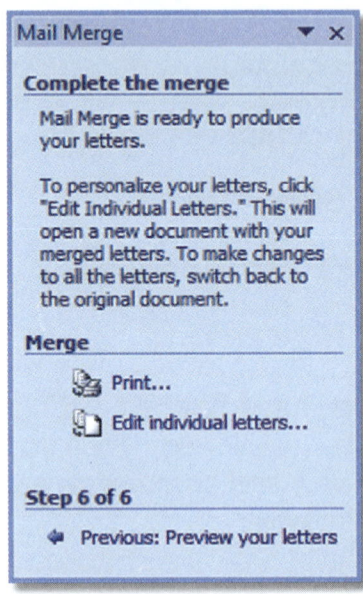

Fig. 5.14 *Step 5 of 6 section of the task pane*

Fig. 5.15 *Completing the merge*

5. Click on **Edit individual letters…** option in the **Merge** section of the task pane. The **Merge to New Document** option box opens (Fig. 5.16).

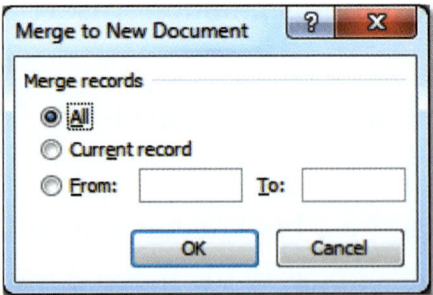

Fig. 5.16 *The merged document*

6. Select the records you want to merge in the **Merge records** section of the **Merge to New Document** dialog box. Click **OK**.

7. Microsoft Word will create a new merged document.

8. To personalise individual documents, scroll to the information you want to edit, and make your changes.

9. Print or save the document just as any other regular word document.

Dear Ramakant,

You are cordially invited to a tea party on the eve of retirement of our Chief Finance Officer, Mr. Kushal Gandhi.

Date: 24 July, 2013
Time: 5:30 p.m.
Venue: 3rd floor, Company Head Office

We look forward to seeing you there.

Regards,

S.R. Das
Human Resource Manager

Dear Sunil,

You are cordially invited to a tea party on the eve of retirement of our Chief Finance Officer, Mr. Kushal Gandhi.

Date: 24 July, 2013
Time: 5:30 p.m.
Venue: 3rd floor, Company Head Office

We look forward to seeing you there.

Regards,

S.R. Das
Human Resource Manager

Dear David,

You are cordially invited to a tea party on the eve of retirement of our Chief Finance Officer, Mr. Kushal Gandhi.

Date: 24 July, 2013
Time: 5:30 p.m.
Venue: 3rd floor, Company Head Office

We look forward to seeing you there.

Regards,

S.R. Das
Human Resource Manager

ACTIVITY

Place the six steps to create a merged document in a correct order on the ladder.

- Complete the merge
- Select starting document
- Preview your letters
- Write your letter
- Select the document type
- Select recipients

GLOSSARY

Address book/Data source: It is the tabular data arranged in the form of rows and columns.

Mail merge: It is the process of merging two files or documents.

Main document: It is the document consisting of a common data that needs to be created in multiple numbers.

Merged document: It is the final document obtained by merging the data source file and the main document.

NOW YOU KNOW

1. Using mail merge, you can create a set of labels or envelopes, a set of form letters, email messages, faxes, or a set of numbered coupons.

2. Form letter is the final invitation card that will be obtained after the data source file and the main document are merged. It is also known as a merged document.

3. For merging mail, use Start Mail Merge drop-down list in the Start Mail Merge group of the Mailings tab.

EXERCISE

A Fill in the blanks.

1. ………………..…… is the process of merging the main document and the data source.

2. Mail Merge is used for creating ……………………..…… , ……………………..……., etc.

3. ……………………..…… can also be taken from the active window.

4. Another name for address book is ……………………..……

5. ……………………..…… to display Mail Merge.

B Give one word for:

1. Merging two files or documents.

2. The tabular data arranged in rows and columns.

3. The document consisting of a common data that needs to be created in multiple numbers.

4. The option in the Mail Merge task pane used when the address book is already created.

5. The dialog box that helps you to insert the fields in the current active document.

C Match the following.

1.	Mailings tab	a.	Can be created in MS Excel
2.	Select document type	b.	An invitation letter
3.	Main document	c.	Mail Merge option
4.	Merged file	d.	Letters, envelops, etc.
5.	Address book	e.	The invitation letter with friend's details

D Answer the following questions.

1. What do you understand by the term Mail Merge?
2. How can Mail Merge help you in everyday life? Give two examples.
3. Write the steps on how a merged document is created after the desired document has been selected.
4. Name the software where an address book can be created.
5. List the different data sources that can be used in Mail Merge.

LAB WORK

A. Create a Diwali greeting card for sending it across to your relatives and friends.
B. Create a notice about a computer science quiz on behalf of your teacher. Send the notice to all your classmates using Mail Merge.

TEACHER'S NOTES

1. Discuss with the students about the benefits of using Mail Merge in the professional world.
2. Ask the students to create a thank you note for their relatives and friends who attended their birthday party last weekend.

6 Advanced PowerPoint 2007

SNAP RECAP

1. You can add and format styles in PowerPoint.
2. Editing a slide requires moving and duplicating text.
3. All formats like font, size, font color, etc. can be copied easily using Format Painter.
4. Graphics can be used for making a presentation more interesting.
5. Slide transition means moving from one slide to another during a presentation.
6. Slide Show runs the slides in 'full screen' mode.

LEARNING OBJECTIVES

You will learn about:
1. creating a presentation using a template
2. creating a presentation using themes
3. Photo Album
4. slide master
5. Custom Animation
6. inserting charts and tables
7. creating hyperlinks
8. reusing slides

Introduction

In MS PowerPoint 2007, you can create presentations using templates or themes, create photo album presentations, modify master slide, add custom animations, charts, tables, hyperlinks, and reuse slides.

Creating a Presentation Using a Template

In MS PowerPoint 2007, a template is a design or a pattern of a slide or group of slides. These templates contain layouts, theme colors, theme fonts, theme effects, background styles, and even content.

Custom templates can be created, stored and used any number of times. You can also share these custom templates with other users. Some free templates are also available online for use.

Steps to create a presentation based on a design template are:

1. Click on the **Office Button** and select **New** option from the drop-down list.
2. The **New Presentation** dialog box appears. Select **Installed Templates** option in the **Templates** section (Fig. 6.1) in the left pane.

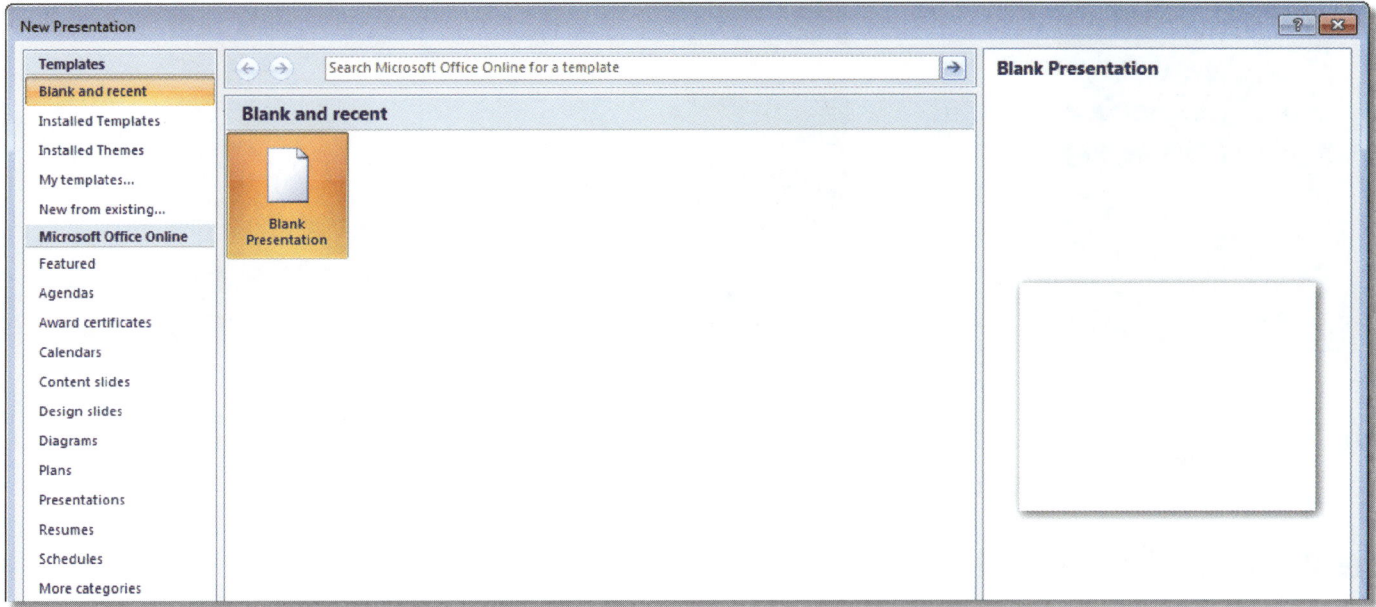

Fig. 6.1 *New Presentation dialog box*

3. Choose a template design from the given set of options in the **Installed Templates** section in the middle pane and click on **Create** button. (Fig. 6.2).

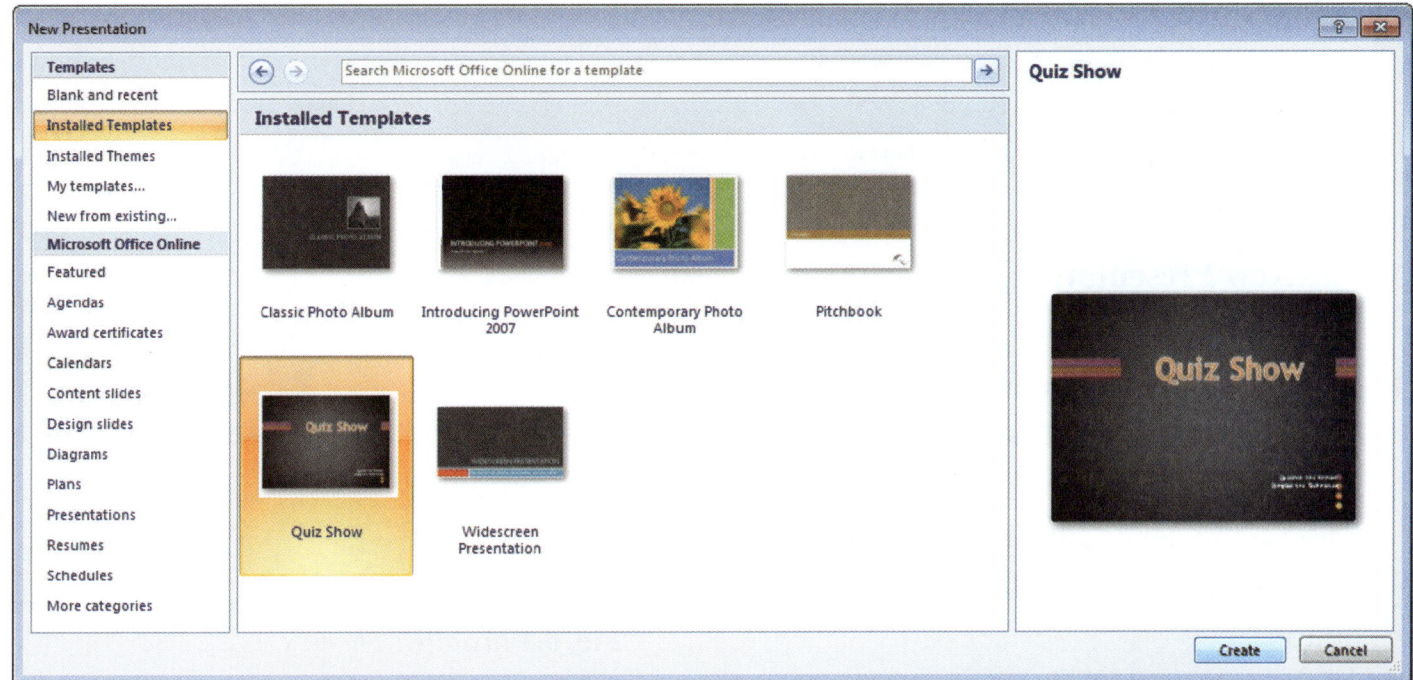

Fig. 6.2 *Installed Templates*

4. The first slide of the blank presentation opens with the template selected (Fig. 6.3).

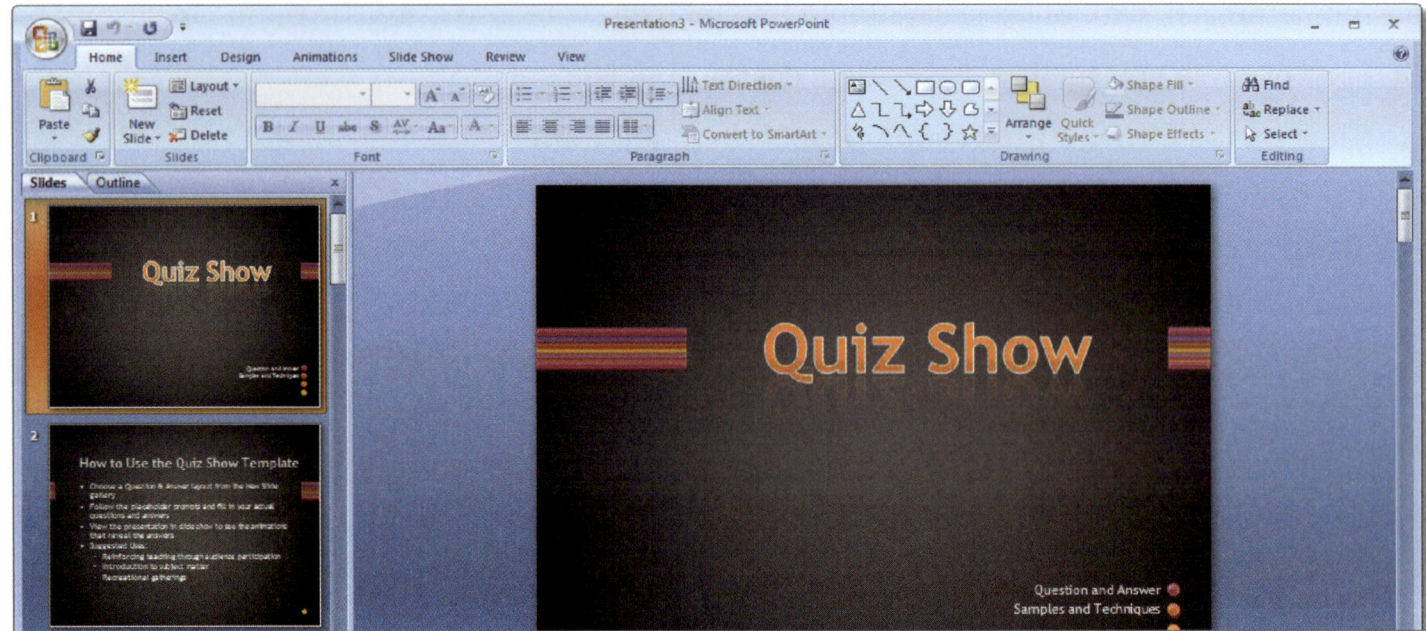

Fig. 6.3 *Selected slide template*

5. In the **Slide** tab, you can scroll up and down to select and change the contents of the slides based on your requirements.

Creating a Presentation Using Themes

A theme is an easy way to make a presentation. An Installed Theme is a set of formatting styles that includes background, fonts, lines, fill effects, etc. that enables the user to make a quick and a professional looking presentation.

Steps to create presentation using Themes

1. Click on the **Office Button** and select **New** option from the drop-down list.
2. The **New Presentation** dialog box appears.
3. Select **Installed Themes** option under **Templates** section (Fig. 6.4). Choose the desired theme and click on **Create** button.

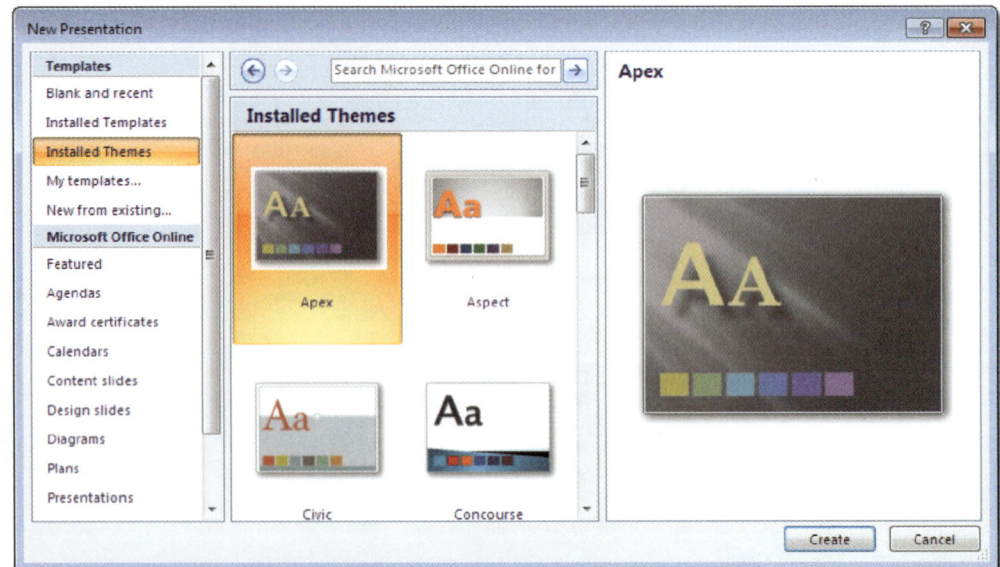

Fig. 6.4 *Installed Themes*

4. A blank presentation opens and the slide appears in the format selected by the user.

Photo Album

Photo Album is a PowerPoint presentation containing photographs to be displayed. A new presentation is created for each photo album created.

Follow these steps to create your own photo album:

1. Click on **Insert** tab ⟹ **Illustrations** group ⟹ **Photo Album** drop-down list ⟹ **New Photo Album…** option (Fig. 6.5).

Fig. 6.5 *New Photo Album option*

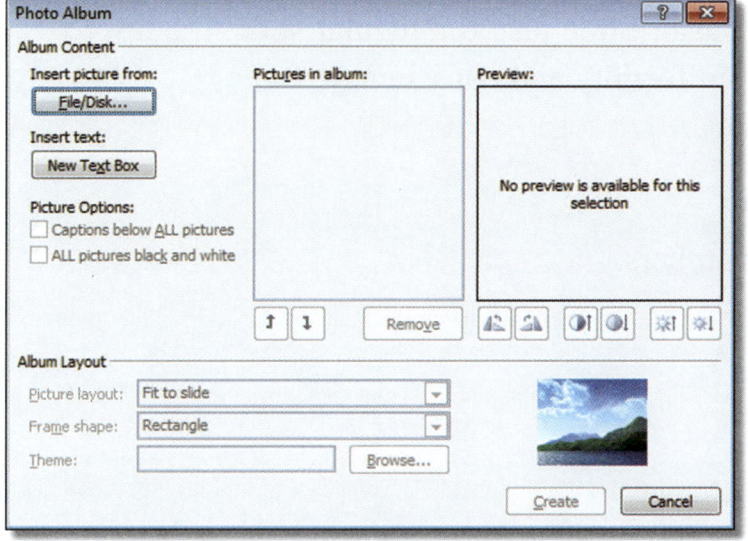

Fig. 6.6 *Photo Album dialog box*

2. The **Photo Album** dialog box appears (Fig. 6.6).

3. Click on **File/Disk…** button in the **Insert picture from:** section. The **Insert New Pictures** dialog box appears (Fig. 6.7). Select a picture from the desired location and click on **Insert** button.

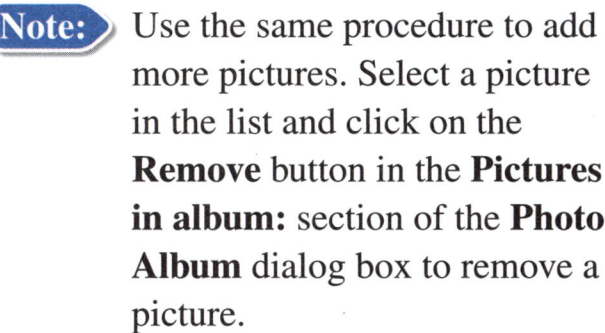 Use the same procedure to add more pictures. Select a picture in the list and click on the **Remove** button in the **Pictures in album:** section of the **Photo Album** dialog box to remove a picture.

4. The list of pictures added in the photo album can be seen in **Pictures in album:** section of the **Photo Album** dialog box. The sequence of pictures can be re-arranged using the up and down arrows given in the lower part of this section. A picture can be rotated or its brightness can also be changed.

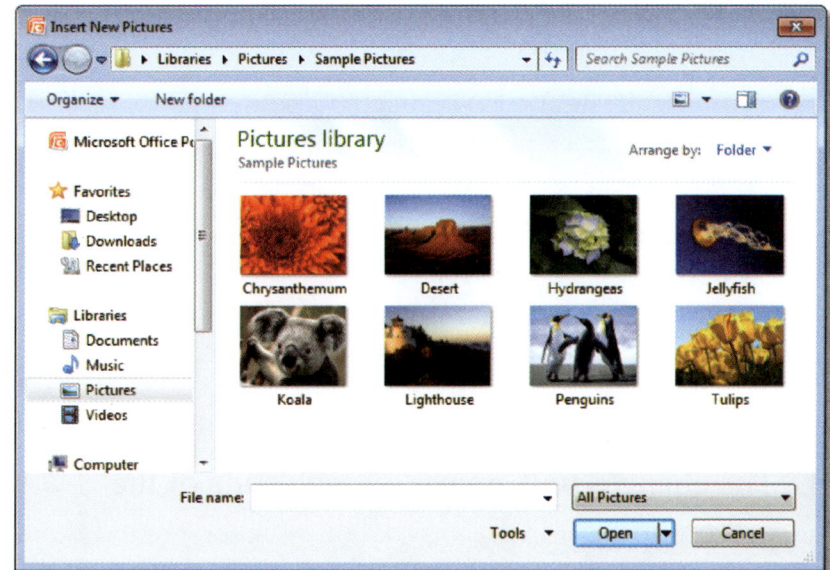

Fig. 6.7 *Insert New Pictures dialog box*

5. Click on **New Text Box** button in the **Insert text:** section to add text to a slide in the presentation.

6. Select the **Picture layout:** and **Frame shape:** using the drop-down lists in the **Album Layout** section.
7. Choose a **Theme:** by clicking on the **Browse...** button. Select the desired theme and click **Select**.
8. Click on **Create** button to create a new presentation titled Photo Album.

Slide Master

You can modify the PowerPoint Slide Master to change the look of all the slides in a presentation. PowerPoint Slide Master is also known as **Master Slide**. It acts just like a template and defines how slides are formatted. You can work on the Master Slide just as a regular slide. It helps to ensure that every slide of the presentation bears uniformity and consistency.

In the Slide Master you are allowed to:
- change the font name, color, size and style.
- change the formatting of the bullets and numbers.
- change the background of the slide.
- add common features like an image, logo, etc.
- add common headers and footers.

You can open the PowerPoint Master Slide as follows:

1. Click on **View** tab ⟹ **Presentation Views** group ⟹ **Slide Master** option (Fig. 6.8).

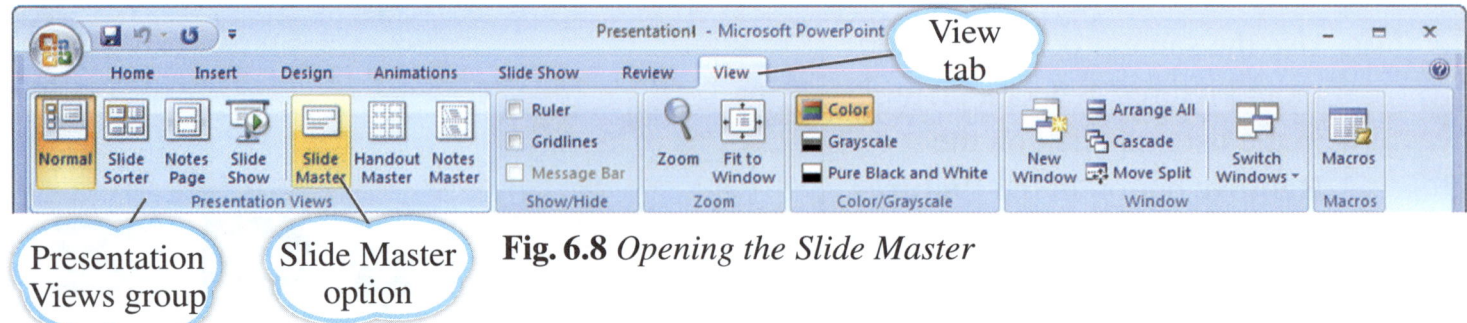

Fig. 6.8 *Opening the Slide Master*

2. It displays the presentation in **Master View**. Make the changes in the Master Slide.
3. The changes will appear on each slide of the presentation.
4. To close the **Master View**, select **Slide Master** tab ⟹ **Close** group ⟹ **Close Master View** option.

   OR

   Select the **View** tab ⟹ **Presentation Views** group ⟹ **Normal** option.

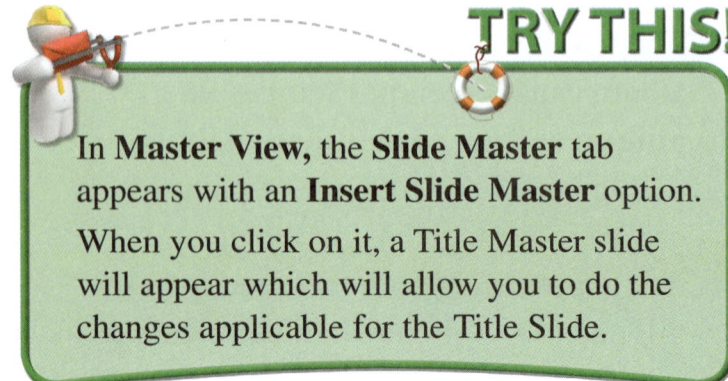

TRY THIS!

In **Master View,** the **Slide Master** tab appears with an **Insert Slide Master** option. When you click on it, a Title Master slide will appear which will allow you to do the changes applicable for the Title Slide.

Notes Master

Notes Page View displays the speaker notes for each slide. They are not a part of the presentation, so the audience will not see them. Notes Pages can be printed with the slides. The text of the notes is regular text that can be formatted. PowerPoint allows you to change the formatting of all the Notes Slides of a presentation. You can make these changes using the **Notes Master** option in **Presentation Views** group of the **View** tab. Whatever changes you can do in Slide Master, can also be done in Notes Master.

FACT FILE

Any headers or footers you add, will not appear on the Notes Master. However, they will appear on the Notes Page view.

Handout Master

Handouts are the printed materials given to the audience during the presentation. You can make changes in the Handout Master slide before printing so that it can be applied to all the handouts of the presentation. The changes may include repositioning and resizing the headers and footers, etc.

Custom Animation

Animation refers to the special effects that are added to the objects and text in a presentation. This is done to capture the viewer's attention. Custom animation gives animated effects to different objects within a slide. Through custom animation you specify how an object or text should appear during the presentation.

Follow these steps to animate the objects in a slide:

1. Select the object to be animated from the slide.
2. Click on **Animations** tab and select **Custom Animation** option in the **Animations** group.
3. The **Custom Animation** task pane appears (Fig. 6.9).

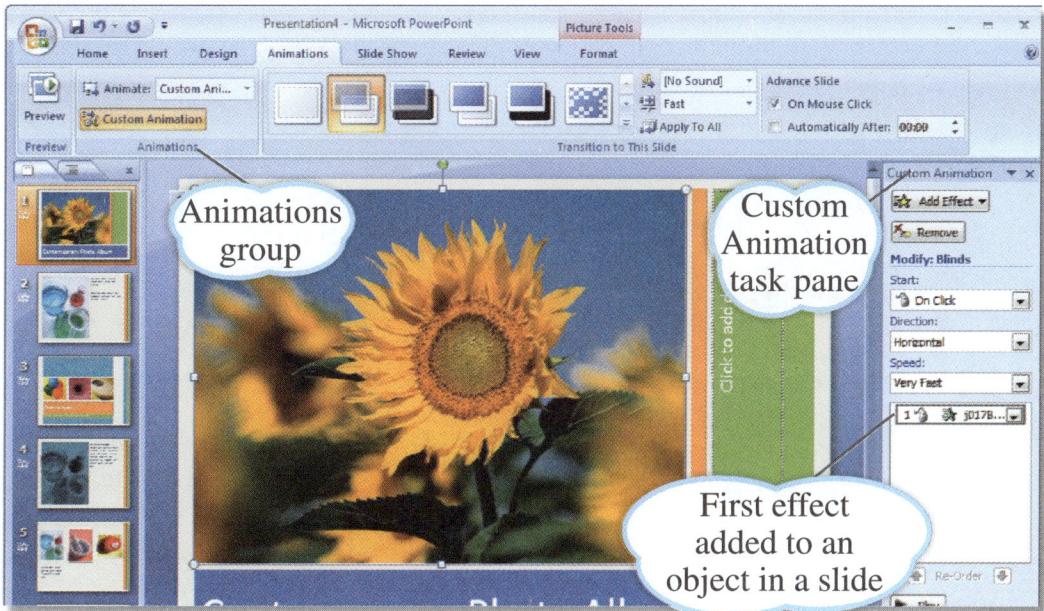

Fig. 6.9 *Custom Animation task pane*

4. Click on **Add Effect** button and choose one or more of the following options from the drop-down list:
   - Effects in the **Entrance** option show how the selected object will enter the slide show.
   - **Emphasis** option adds an effect to the selected object on the slide.
   - **Exit** option shows how the selected object leaves the slide.
   - **Motion Paths** option adds an effect to make the selected object move in a specified path.
5. To specify the start time of an animation select an appropriate option from the **Start:** drop-down list in the **Modify:** section.
   - Select **On Click** option to start the animation only on clicking the slide.
   - Select **With Previous** option to start an animation simultaneously with the previous one.
   - Choose **After Previous** option to start an animation immediately after the previous one.

   Repeat this step for each animation.
6. Select the **Direction:** and **Path:** drop-down lists to specify the direction/path of movement of the object (Fig. 6.10).
7. The speed of each animation can be chosen from the **Speed:** drop-down list.
8. Repeat the above steps for all the objects on the slide.
9. The objects appear in a list in the **Custom Animation** task pane

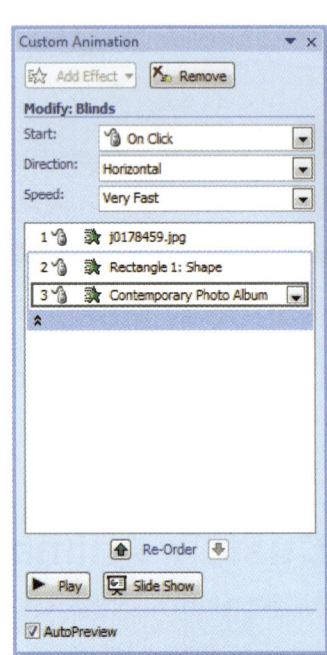

Fig. 6.10 *Selecting effects*

(Fig. 6.11). You can change the order of appearance of the animations during the slide show. Select and drag an animation up or down in the list to change the order.

10. Click on **Play** and **Slide Show** buttons to see the effects.
11. Close the task pane.

Fig. 6.11 *List of objects*

Select an animation in the **Custom Animation** task pane. Click the drop-down list on the extreme right of a particular animation. Choose the **Start:** time for the animation from the list. You can also remove an animation by selecting it and clicking the **Remove** button.

ACTIVITY

Complete the following activity based on the instructions given.

1. Create a presentation on 'Importance of water' and save it as Science.pptx.
2. Apply custom animation to all the important objects on your slides.
3. Also apply slide transitions with each slide advancing automatically after 3 seconds.
4. Save the changes.
5. Run your presentation.

Inserting Charts and Tables

Inserting Charts

If you want to display or analyse the data in a pictorial format you can use charts in MS PowerPoint 2007.

To insert a chart in MS PowerPoint 2007, you need to follow a few steps:

1. Click on **Insert** tab ⟹ **Illustrations** group ⟹ **Chart** option.
2. The **Insert Chart** dialog box appears. Select a category in the left pane and choose a type from the right pane. Click **OK**.
3. The chart will be displayed on the slide along with a data sheet (Fig. 6.12).

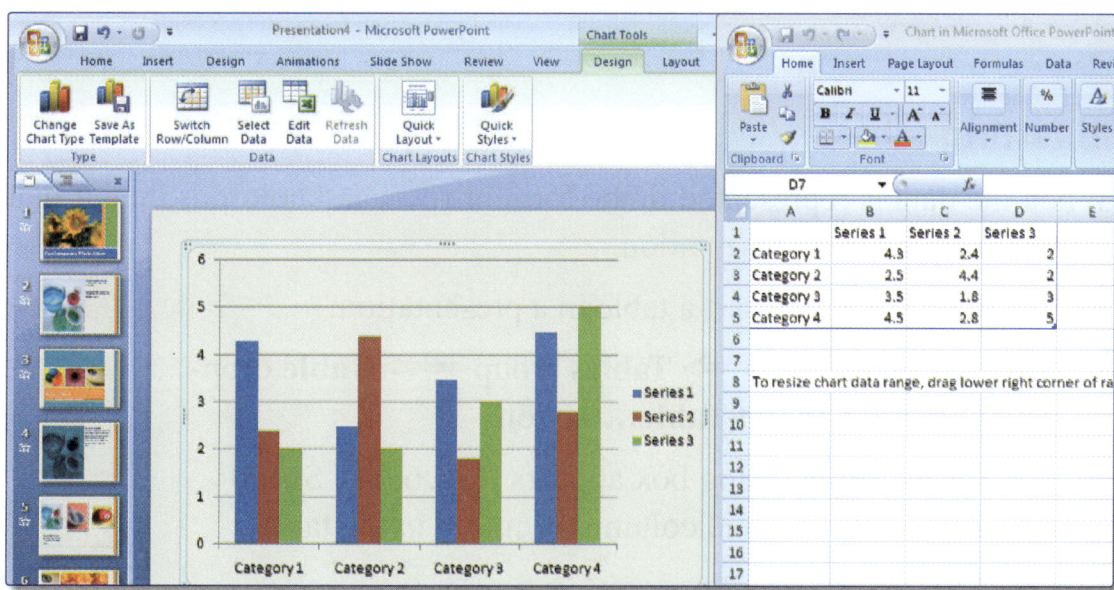

Fig. 6.12 *Inserting a chart*

The data sheet contains default data and values which can be changed as required. You may close the datasheet once the data and values have been entered. To view it again, right click on the chart and select **Edit Data...** option from the shortcut menu.

4. You can also change the chart type for the same values. Right click on the chart and select **Change Series Chart Type…** option from the shortcut menu. The **Change Chart Type** dialog box appears (Fig. 6.13). Select the new chart type and click **OK**.

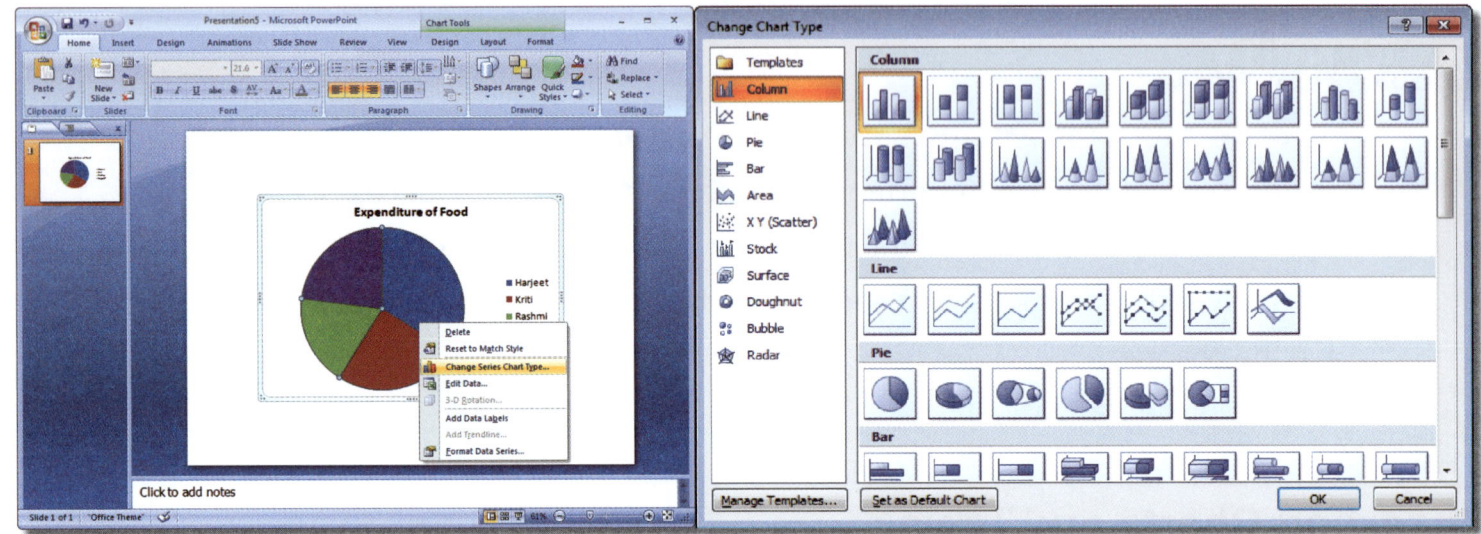

Fig. 6.13 *Changing the chart type*

TRY THIS!

Right click on the chart and explore the other options in the shortcut menus like **3-D Rotation…**, **Format Data Labels…** and **Format Data series…** in the shortcut menu. Try the different options to bring variations in your chart.

Inserting tables

When the data is represented in the form of rows and columns then it makes a table. Tables can also be inserted in a presentation.

Follow these steps to insert a table in a presentation:

1. Click on **Insert** tab ⟹ **Tables** group ⟹ **Table** drop-down list ⟹ **Insert Table…** option.
2. The **Insert Table** dialog box appears (Fig. 6.14). Specify the number of rows and columns required in the table.

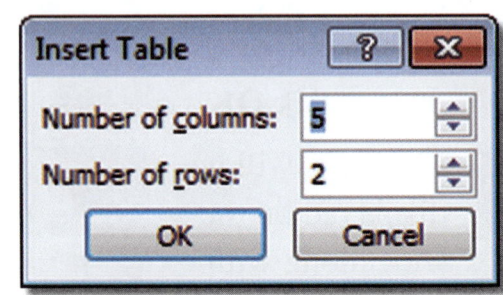

Fig. 6.14 *Insert Table dialog box*

3. Table with specified columns and rows will be inserted in the slide (Fig. 6.15).

Fig. 6.15 *Inserting table in a slide*

4. Two new tabs appear in the Ribbon, **Design** and **Layout,** both under **Table Tools**. The table can be formatted using the options given under different groups of the two tabs. The different tools are explained in Table 6.1 and Table 6.2.
5. Click on the table and insert values.

Table 6.1 *Options in Design tab*

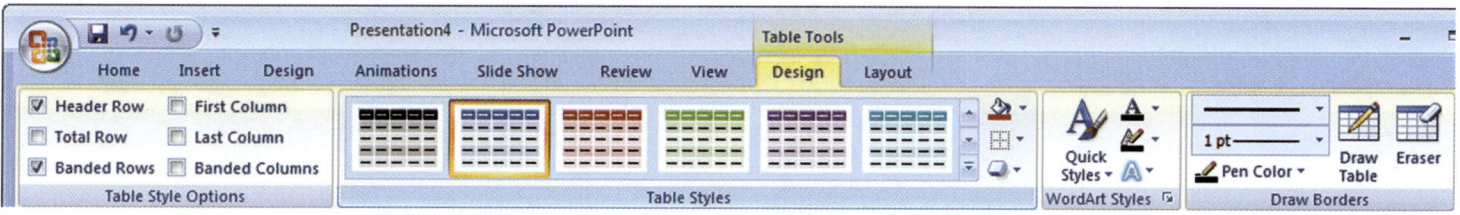

Option	Icon	Description
Table Style Options	☑ Header Row ☐ First Column ☐ Total Row ☐ Last Column ☑ Banded Rows ☐ Banded Columns	Creates a customised table with specific color scheme, shading and bands depending upon the requirements
Table Styles		Creates tables with a particular style and color scheme
Shading		Selects a type of shading or fill color for the selected table cells
Borders		Assigns borders or lines to the selected table cells
Effects		Adds visuals effects like shadow and reflection to the table
WordArt Quick Styles		Types the text in the chosen WordArt style
Text Fill		Text is written with the selected solid color, gradient, picture, or texture
Text Outline		Assigns a specified color, width and line style to the text outline
Text Effects		Adds visuals effects like shadow, glow, reflection, or 3-D rotation to the text
Pen Style		Assigns a style to the line used for drawing borders
Pen Weight	1 pt	Changes thickness of the lines forming the borders

Pen Color	Pen Color	Selects color from the color palette, the color of the border, for the next table or line drawn
Draw Table		Creates borders of tables
Eraser		Deletes unnecessary lines and borders from a table

Table 6.2 *Options in Layout tab*

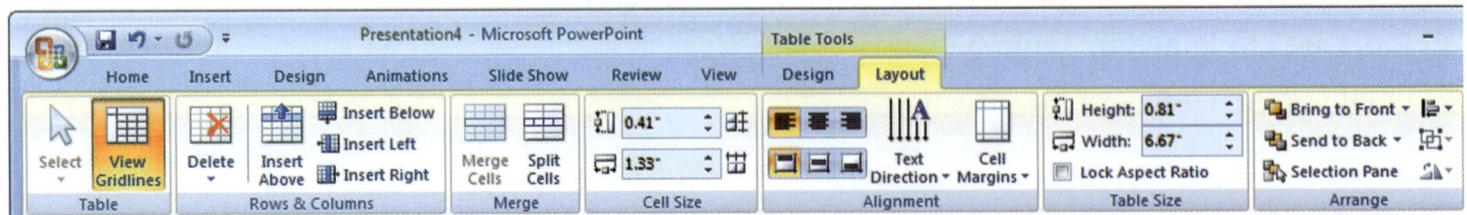

Option	Icon	Description
Select		Selects a row, a column or the entire table
View Gridlines		Displays or hides the gridlines in a table
Delete		Deletes the rows and columns in a table
Rows & Columns		Inserts rows above and below, and inserts columns on the right and left
Merge Cells		Combines the selected cells into the specified number of rows and columns
Split Cells		Splits the selected cells into the desired number of cells
Cell Height and Cell Width		Adjusts the cell height and width according to the specified measurements
Distribute Rows		Adjusts all the rows in the current selection to the same row height
Distribute Columns		Adjusts all the columns in the current selection to the same column width
Text Alignments		Aligns text to the center, left, or right, and top, middle, or bottom in the cell
Text Direction		Changes the orientation of the table text
Cell Margins		Adjusts the margins of cells based on the measurements specified
Table Size		Adjusts height and width of the table

78

Bring to Front		Brings the selected object to the front
Send to back		Sends the selected object at the back of all the others
Selection Pane		Changes the order and visibility of the selected object based on changes made in the Selection Pane

Creating Hyperlinks

Hyperlinks create a link to a slide, a web page, an email or any other program.

FACT FILE

When a website address or an email address is typed, PowerPoint changes it automatically to blue color and underlines it, thus making it a hyperlink.

Follow these steps to create a hyperlink in MS PowerPoint 2007:

1. Select the word or a sentence which is to be made a hyperlink.
2. Click on **Insert** tab ⟹ **Links** group ⟹ **Hyperlink** option (Fig. 6.16).

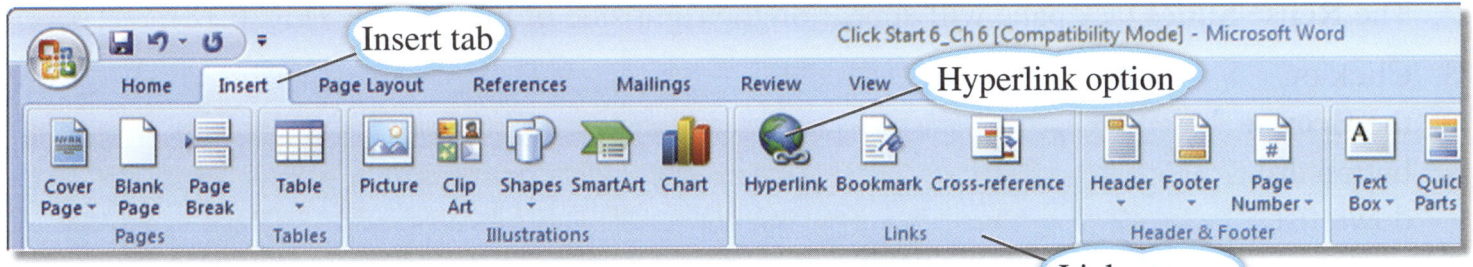

Fig. 6.16 *Inserting a Hyperlink*

3. The **Insert Hyperlink** dialog box appears (Fig. 6.17).
4. In the **Text to display:** box the selected word will be displayed.
5. In the **Address:** box, you enter the address of the website to which a hyperlink is to be created. For example, www.cambridgeindia.org.

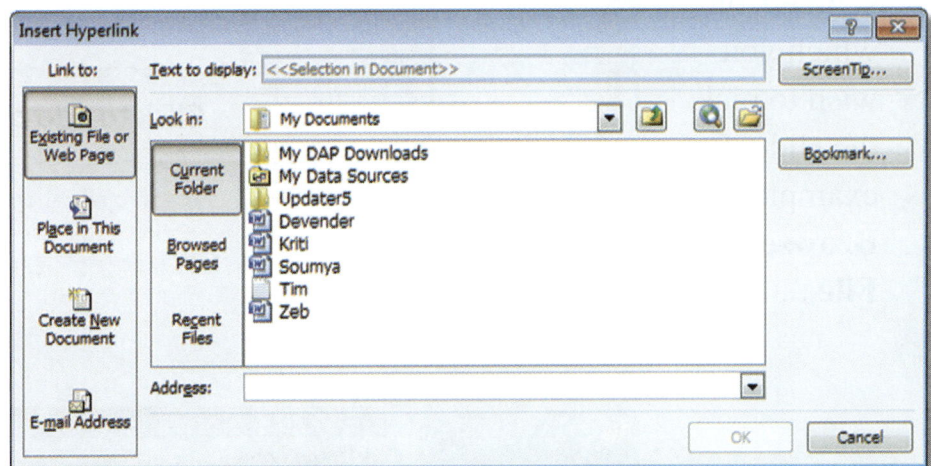

Fig. 6.17 *Insert Hyperlink dialog box*

6. You can also select a slide from the current presentation or another presentation from the listed ones.
7. Click on **OK**.
8. Run the presentation and click on the hyperlink. You will see the file or slide linked opening automatically.

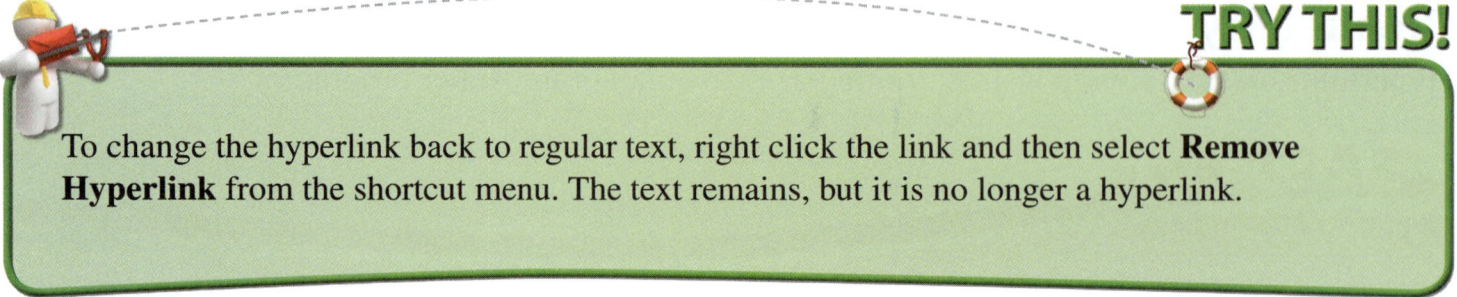

TRY THIS!

To change the hyperlink back to regular text, right click the link and then select **Remove Hyperlink** from the shortcut menu. The text remains, but it is no longer a hyperlink.

Reusing Slides

Sometimes you require data from an already saved presentation. In such a case, you can reuse the slides in the existing presentation.

To reuse slides from an another existing presentation you need to follow a few steps. They are:

1. Click on **Home** tab ⟹ **Slides** group ⟹ **New Slide** drop-down list ⟹ **Reuse Slides...** option.
2. The **Reuse Slides** task pane will appear on the right side of the window (Fig. 6.18).
3. Click on the **Browse** button drop-down list.
4. Select the source from which you wish to pick the slide. For example, **Browse File....**

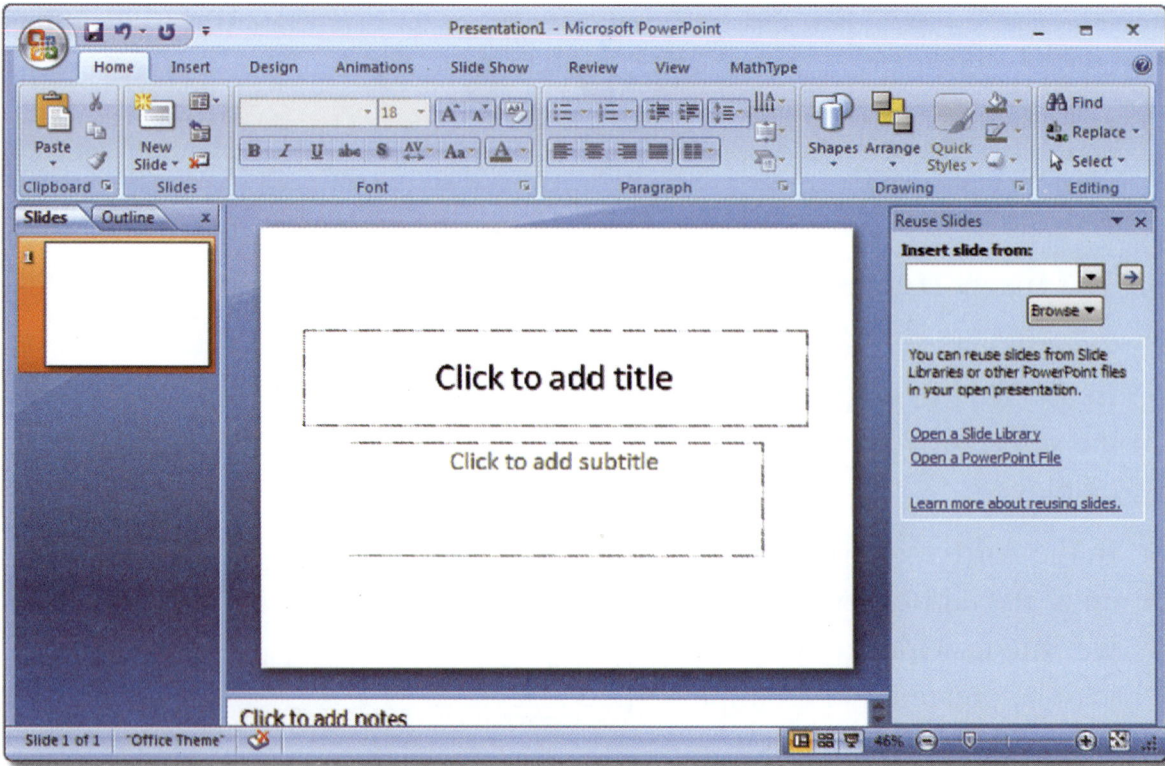

Fig. 6.18 *Reuse Slides task pane*

5. The **Browse** dialog box will appear. Click on the destination folder in the left pane and select the presentation from which you wish to reuse the slide in the right pane. Click on **Open** (Fig. 6.19).

6. After selecting the presentation the slides of the presentation will be displayed in the **Reuse Slides** task pane.

7. Click on the slide you wish to reuse (Fig. 6.20).

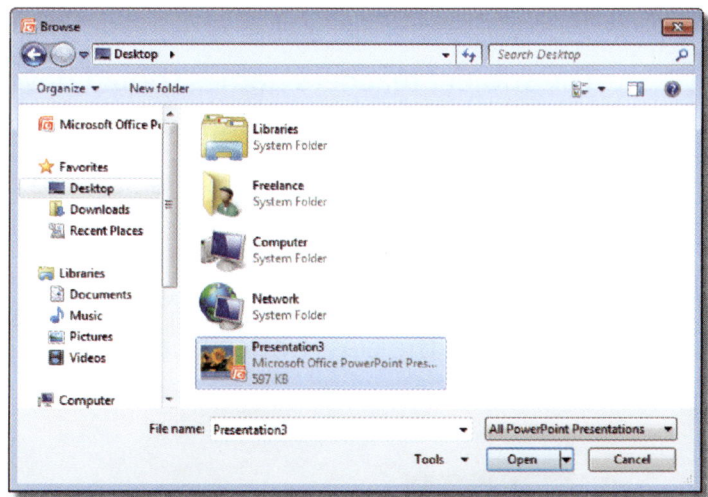

Fig. 6.19 *Browse dialog box*

Fig. 6.20 *Reusing a slide*

ACTIVITY

Complete the following activity.

1. Create your presentation on 'My Class'.
2. The presentation should have slides on class teacher, class location in the school premises, subjects taught and subject teachers' details, class strength and children's details, etc.

3. The subject teacher's names should have a hyperlink to a Word 2007 file. That Word file should contain some points on the subject teachers.
4. Import relevant slides from the Science.pptx which was created earlier, into this current presentation.
5. Save the changes.
6. Place it on the class notice board.

GLOSSARY

Theme: It is a blank presentation with already designed colors and graphics for the slides.

Animation: It refers to the special effects added to the objects and text in a presentation.

Template: It is a facility which provides ideas for the presentation through suggested content and layout.

Handouts: It is the material given to the audience during a presentation.

Notes Page View: It displays the speaker notes for each slide.

Photo Album: It is a newly created PowerPoint presentation containing photographs.

Slide Master: It a slide that can change the look of all the slides in a presentation.

NOW YOU KNOW

1. Notes Page can be printed with the slides.
2. Custom animation means giving animated effects to different objects within a slide.
3. Charts are used to display or analyse data in the pictorial format.
4. Photo Album is a new PowerPoint presentation containing photographs.
5. When data is represented in the form of rows and columns it forms a table. Tables can also be inserted in a presentation.
6. Hyperlinks create a link to a slide, a web page, an email or any other program.
7. Slides can be reused from an existing presentation.

EXERCISE

A. Fill in the blanks.

1. For every photo album, a new ………………………………. is created.
2. You can ………………………………. slides from an another presentation.
3. By using ………………………………., the text is created as a link to open some other file or a website.
4. You can animate the objects present on the slide by using ……………………………….
5. ………………………………. helps you to advance your slide by either using mouse-click or automatically after few seconds of interval.

B. Give one word for: HOTS

1. A link to a slide, a web page, an email or any other program.
2. A menu where Table option is present.
3. Option with which slides can be picked from another presentation.
4. The reading material given to the audience during the presentation.
5. Special effects that are added in a presentation.

C. Give the difference between:

1. Slide Transition and Slide Animation
2. Template and Theme
3. Notes Page Master and Slide Master

D. Answer the following questions.

1. What is a template?
2. How would you show an external document in a running presentation?
3. Why do you need to reuse slides in PowerPoint 2007? HOTS
4. What is Custom Animation?
5. Explain the changes that can be made using Master Slides available in PowerPoint 2007.

LAB WORK

A. **Prepare a presentation on 'My ambition in life'.**
   1. The presentation should basically cover what you plan to do when you grow up.
   2. Give transition effects and animations in your slides.
   3. Insert pictures and ClipArt wherever required.

B. **Prepare a presentation on the 'Harappan Culture' with the help of the Internet.**
   1. Insert pictures, wherever required.
   2. Give transition and animation effects to your slides.

MS Office 2010 Updates

In PowerPoint 2010:

- You can broadcast your slideshow by uploading your presentation on free PowerPoint Broadcast Service. You just need a Windows Live ID to sign in to send a private URL to various users via email who just have to click on the link to watch the presentation.

- You can convert your presentation into a video that has completely synchronised audio and animations that you used in the presentation.

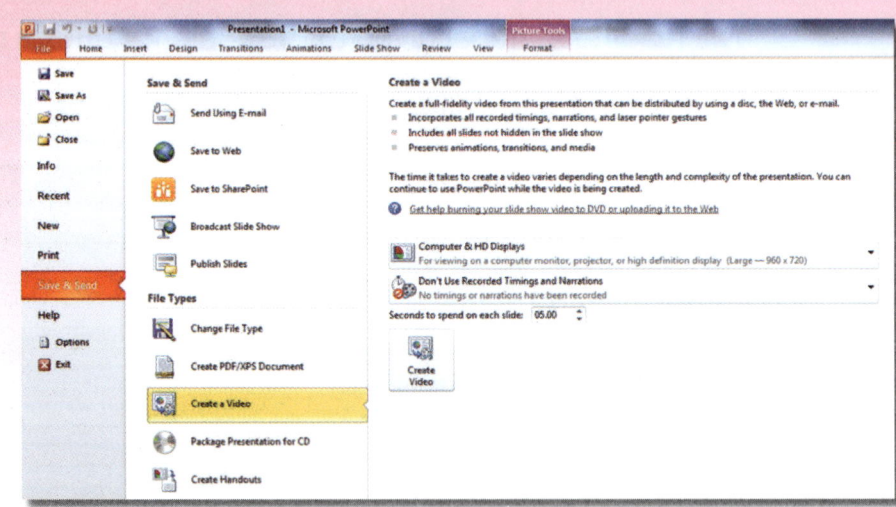

TEACHER'S NOTES

1. Ask the students to choose a topic from their Computer Science coursework and prepare a presentation on it. They should use at least four features learnt in this chapter.

2. Ask the students to prepare a presentation on their favourite things. For example, favourite food, color, sport player, part time, etc.

7 More about MS Excel 2007

SNAP RECAP

1. You can format data in MS Excel 2007 using different formatting tools.
2. You can use the Auto Fill option to automatically fill the cells either as a series or copy them.
3. You can adjust row and column sizes, and also insert or delete cells whenever required.

LEARNING OBJECTIVES

You will learn about:
1. formatting numbers
2. modifying and formatting data
3. creating custom lists
4. formulas and functions

Introduction

In this chapter, you will learn about several formatting features that are used in MS Excel 2007 and the functions that are used to do various calculations.

Formatting Numbers

Numbers entered in MS Excel 2007 could be a value, date or time. You can choose the format of the digits by following a few steps:

1. Select the range of cells that you wish to format (Fig. 7.1).

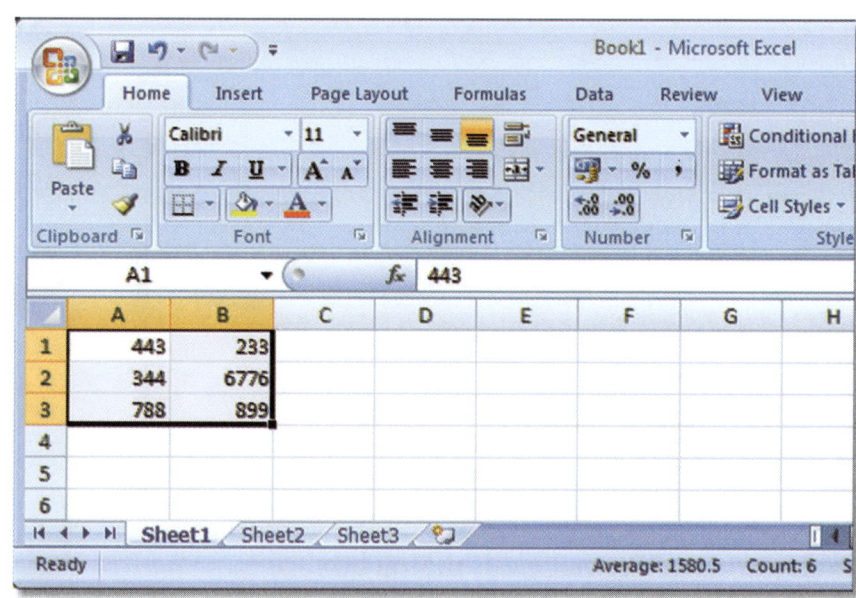

Fig. 7.1 *Selecting a range*

2. Click on **Home** tab ⟹ **Number** group ⟹ **Number Format** drop-down list. Select the desired format from the drop-down list (Fig. 7.2a).

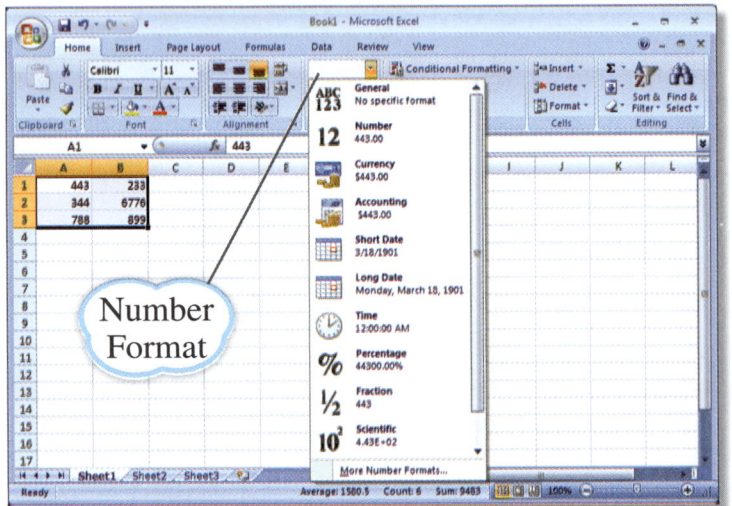

a. Number format drop-down list

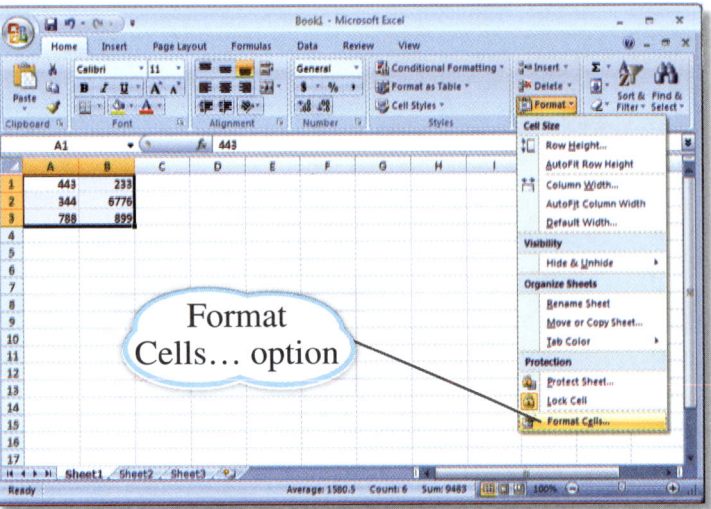

b. Using Format option

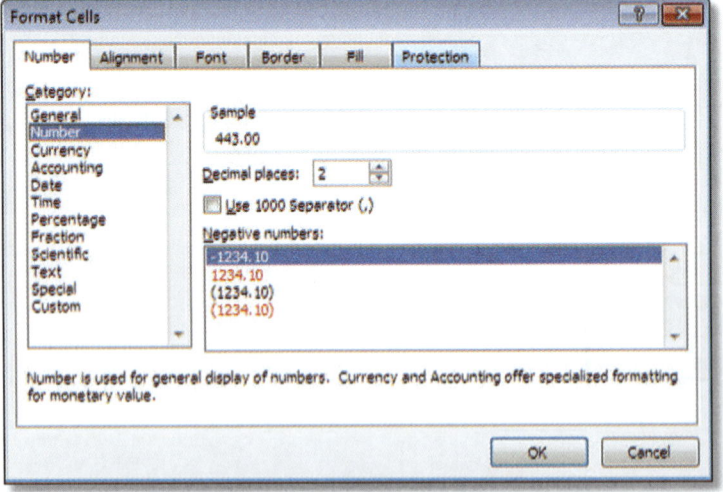

c. Format Cells dialog box

Fig. 7.2 *Formatting numbers*

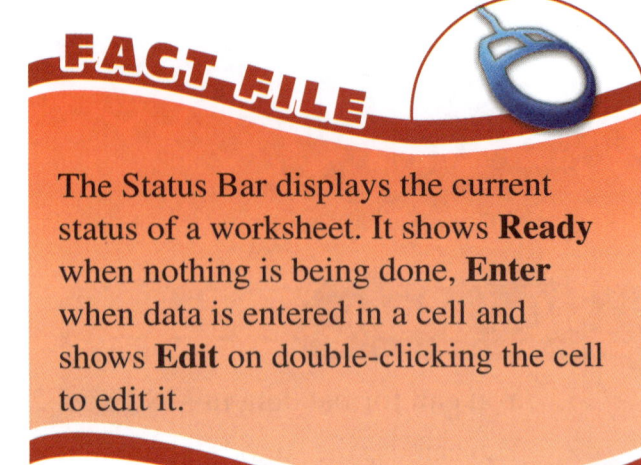

The Status Bar displays the current status of a worksheet. It shows **Ready** when nothing is being done, **Enter** when data is entered in a cell and shows **Edit** on double-clicking the cell to edit it.

Click on **Home** tab ⟹ **Cells** group ⟹ **Format** drop-down list ⟹ **Format Cells...** option (Fig. 7.2b). **Format Cells** dialog box opens. In the **Number** tab, select the desired style from the **Category:** section and click **OK** (Fig. 7.2c).

Right click the mouse and select **Format Cells....** option from the shortcut menu. **Format Cells** dialog box opens. In the **Number** tab, click on the desired format in the **Category:** section and click **OK**.

3. Data in the selected range of cells will now appear in the selected format.

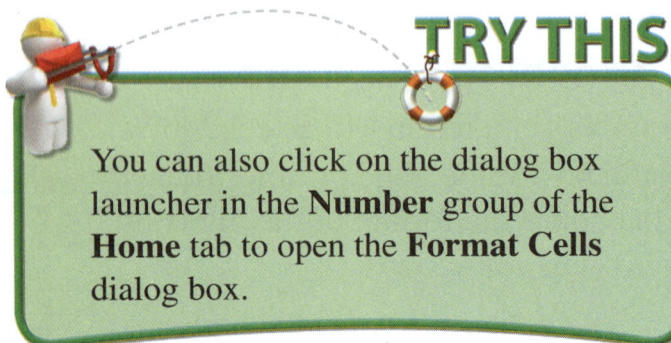

You can also click on the dialog box launcher in the **Number** group of the **Home** tab to open the **Format Cells** dialog box.

Modifying Data

The data entered in a MS Excel 2007 worksheet can be modified. To change the data already typed in the cells, follow the steps given below:

1. Click on the cell having the data that needs to be changed.

Note: Click once to select the cell if the entire data of the cell has to be changed; double-click the cell if a part of the data is to be changed.

2. Replace it with the new data.
3. Press the **Enter** key on the keyboard. You may also click on the **Enter** button on the **Formula Bar** (Fig. 7.3).

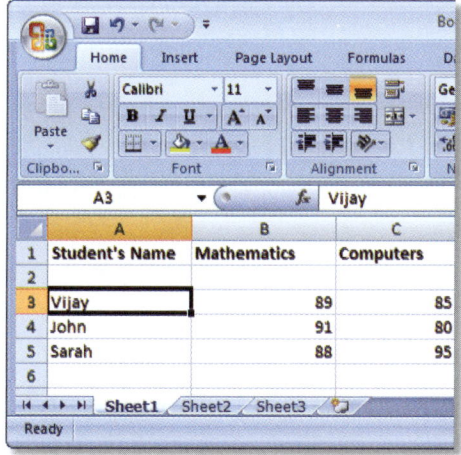
Data to be modified

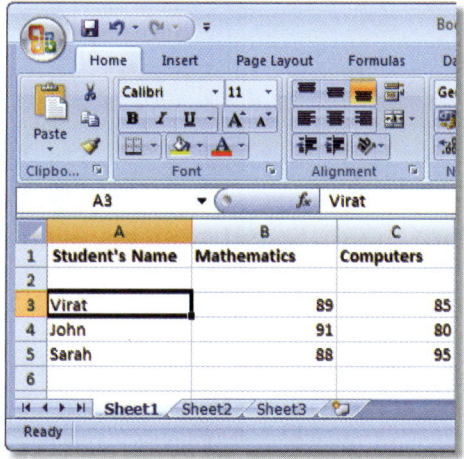
Overwriting data

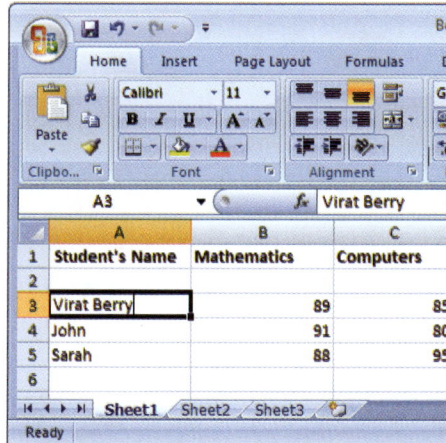
Data partially modified

Fig. 7.3 *Modifying data*

Formatting Data

You have already learned in your earlier classes to format text in MS Excel 2007. Now you will learn to change fonts, format border, apply pattern and color, to a cell.

Formatting the fonts

Follow these steps to change the font style used for the text in a worksheet:

1. Select the cell or range of cells.
2. Right click on the mouse and select **Format Cells...** option from the shortcut menu.
3. The **Format Cells** dialog box appears.
4. Click the **Font** tab in the dialog box (Fig. 7.4).
5. You may select the required formats for the fonts to be used. Such as **Font:**, **Font style:**, **Size:**, **Color:**, etc.

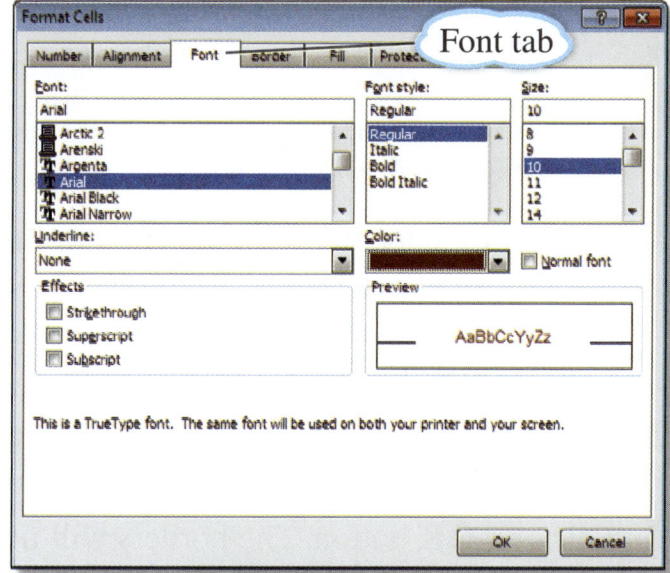
Fig. 7.4 *Font tab*

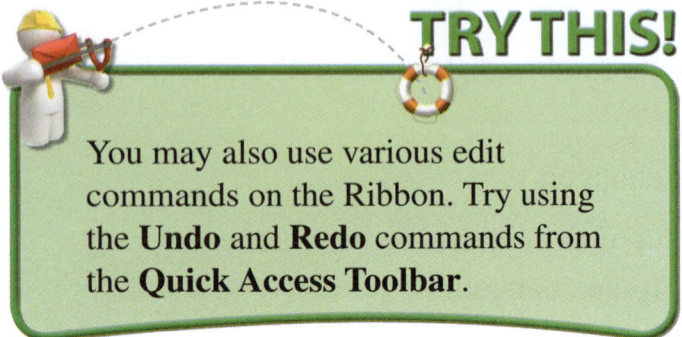

TRY THIS!

You may also use various edit commands on the Ribbon. Try using the **Undo** and **Redo** commands from the **Quick Access Toolbar**.

6. Click on **OK** button. The data is now formatted based on the selections made (Fig. 7.5).

1. Select the cell or range of cells.
2. Click on **Home** tab ⟹ **Font** group.
3. Choose the desired formats from the different options available.

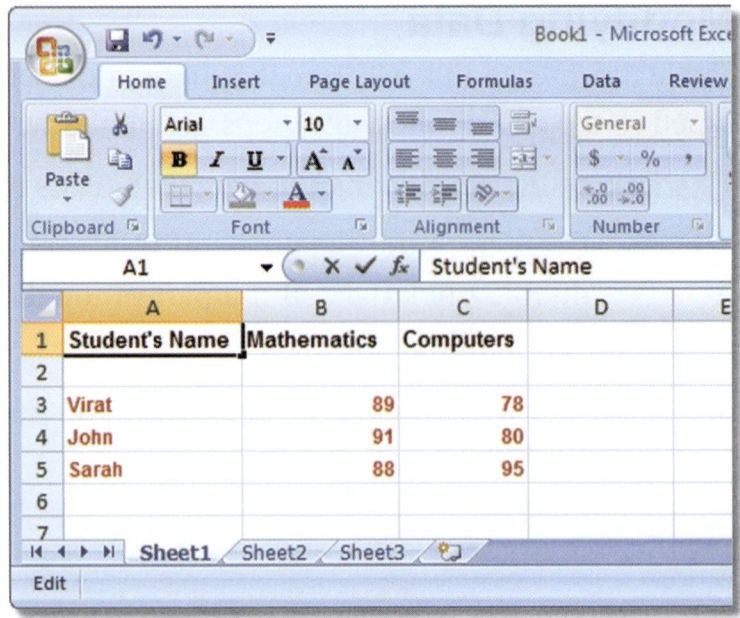

Fig. 7.5 *Formatting data*

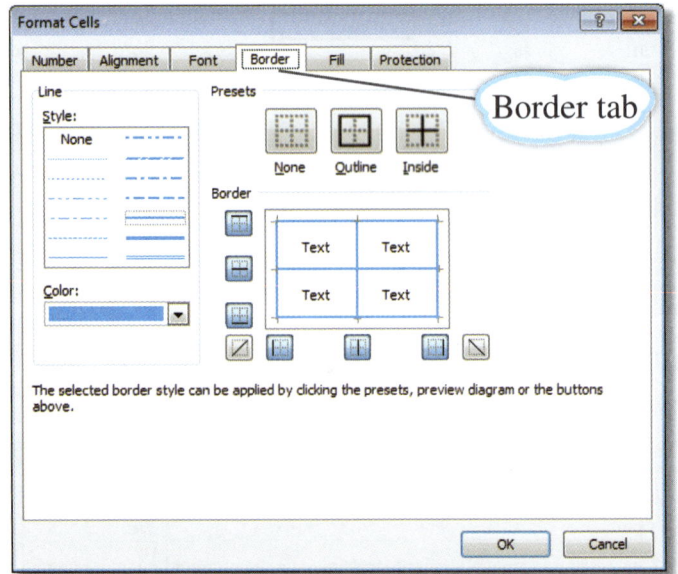

Fig. 7.6 *Formatting borders*

Border formatting

Follow these steps to format the border of the cells:

1. Select the cells for which the border is needed.
2. Right click on the mouse and select **Format Cells...** option from the shortcut menu.
3. The **Format Cells** dialog box appears. Click on the **Border** tab (Fig. 7.6).

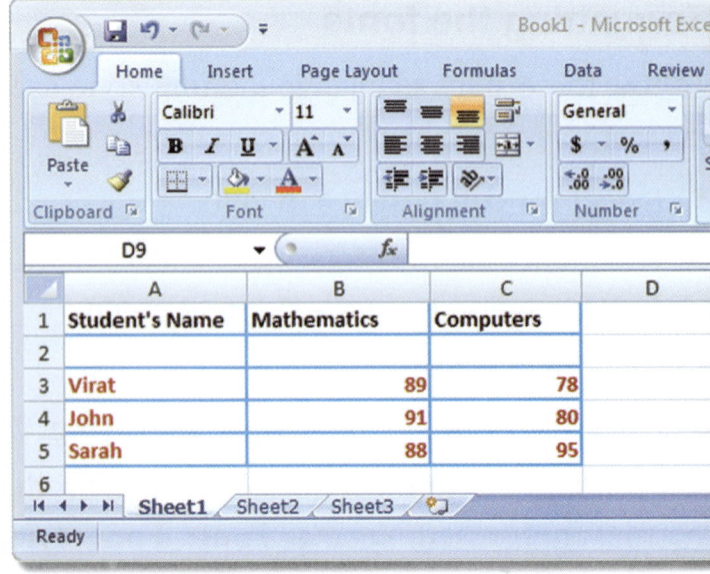

4. In this tab, select the style for lines of the border from **Style:** in the **Line** section . You can also choose different colors from the **Color:** drop-down list.
5. Select the borders from **Presets** and **Border** sections.
6. Click on **OK** button. The borders will now appear formatted (Fig. 7.7).

Fig. 7.7 *Formatted borders*

Formatting cells

You can also change the pattern and the background color of the cells in a worksheet. You need to follow the steps given below:

1. Select the cell or range of cells.
2. Right click the mouse and select **Format Cells...** option from the shortcut menu.
3. The **Format Cells** dialog box appears. Click on the **Fill** tab (Fig. 7.8).

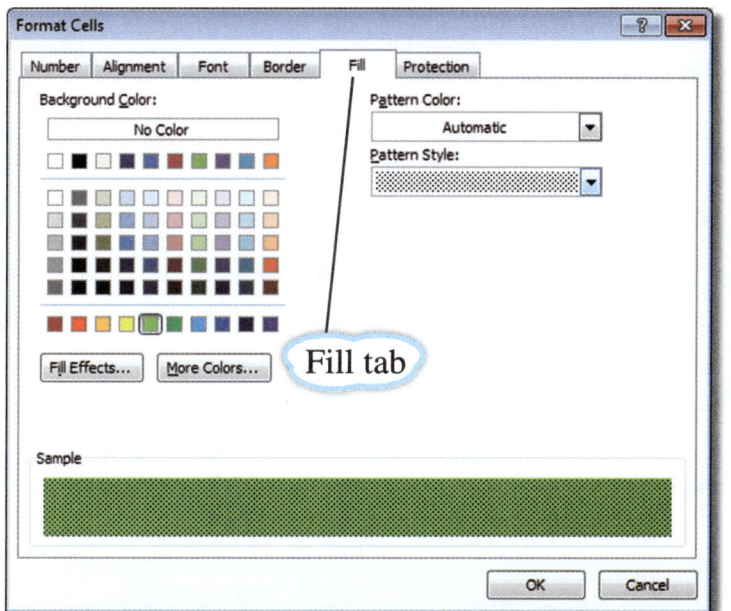

Fig. 7.8 *Selecting pattern for cells*

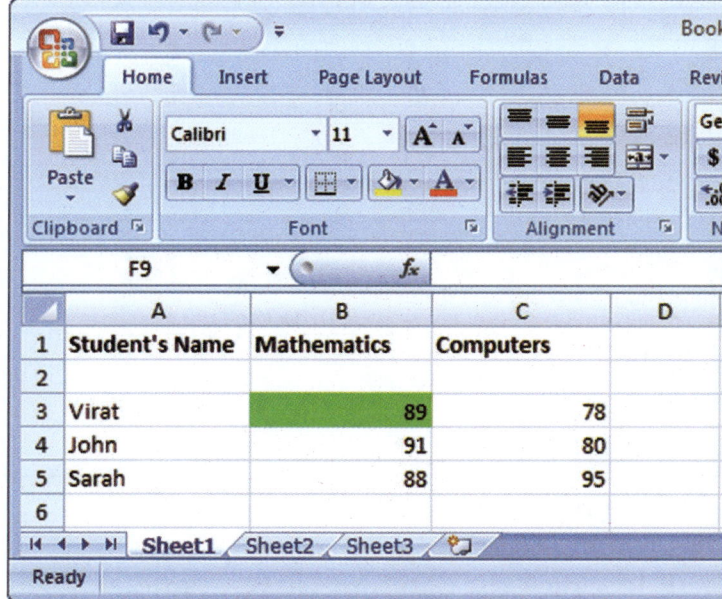

Fig. 7.9 *Pattern applied to cells*

4. Choose the required pattern and background color for the cells from **Pattern Color:**, **Pattern Style:** and **Background Color:** sections.
5. Click on **OK**. The changes are reflected in the worksheet (Fig. 7.9).

FACT FILE

You can also format the cells, text, fonts, patterns, and cell borders directly from the options given on the Ribbon.

Creating Custom Lists

In Excel, you can also create your own Custom list. This is done to save a set of items that can be filled in a selected range of cells automatically, whenever required. To create a Custom list in MS Excel 2007, follow the steps given below:

1. Click on **Office Button**.

2. Click on **Excel Options** button (Fig. 7.10).
3. The **Excel Options** dialog box appears (Fig. 7.11).

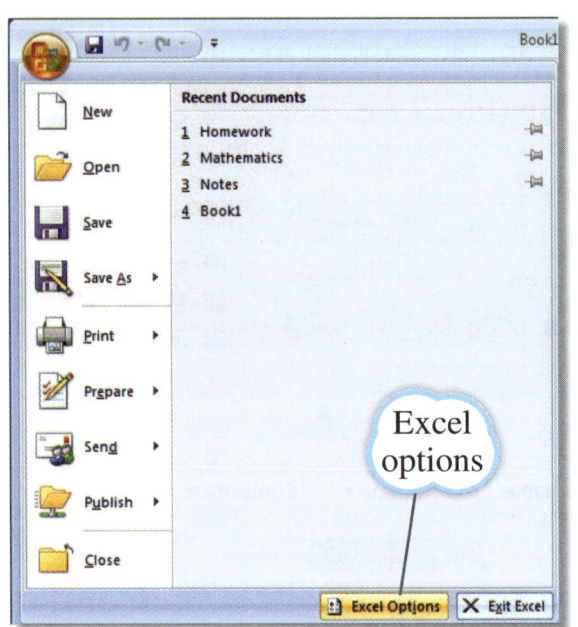

Fig. 7.10 *Selecting Excel Options*

Fig. 7.11 *Excel Options dialog box*

4. Click on **Edit Custom Lists...** button. The **Custom Lists** dialog box opens (Fig 7.12).

5. Enter the desired list under the **List entries:** section. Click on **Add** button and then click **OK**.

6. You may also import data by clicking on the **Import** button, and select the data from another worksheet.

7. Click on **OK**.

8. Use the list created with the **Fill Handle**.

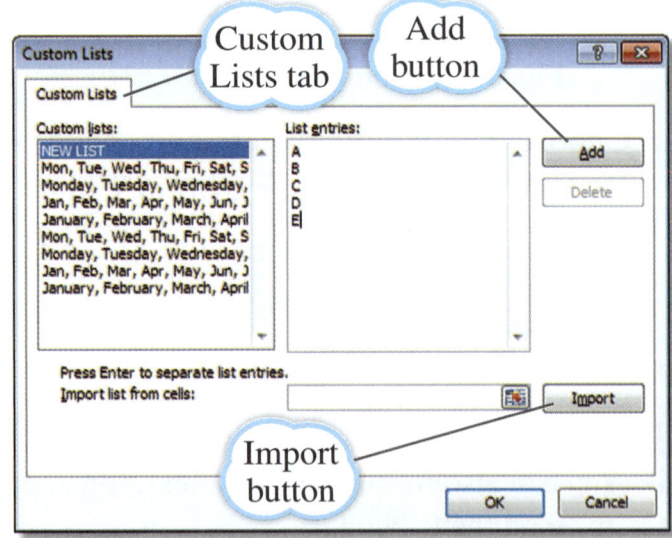

Fig. 7.12 *Custom Lists dialog box*

Formulas and Functions

The unique feature of an MS Excel spreadsheet program is that it allows you to create mathematical formulas and execute functions. Moreover, if any number used in the formula changes, the entire spreadsheet is automatically updated. Here you will learn how to add, divide, multiply and subtract by typing formulas into an Excel worksheet.

Formulas

A formula in general is made up of an operand and an operator. The MS Excel 2007 formula however, can be a set of values, cell references, functions, given with or without an operator. Any formula can be created in Excel. They are entered on the worksheet cell and must begin with an equal to sign '='. After the formula has been typed into the cell, the calculation executes immediately and the formula itself is visible in the **Formula Bar**.

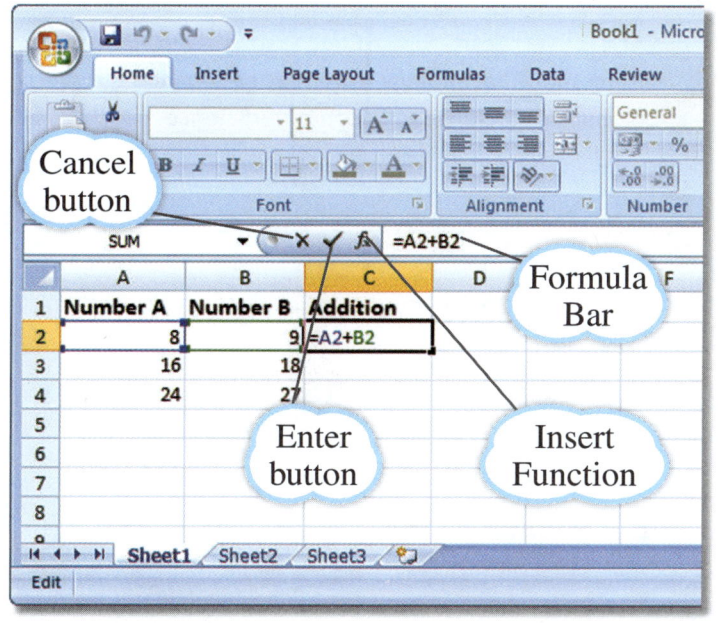

Fig. 7.13 *Creating a list of numbers*

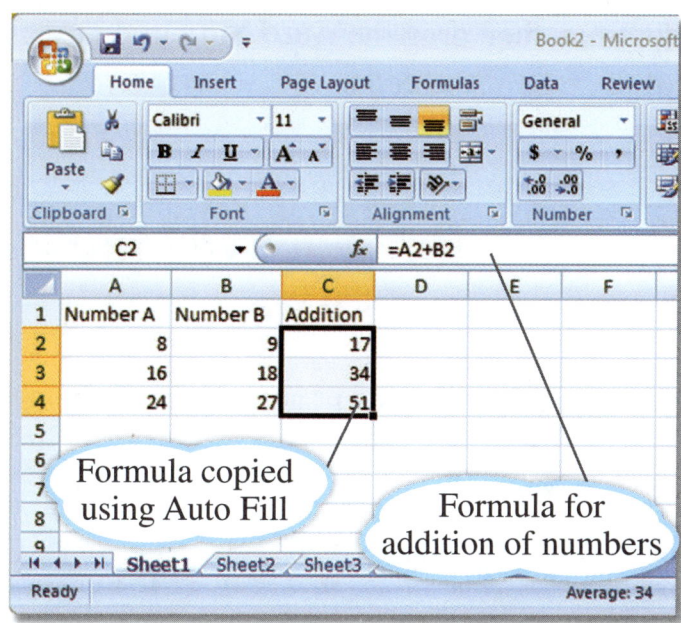

Fig. 7.14 *Calculating all the values in a list using Auto fill option*

In case you do not write an '=' sign then Excel treats the formula as a normal text entry.

Let us create a list of numbers (Fig. 7.13). To do various calculations in MS Excel 2007, follow the steps given below:

1. You may either enter the formula directly in the Formula Bar or double-click the cell where you wish to get the result and type the formula.

2. Drag down the **Auto Fill** option to do the calculations automatically for all the values that you enter (Fig. 7.14). The formula entered initially is followed automatically for all the other values in the list.

Special case

You may even add the text using the text formulas in MS Excel. Few special cases are given below.

Case I: To add two strings or text values (called **concatenation of strings**) using ampersand (&) as an operator you can:

- Type the formula and click enter on the Formula Bar (Fig. 7.15).
- Type the text within " " and add them using '&'. For example, "Click" & " Start" will give Click Start on pressing the Enter button.

You may then drag the **Auto Fill** option to fill the rest of the cells.

Result displayed using Auto Fill

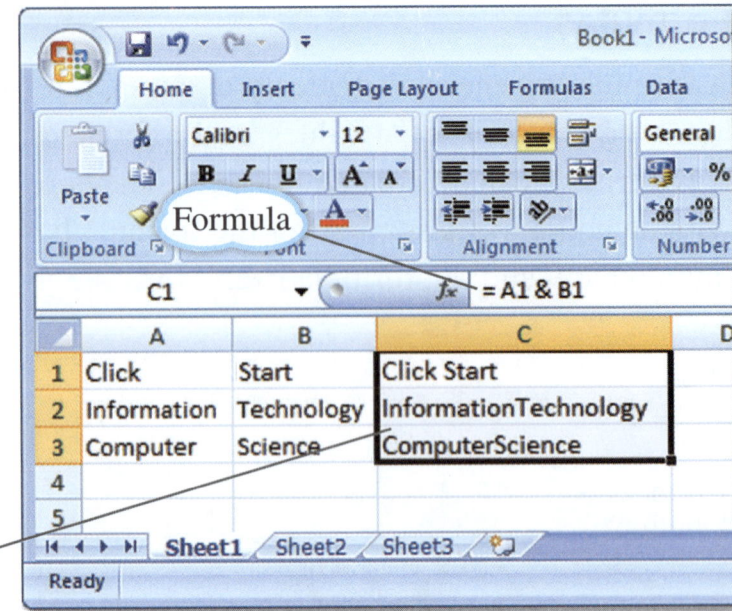

Fig. 7.15 *Concatenating text*

Case II: To get the result along with the text see the following example (Fig. 7.16).

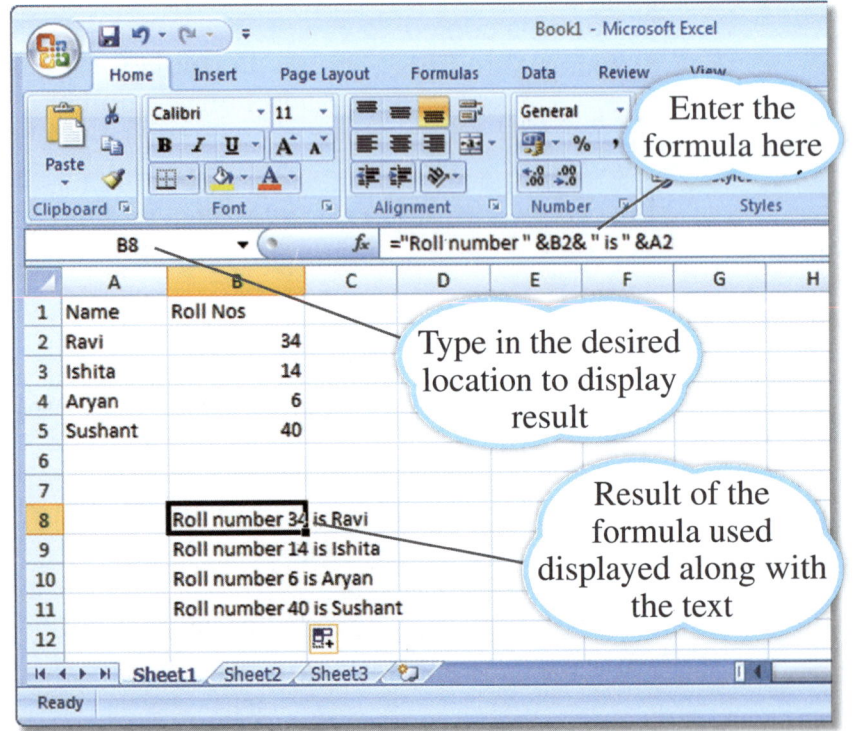

Fig. 7.16 *Getting text values as a formula*

FACT FILE

MS Excel strictly follows the BODMAS rule. The various arithmetic operators used in a numeric formula are:

- Exponent (^)
- Multiplication (*)
- Division (/)
- Addition (+)
- Subtraction (−)

Error results

Sometimes errors are displayed in the working cells or the Formula Bar in place of the results.

A list of some common errors displayed in MS Excel 2007, and their possible reasons are given in Table 7.1.

Table 7.1 *Errors Displayed in MS Excel*

Error message displayed	Possible reasons
#####	The column is not wide enough to display the result or the value
#DIV/0!	Division by zero error (Invalid operation)
#N/A	Data unavailable
#VALUE!	Invalid data
#NAME!	When text is not recognised
#REF!	Invalid cell reference
#NULL!	Ranges do not intersect or the user is using an invalid range operator

Basic functions

In MS Excel, functions are pre-defined formulas that perform specific calculations. Some of the basic functions available are Sum( ), Max( ), Min( ), Count( ), Average( ).

Using functions can be a more efficient way of performing mathematical operations than formulas. For example, if you want to add the values of cells D1 through D10, you would type the formula:

= D1 + D2 + D3 + D4 + D5 + D6 + D7 + D8 + D9 + D10

Alternatively, you may use the SUM( ) function and simply type: =SUM(D1:D10)

These commonly used functions and their examples are given below.

SUM( )

It adds up all the values in a range of cells (Fig. 7.17).

For example, the formula:

=SUM(A1:A10) finds the sum of cells A1 through A10
=SUM(G1,F6) finds the sum of two cells
=SUM(6,23,D3) finds the sum of two constants and a cell.

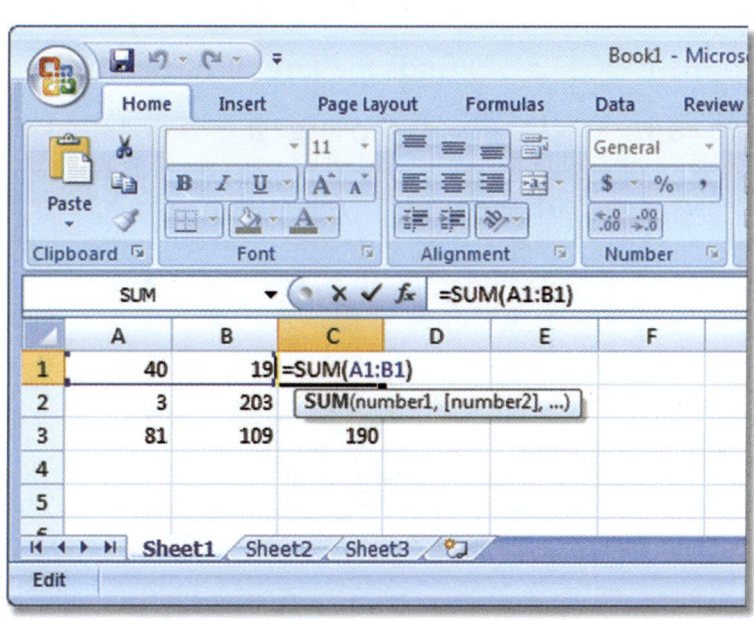

Fig. 7.17 *Using SUM( ) function*

AVERAGE( )

It calculates the average of the cell values (Fig. 7.18). For example, the formula:

=AVERAGE(B1:B10) finds the average of cells B1 through B10

=AVERAGE(B2,B7) finds the average of two cells

=AVERAGE(6,23,D3) finds the average of two constants and a cell.

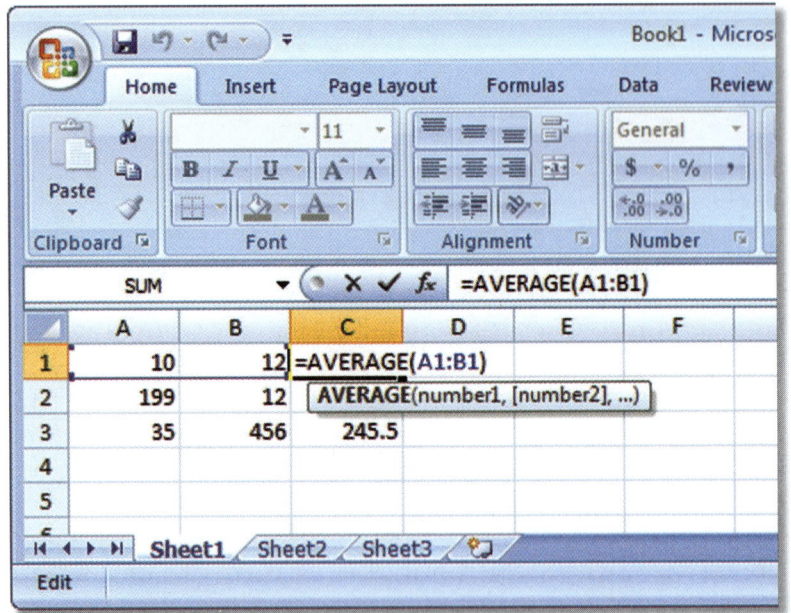

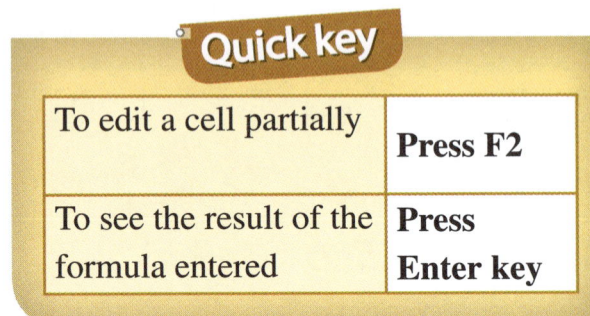

Fig. 7.18 *Using AVERAGE( ) function*

MAX( )

It finds the largest number in the selected range of the cell values (Fig. 7.19). For example, the formula:

=MAX(C1:C10) finds the largest number from cells C1 through C10

=MAX(D2,E2) finds the largest of two cells

=MAX(6,D3) finds the largest of a constant and a cell.

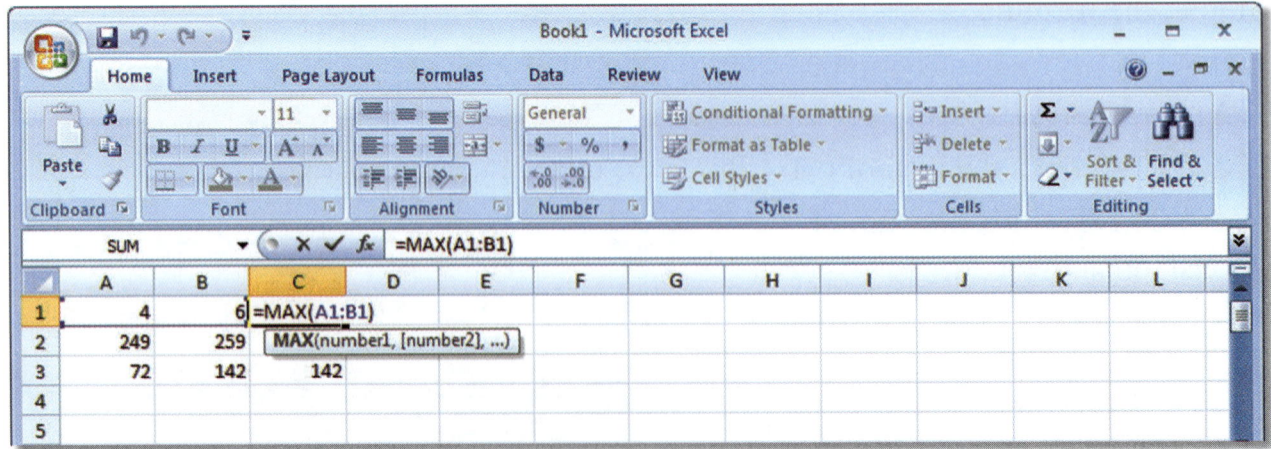

Fig. 7.19 *Using MAX( ) function*

MIN( )

It finds the lowest number in the selected range of the cell values (Fig. 7.20). For example, the formula:

=MIN(C11:C15) finds the minimum number from cells C11 through C15

=MIN(D12,E12,F12) finds the minimum of three cells

=MIN(6,D13) finds the minimum of a constant and a cell.

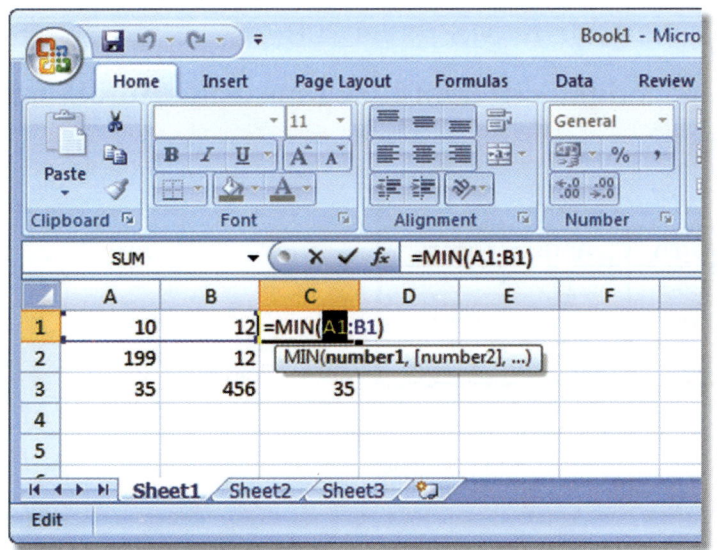

Fig. 7.20 *Using MIN( ) function*

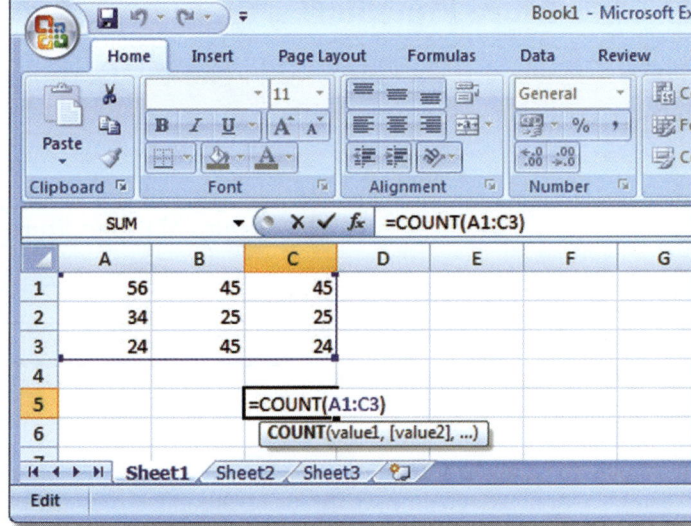

Fig. 7.21 *Using COUNT( ) function*

COUNT( )

It counts the cell values (Fig. 7.21). For example, the formula:

= COUNT(A11:C15) finds the count of values from cells A11 through C15

= COUNT(H9,F5,F6) finds the count of values of three cells

= COUNT(6,G3) finds the count of values of a constant and a cell

ACTIVITY

Complete the following activity.

1. Create a MS Excel 2007 file to show the scores of students in a class.
2. Make a new column as total of activity and internal marks.
3. Copy the formula for the rest of the subjects down the column using Auto Fill feature.
4. Count the total number of subjects using Count( ).
5. Find out the highest total marks.
6. Find out the lowest total marks.

AutoSum

This feature is used to add numbers. It is also used to find the sum, average, maximum, minimum and count of numbers.

The AutoSum can be accessed at the following locations:

1. Click on **AutoSum** drop-down list in the **Editing** group of the **Home** tab or in the **Function Library** of the **Formulas** tab.
2. Click **More Functions…** to see more functions available in MS Excel 2007.

The following data (Fig. 7.22) can be used to understand the different functions using AutoSum feature.

	A	B	C	D
1			Month	
2	Nature of Expenditure	March	April	May
3	Food	2300	2275	3450
4	Electricity	1480	1495	1855
5	Entertainment	1275	1230	1340

Fig. 7.22 Sample data

SUM( )

1. Select E3.
2. Click on **AutoSum** option. A marquee (dashed border) will appear from B3 to D3 (Fig. 7.23).
3. Click on **AutoSum** option once again or press **Enter** key to get the result in E3.

	A	B	C	D	E	F
1			Month		Total	
2	Nature of Expenditure	March	April	May		
3	Food	2300	2275	3450	=SUM(B3:D3)	
4	Electricity	1480	1495	1855	SUM(number1, [number2], …)	
5	Entertainment	1275	1230	1340		

Fig. 7.23 Using SUM() function

AVERAGE( )

1. Select E3.
2. Click on **AutoSum** drop-down list and select **Average**. A marquee will appear from B3 to D3 (Fig. 7.24).
3. Click on **Enter** key.

	A	B	C	D	E	F
1			Month		Average	
2	Nature of Expenditure	March	April	May		
3	Food	2300	2275		=AVERAGE(B3:D3)	
4	Electricity	1480	1495	1855	AVERAGE(number1, [number2], …)	
5	Entertainment	1275	1230	1340		

Fig. 7.24 Using AVERAGE() function

MAX( )

1. Select E3.
2. Click on **AutoSum** drop-down list and select **Max**. A marquee will appear from B3 to D3 (Fig. 7.25).
3. Click on **Enter** key.

	A	B	C	D	E	F
1			Month		Maximum	
2	Nature of Expenditure	March	April	May		
3	Food	2300	2275	3450	=MAX(B3:D3)	
4	Electricity	1480	1495	1855	MAX(number1, [number2], ...)	
5	Entertainment	1275	1230	1340		

Fig. 7.25 *MAX() function*

MIN( )

1. Select E3.
2. Click on **AutoSum** drop-down list and select **Min**. A marquee will appear from B3 to D3 (Fig. 7.26).
3. Click on **Enter** key.

	A	B	C	D	E	F
1			Month		Minimum	
2	Nature of Expenditure	March	April	May		
3	Food	2300	2275	3450	=MIN(B3:D3)	
4	Electricity	1480	1495	1855	MIN(number1, [number2], ...)	
5	Entertainment	1275	1230	1340		

Fig. 7.26 *MIN() function*

Note: Drag to use **Fill Handle** to make similar calculations for the other cells using the specific formula.

This tool can be used for making calculations across rows or columns.

The formula seen on using the AutoSum feature can be manually edited/changed also.

Function Library

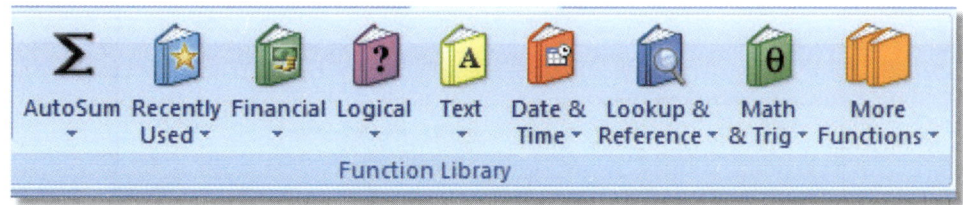

Function Library is a group in the **Formulas** tab of MS Excel 2007. Here different text, date and time, financial, logical functions have been grouped under different options.

We have already learnt about the **AutoSum** option belonging to this group. The **Math & Trig** option can be used to find the H.C.F. and L.C.M. of two or more integers.

H.C.F. (Highest Common Factor)

It is also called as the GCD (Greatest Common Divisor). It is the largest common integer that can divide two or more numbers without leaving a remainder.

Follow these steps to find the H.C.F. of two or more numbers.

1. Enter the numbers in two simultaneous/adjacent cells of the worksheet.
2. Select the simultaneous/adjacent cell (Fig. 7.27).

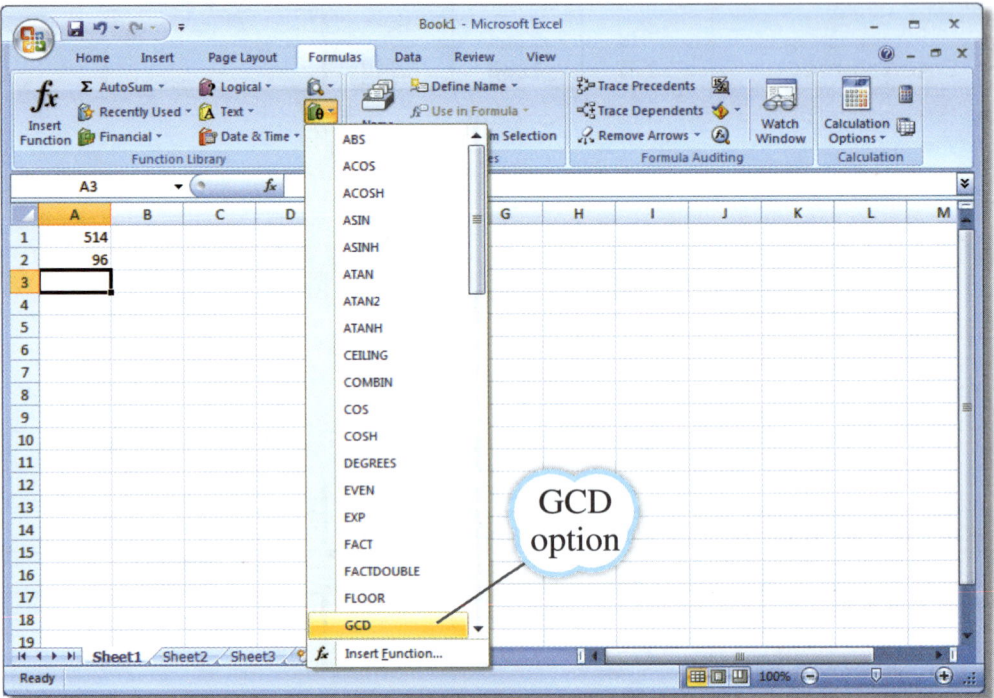

Fig. 7.27 *Function Arguments dialog box*

3. Click on **Formulas** tab ⟹ **Function Library** group ⟹ **Math & Trig** drop-down list ⟹ **GCD** option. The **Function Arguments** dialog box opens (Fig. 7.28).

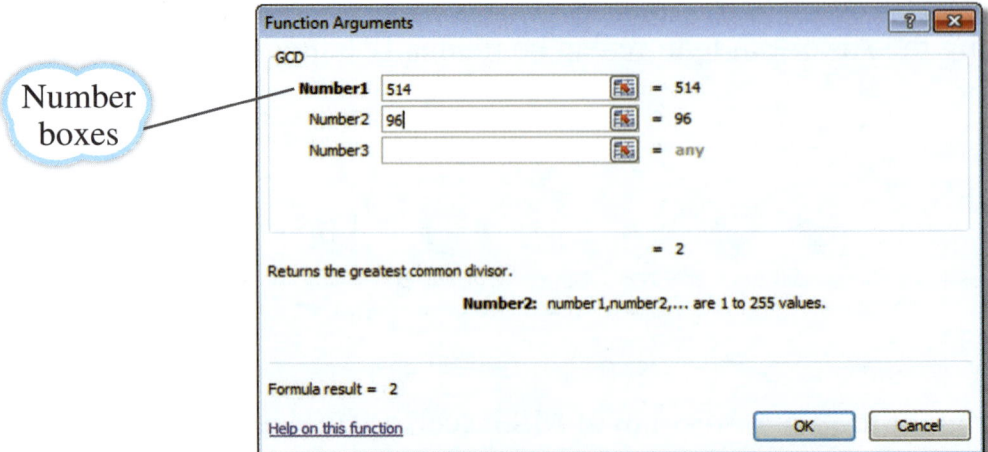

Fig. 7.28 *Function Arguments dialog box*

4. Click and type the first number in the **Number 1** box and second number in **Number 2** box respectively. Additional values can be entered in the subsequent boxes. Click **OK.**

5. The highlighted cell in the worksheet will show the answer.

The same steps can be followed for calculating the **L.C.M. (Lowest Common Factor)** of two or more numbers. Select **LCM** option in the **Math & Trig** drop-down list and enter the values in the **Function Arguments** dialog box.

GLOSSARY

Ampersand (&): It is the operator used to add strings.

Concatenation: It is the process of adding text or string characters.

Formula: It is written with an operand and an operator.

Function: It is a pre-defined formula of MS Excel.

NOW YOU KNOW

1. You can choose a format to enter numbers in MS Excel 2007.

2. The data entered can either be completely replaced by selecting the cell or partially modified by double-clicking on the cell.

3. You can format data by changing fonts and font size, creating borders to a range of cell or giving a pattern to cells.

4. Data list can also be customised and entered in an MS Excel 2007 document automatically.

5. MS Excel formula can be a set of values, cell references, functions, with or without an operator.

6. Once a formula is typed into a cell, the calculation executes immediately and the formula itself is visible in the Formula Bar.

7. Two strings or text values are added using ampersand (&) as an operator.

8. Sometimes errors are displayed in the working cells or the Formula Bar in MS Excel 2007.

9. Some of the basic functions in MS Excel are Sum, Max, Min, Count, Average.

10. AutoSum is a feature of MS Excel 2007 to find the sum, average, maximum, minimum and the count of numbers.

EXERCISE

A **State whether the following sentences are True or False.**

1. You cannot add borders to cells in MS Excel 2007.

2. ##### is a valid formula.

3. It is not important to type '=' before a formula or a function.

4. AutoSum feature calculates the lowest value in the list.

5. Adding of two strings is called concatenation.

B **Write the formula to get the following result:**

1. Add the values from cell A2 to D2 and display result in E2.
2. Find the maximum value from the numbers given in row A from A2 to A5.
3. Find the average of values from C2 to E2.
4. Find the minimum value from the numbers given in row B from B1 to B6.
5. Find the count of values from cells A5 through E12.

C **What happens when:** HOTS

1. The width of the column to display the output is less.
2. The value given for division is divided by 0.
3. You double-click any active cell in MS Excel 2007.
4. You forget to put '=' symbol before the formula.
5. You use an invalid operator.

D **Answer the following questions.**

1. Write the steps to format numbers in MS Excel 2007.
2. What happens if the formula or a function is typed incorrectly? Give some common errors displayed in MS Excel 2007 and their possible reasons.
3. What is the purpose of Count( ) function.
4. Why do you use AutoSum feature?
5. What is a Function Library? List the various options available in it.

LAB WORK

A. **Design an Excel sheet for the employees of a company and their salaries. Calculate:**

1. The average salary of an employee for all the departments.
2. Count the number of employees in the list.
3. Format the department column with a different color.
4. Write the name of the employees who receive salary >100000 in a different font color.

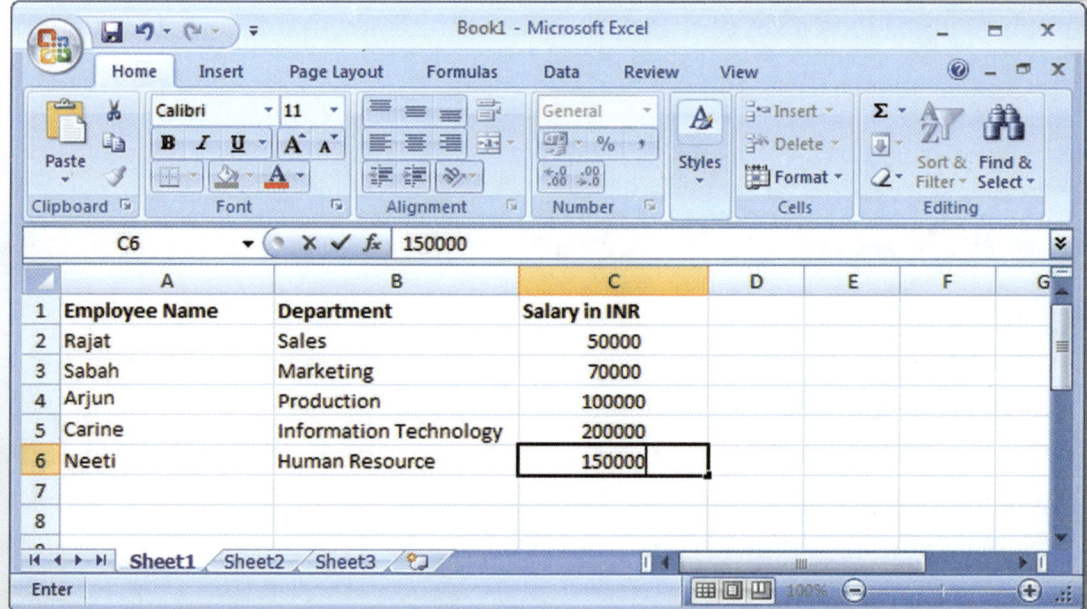

B. **Create a custom list of items purchased at home every month. Show records of the money spent on them for at least four months.**

TEACHER'S NOTES

1. Ask the students to imagine themselves as shopkeepers. Ask them to prepare a list of commodities available at their shop, cost per item, sale of each item per month, etc. in Excel 2007. They should perform all calculations using AutoSum.
2. Ask the students to prepare a list of areas/fields from everyday life where they can use the MS Excel 2007 features studied in this chapter.

8 Introduction to QBASIC

SNAP RECAP

1. A computer language is a set of instructions or commands that a computer understands.

LEARNING OBJECTIVES

You will learn about:
1. QBASIC
2. components of a QBASIC window
3. writing and executing a program
4. how to open a program
5. how to save a program
6. how to exit QBASIC

QBASIC

QBASIC is a programming language. **BASIC** stands for **Beginner's All-purpose Symbolic Instruction Code**. It belongs to the category of high-level programming languages. In 1985, Microsoft released a version of BASIC language called QBASIC (Quick Basic) with its MS DOS 5.0 operating system. It basically supports Character User Interface (CUI). Quick BASIC is an easy-to-use version of the original BASIC. QBASIC became very popular as a programming language because it uses simple statements as commands. There are various versions of Basic like GWBasic, Power Basic, Visual Basic, etc. that are available in the market.

Starting QBASIC

To start QBASIC, you have to run the QBASIC.exe file stored in your computer. The QBASIC window appears with a **Welcome** dialog box (Fig. 8.1).

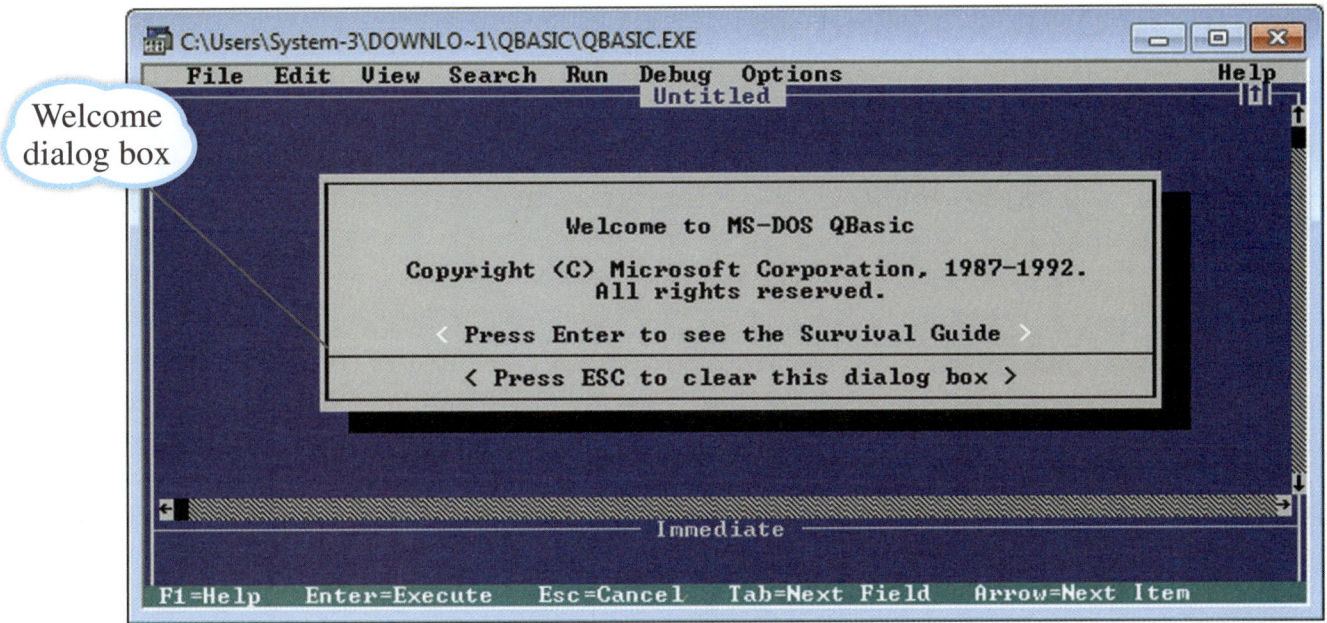

Fig. 8.1 *A QBASIC window*

Press the **Escape** (**Esc**) key to clear the **Welcome** dialog box. The main screen of QBASIC window is revealed (Fig. 8.2).

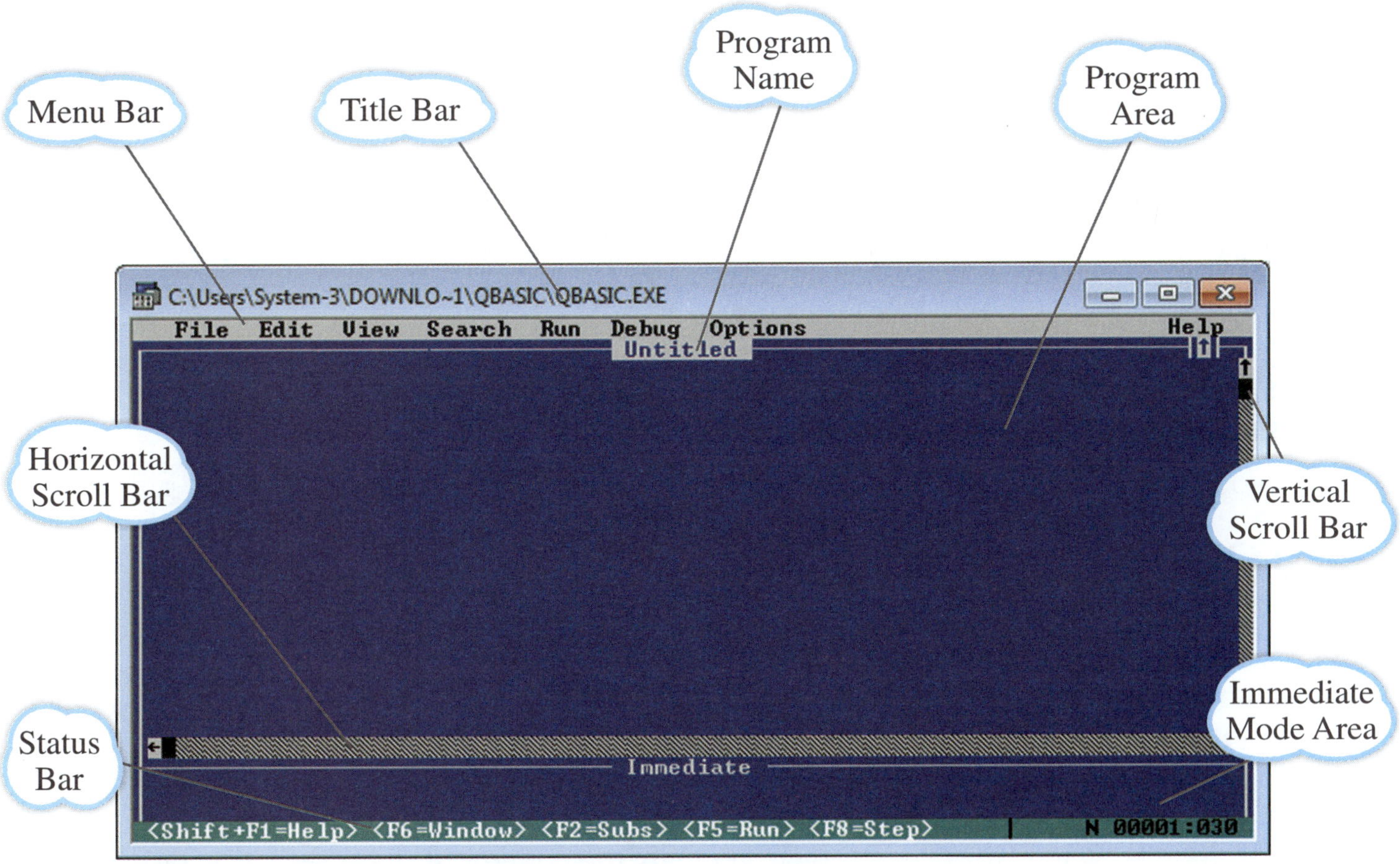

Fig. 8.2 *Components of a QBASIC window*

Components of QBASIC Window

Let us get familiar with the different components of QBASIC window (Fig. 8.2).

Title Bar
The bar present on the top of the window is the Title Bar. It displays the name of the program running along with the file name.

Menu Bar
The Menu Bar is present just below the Title Bar. The Menu Bar has the following menus: File, Edit, View, Search, Run, Debug, Options and Help. You can select the desired menu with a mouse click.

Program Name
It is displayed just below the Menu Bar. By default, it displays 'Untitled'.

Program Area
It is the actual workspace where you type a program. The cursor blinks to show that it is ready to accept the input from the user. Use the various keys on the keyboard to provide the input.

Horizontal scroll bar
It helps to scroll either to the left or to the right of the screen to see a part of the program that is not visible.

Vertical scroll bar
It helps to scroll either to the beginning or to the end of the screen to see the lines that are not visible.

Status Bar
It displays the current position of the cursor. It also displays the shortcut keys for the frequently used commands.

Immediate Mode Area
It is the mode in which a QBASIC statement is executed as soon as the Enter key is pressed.

Using QBASIC for Programming

By now you have already learnt that a set of instructions given to the computer is called a **program**. These instructions are called **commands**. Let us now learn, how to write a simple program in QBASIC using PRINT and CLS commands. However, you must first understand how to use these commands and their respective funtion(s).

CLS command
The CLS command stands for Clear Screen. It clears the content of the screen. To start a program with a fresh screen you can use the CLS as the first line of every program. However, this command can be used anywhere in a program.

PRINT command

The PRINT command as the name suggests is used for displaying the output on the screen. After writing PRINT, the text should be written within double quotes. Numeric values can be written without double quotes.

A PRINT command with no text, displays an empty line on the output screen.

Executing a program

1. Use PRINT and CLS commands to write a simple program. Figure 8.3 showcases one such program.

Fig. 8.3 *Input screen*

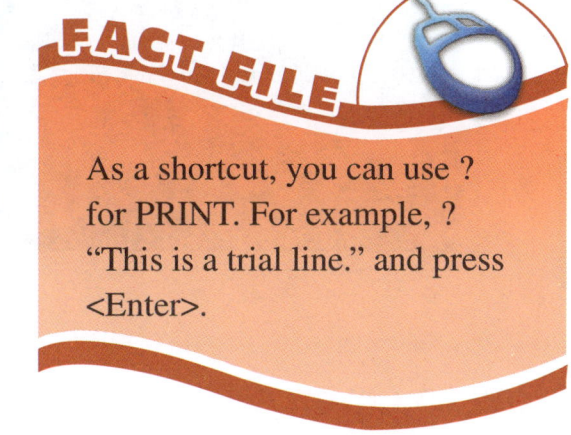

As a shortcut, you can use ? for PRINT. For example, ? "This is a trial line." and press <Enter>.

2. To execute or to run a QBASIC program click on **Run** menu ⟹ **Start** option (Fig. 8.4).

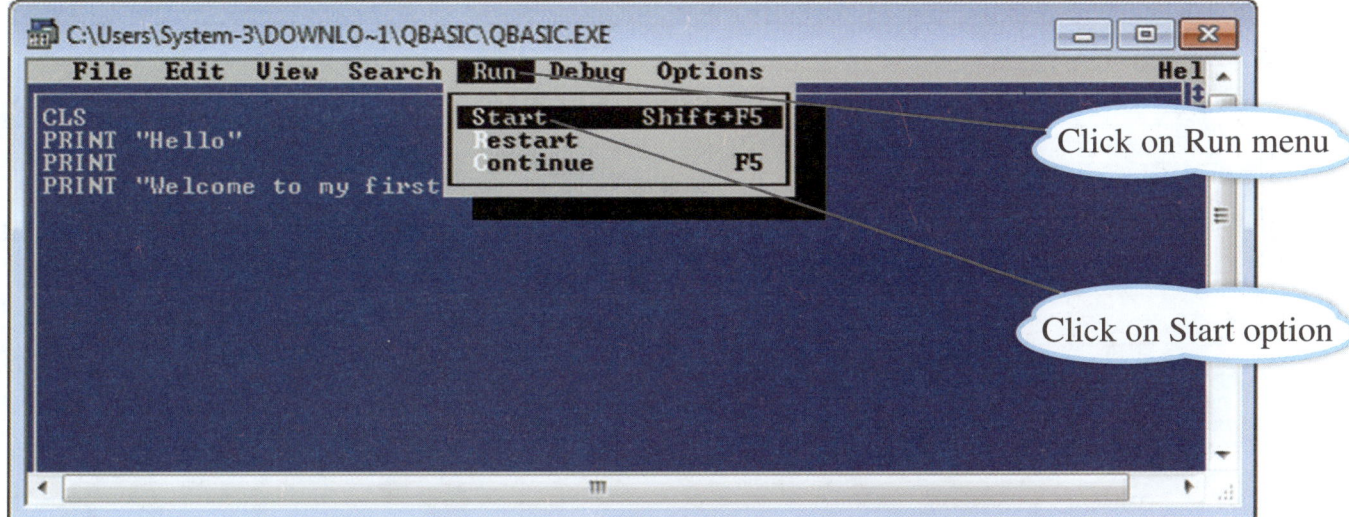

Fig. 8.4 *Using Run menu to execute a QBASIC command*

3. The following output screen occurs (Fig. 8.5).

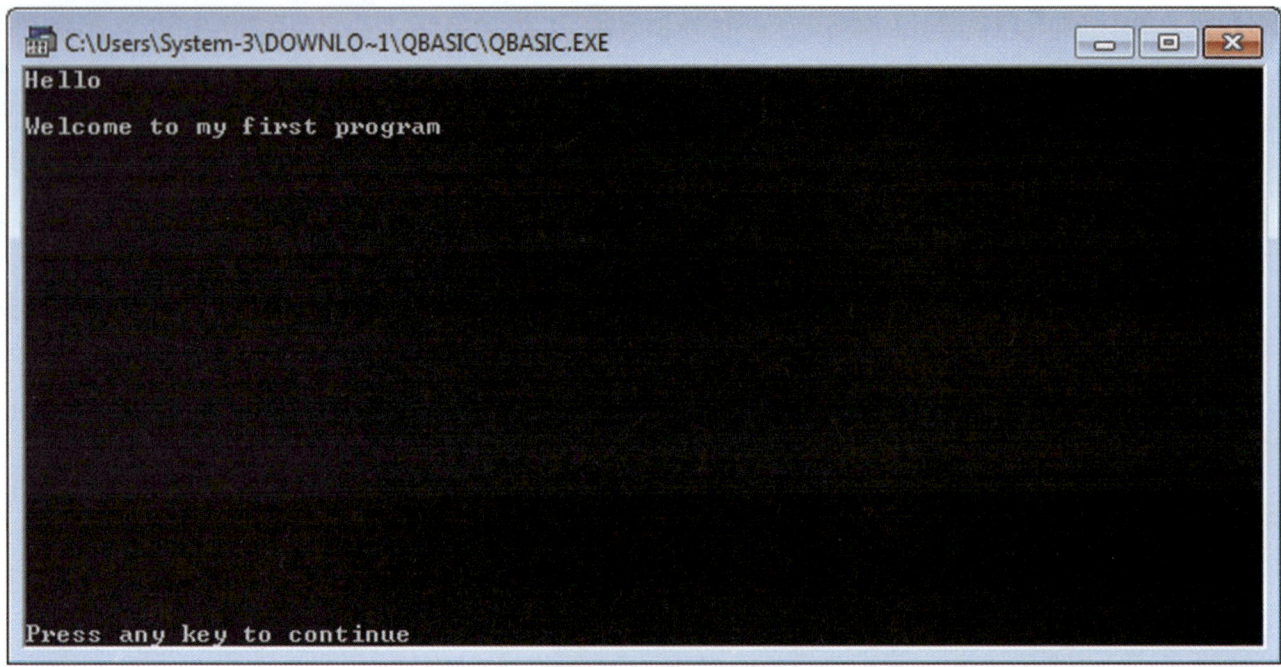

Fig. 8.5 *Output screen*

How to Open a Program

To open an already stored program, follow the steps given below:

1. Click on **File** menu ⟹ **Open...** option (Fig. 8.6).

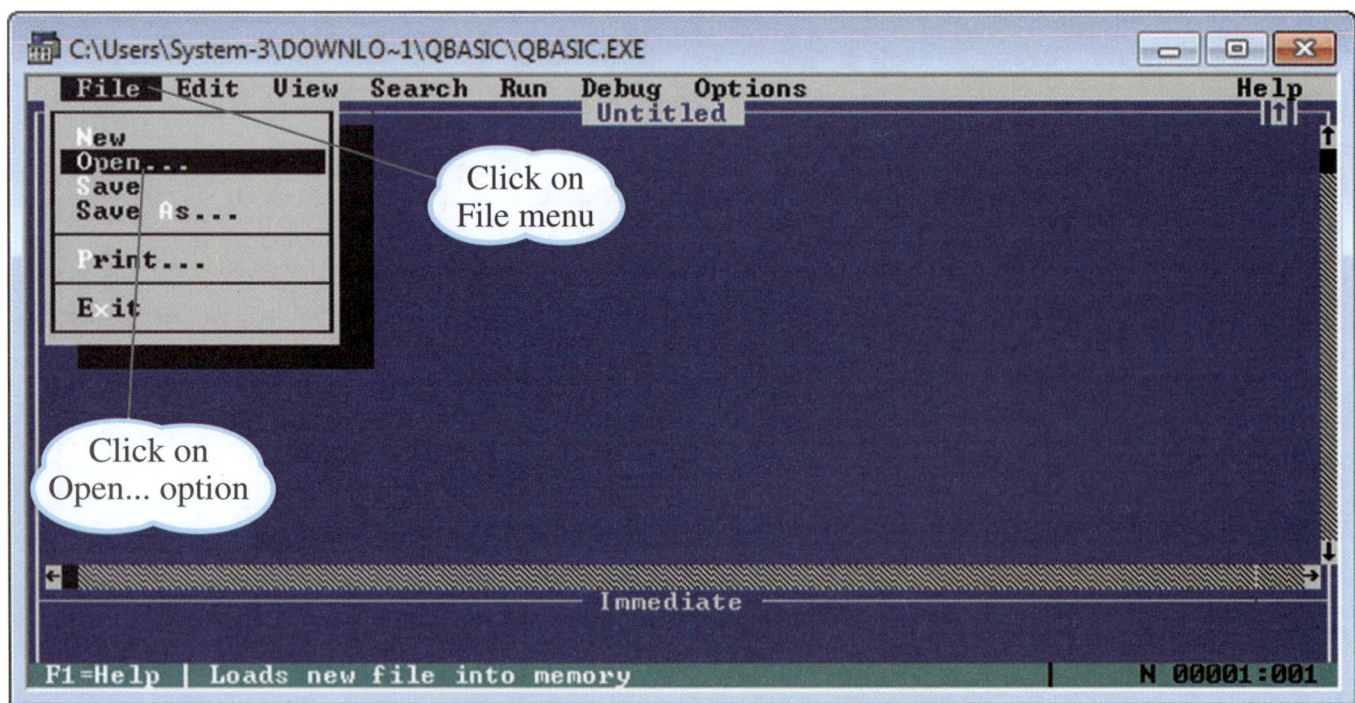

Fig. 8.6 *Opening an already saved program*

2. The **Open** dialog box appears (Fig. 8.7).
3. To open a new program, click **File** menu ⟹ **New** option (Fig. 8.8).

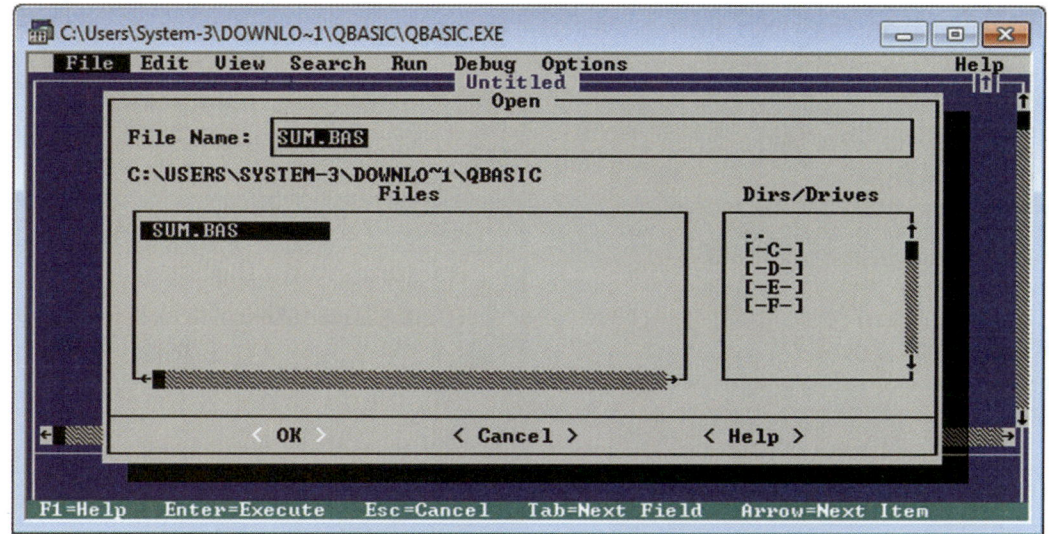

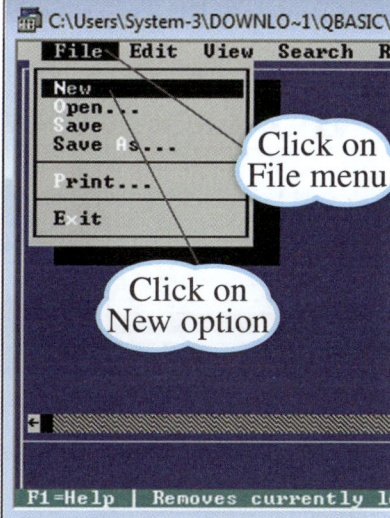

Fig. 8.7 *Open dialog box*

Fig. 8.8 *Opening a new program*

How to Save a Program

After writing a program you can store it in a secondary storage device. If you are saving a file for the first time, you need to use **Save As** option. It helps you to give a name to an untitled program.

The steps to save a program in QBASIC are given here:

1. Click on **File** menu ⟹ **Save As**… option (Fig. 8.9).
2. The **Save As** dialog box appears (Fig. 8.10). Give an appropriate file name. Select the location where you wish to save the program.

Note: A QBASIC program should be saved with the extension of .BAS.

Fig. 8.9 *Saving a program*

Fig. 8.10 *Save As dialog box*

3. Click on **OK**.
4. To save the changes in the existing program file, use **Save** option from the **File** menu.

How to Exit QBASIC

You can quit QBASIC by following the steps given here:

1. Click on **File** menu ⇒ **Exit** option (Fig. 8.11).

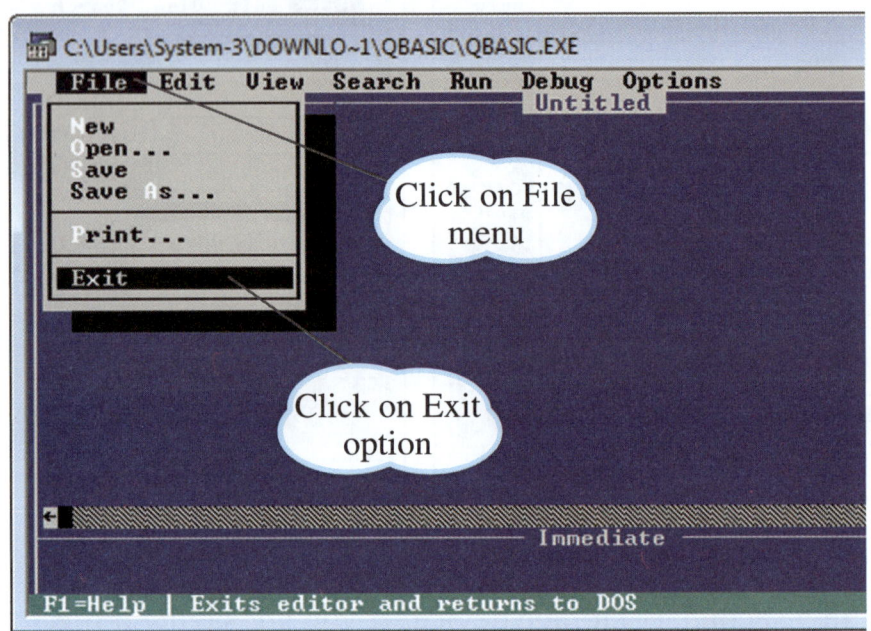

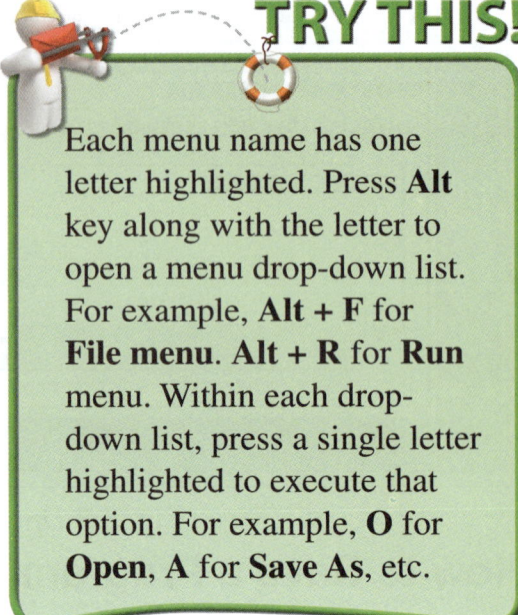

TRY THIS!

Each menu name has one letter highlighted. Press **Alt** key along with the letter to open a menu drop-down list. For example, **Alt + F** for **File menu**. **Alt + R** for **Run** menu. Within each drop-down list, press a single letter highlighted to execute that option. For example, **O** for **Open**, **A** for **Save As**, etc.

Fig. 8.11 *How to exit QBASIC*

2. If the opened file is not saved, it asks if you want to save the file (Fig. 8.12). Select the desired option.

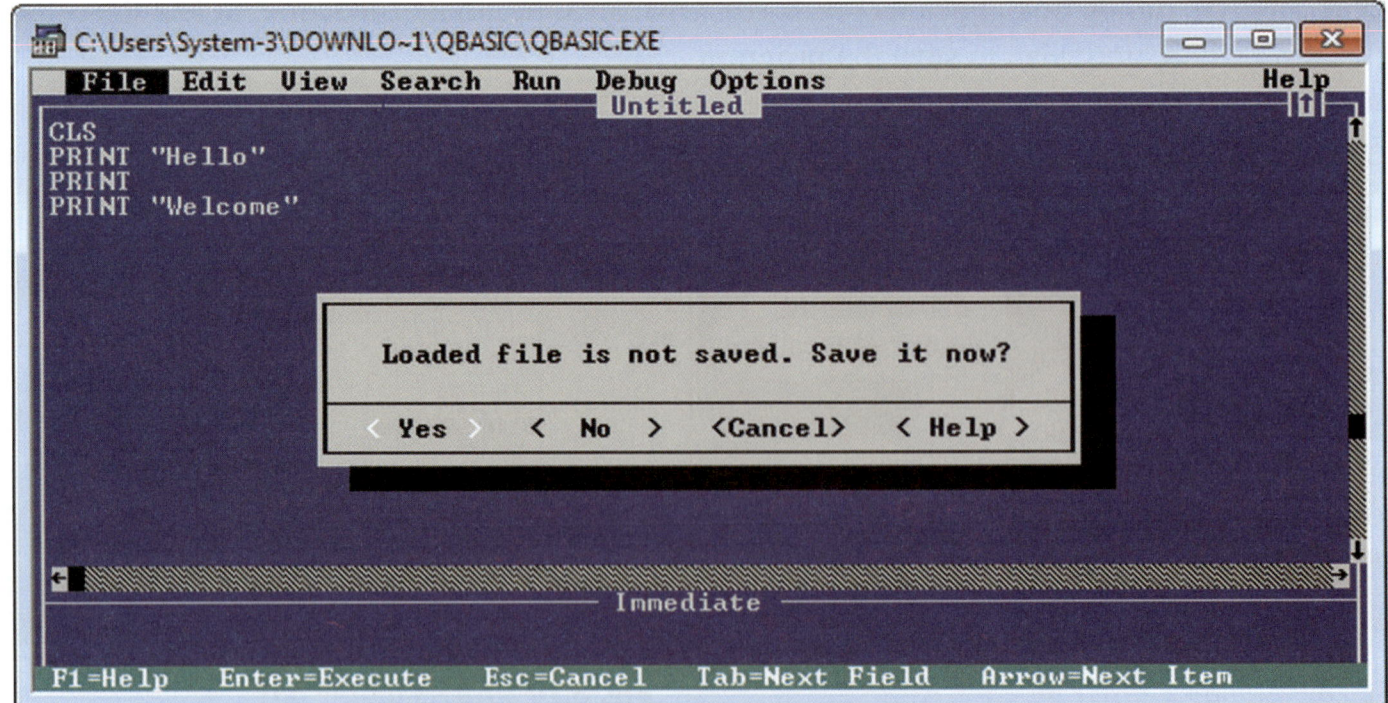

Fig. 8.12 *Saving a file before exiting QBASIC*

ACTIVITY

Rita is writing a program using QBASIC. She writes the following programs. However, they either fail to execute or give a wrong output. Find out the error in her programs.

1. CLS
   Print "My name is Rita"
   "Print" I study in class six

2. CLS
   PINT "Hello"

GLOSSARY

Horizontal scroll bar: It helps to scroll either to the left or the right of the screen.
Immediate Mode Area: It is the area where a QBASIC statement is executed when Enter key is pressed.
Menu Bar: It is the bar present just below the Title Bar.
Program Area: It is the actual workspace where the program is typed.
Program Name: It is displayed just below the Menu Bar.
QBASIC: It stands for Beginner's All-purpose Symbolic Instruction Code.
Status Bar: It displays the status of the current position of the cursor and the shortcut keys for frequently used commands.
Title Bar: It displays the name of the program running and the file name.
Vertical scroll bar: It helps to scroll either to the beginning or to the end of the screen.

NOW YOU KNOW

1. QBASIC is a programming language. It belongs to the category of high-level programming languages.
2. Quick BASIC is an easy-to-use version of the original BASIC.
3. QBASIC screen has different elements: Title Bar, Menu Bar, Program Name, Program Area, Immediate Mode Area, Horizontal and Vertical scroll bars, Status Bar.
4. The CLS command stands for Clear Screen. It helps to clear the content of the screen.
5. The PRINT command is used to display the output on the screen.
6. For executing a program, click on Run menu ⟹ Start option.
7. When saving a file for the first time, it should be saved with the Save As option as it enables to give a name to an untitled program. To save the changes in the existing program file, use Save option.
8. You can quit QBASIC by clicking on File menu ⟹ Exit option.

EXERCISE

A. Fill in the blanks.

1. .... is the extension of QBASIC program.
2. .... option is used to save the changes in the program file.
3. QBASIC is designed from .... language.
4. By default, the name of the program file in QBASIC is ....
5. To exit from QBASIC, you use .... option present in the File menu.

B. Match the following.

1.	QBASIC	a.	Runs a program
2.	Shift + F5	b.	Designed by Microsoft
3.	Save As	c.	File extension in QBASIC
4.	Save	d.	Helps to give a name to a file
5.	.BAS	e.	Changes are saved

C. Label the following picture.

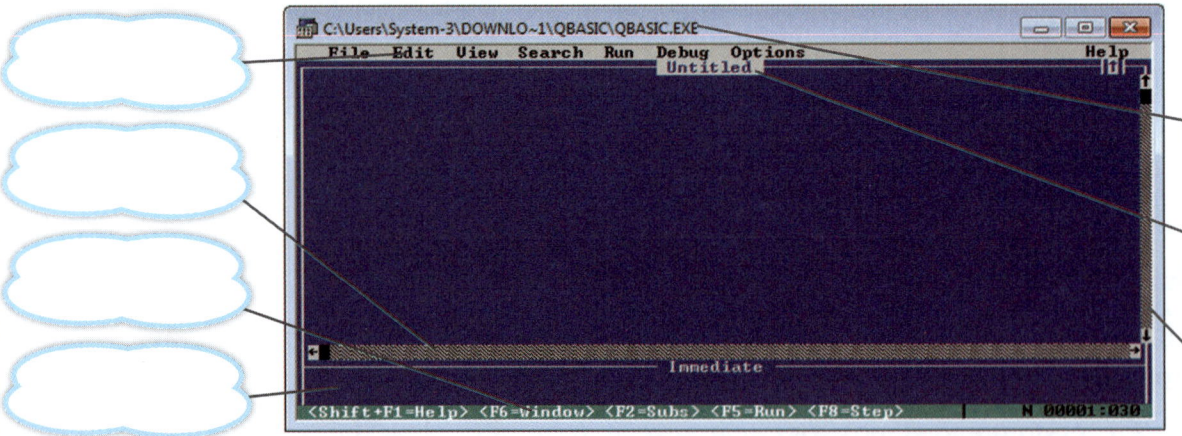

D. Answer the following questions.

1. What is QBASIC?
2. Name the different components of the QBASIC window.
3. What command do you give to clear the output screen? **HOTS**
4. How do you execute a program in QBASIC?
5. What is the full form of BASIC?

LAB WORK

A. **Find out the output of the following programs:**

1. ```
   CLS
   PRINT "******"
   PRINT "****"
   PRINT "**"
   PRINT "*"
   ```

2. ```
   CLS
   PRINT "HI FRIENDS"
   PRINT
   PRINT "QBASIC IS AN INTERESTING LANGUAGE"
   PRINT
   PRINT "TRY OUT YOURSELF"
   ```

B. Find out the options present in the File, Edit, View and Run menu. Make separate lists for all, and write at least a line about each of them.

TEACHER'S NOTES

1. Ask the students to create a short dialogue between them and their best friend using the the QBASIC program.
2. Explain the difference between Windows based QBASIC interpreter and DOS based QBASIC interpreter.

9 QBASIC Statements

SNAP RECAP

1. QBASIC is a programming language.
2. The CLS command stands for Clear Screen. It clears the content on the screen.
3. The PRINT command is used for printing any text on the screen.

LEARNING OBJECTIVES

You will learn about:
1. character set, constants and variables
2. QBASIC statements such as: PRINT, LET, INPUT, REM

Introduction

As with ordinary languages such as English, French, etc. programming languages also have rules of syntax, grammar and spelling. In fact, the application of these rules in a programming language is more strict. This is because a program has to be explicit, as it is a precise statement of the actions to be taken.

QBASIC is a programming language. Just like any other programming language, the elements of QBASIC consist of the character set, the constants, the variables, the operators, and the statements. Let us study about some of these elements here.

Character Set

QBASIC commands are written using some characters and symbols. These can be digits, letters and special characters. The character set used in QBASIC is given below:

1. *Numeric digits:* 0 1 2 3 4 5 6 7 8 9
2. *Letters:* A–Z, a–z
3. *Special characters:* !, @, #, $, %, ^, &, *, (,), >, <, ?, :, ", }, {, [,], etc.

Constants

Constants are such values that do not change during the execution of the program. These can be of the following types.

Numeric constants

These are the numeric digits, that is, integers or real numbers, and can either be positive or negative numbers. Numeric constants can be used in arithmetic calculations. They do not include any special character. For example, 1287, 0.99, 8.45, –7, etc. are all valid numeric constants whereas "764", 67!, 5/6, 4R5, etc. are invalid numeric constants.

String constants

These are the set of characters that include the letters, and can also be combined with the numeric digits, blank spaces and the special characters. String constants are always enclosed within double quotes (" "). For example, "Sachin", "123", "P_Q", etc.

String constants are generally used for comparison and references made in a program and not for the arithmetic calculations.

Variables

A variable is a named memory location that contains a value which may or may not change during program execution. A variable can hold only one value at a time. However, a variable name cannot be a reserved word and can have a maximum of 40 characters. A variable name should always begin with a letter and can have letters, numbers, decimal point but with no space. Variables are of two types. These are: Numeric and String variables.

Numeric variable

It stores only the *numeric values*. The name of the variable can include letters and numeric digits only. A few examples are given below.

    MG = 8 is valid

    LS7 = 6 is valid

    M,L = 9 is invalid

    A @ = 10 is invalid

String variable

It is used for storing *string* values (character set within double quotes). The string variables can be named using letter and numeric digits followed by a '$' sign. These always start with a letter.

A few examples of string variables are given below:

Var$ = "Name" is valid

V56$ = "Name" is valid

%GSV$ = "Name" is invalid

G%$ = "Name" is invalid

ACTIVITY

Write the following as valid or invalid.

String Variable		Numeric Variable	
Click$		5GS5	
3Start$		C-36	
Kite3$		Var2$	
Name		Ch4	

PRINT Statement

PRINT statement is used for displaying a value, message or an output on the monitor.

PRINT "text/message"

This statement prints a text/message on the monitor. The text should be enclosed within double quotes (" ").

For example, the input (Fig. 9.1) and the corresponding output (Fig. 9.2) to display 'Hello' is given here.

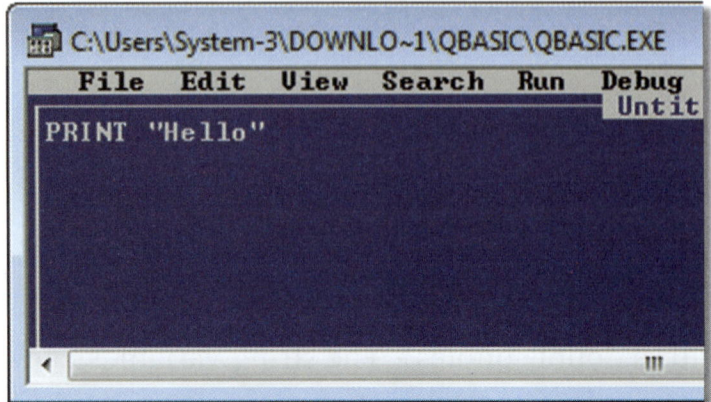

Fig. 9.1 *Input screen*

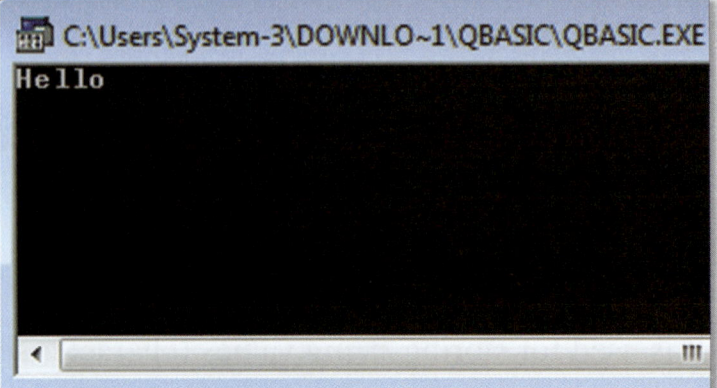

Fig. 9.2 *Output screen*

PRINT <any number>

This statement prints a number. If a number is to be displayed, quotations are not used.

For example, the input and the corresponding output to display '5' is given in Table 9.1.

Table 9.1 *Input – Output*

Input	Output
PRINT 5	5

PRINT "text", <any number>

This statement prints both text message and number. The text and numbers that are to be displayed are separated by a comma (,).

For example, the input and the corresponding output to display 'The sum of given numbers is 15' is given in Table 9.2.

Table 9.2 *Input – Output*

Input	Output
PRINT "The sum of given numbers is", 15	The sum of given numbers is 15

PRINT

PRINT statement without anything is used to display a blank line.

For example, the input and the corresponding output to display a blank line is given in Table 9.3.

Table 9.3 *Input – Output*

Input	Output
PRINT "Hello Friends" PRINT PRINT "Enjoying QBASIC"	Hello Friends Enjoying QBASIC

PRINT with separators

More than one expression list can be printed in one PRINT statement but a separator must be used.

Comma separator (,): It is similar to a Tab key. A comma when used between the two printing statements with one PRINT command leaves a gap of one tab space. For example, for the given input, the output is shown in Table 9.4.

Table 9.4 *Input – Output*

Input	Output
PRINT "The sum of given numbers is", 15	The sum of given numbers is 15

Semicolon separator (;): It is similar to pressing Space Bar key once. A semicolon when used between two printing statements with one print command leaves a gap of one space. For example, for the given input, the output is shown in Table 9.5.

Table 9.5 *Input – Output*

Input	Output
PRINT "The sum of numbers is"; 15	The sum of numbers is 15

ACTIVITY

Make a small program that:

1. Prints your name, skips the next line, then prints your address.
2. Use multiple PRINT commands to print your street address and your city.
3. Run it and then replace semicolons with commas or vice versa to see the difference in the output.

LET Statement

LET statement is used for assigning a value to a variable within a program whose value may change during the program execution.

For example, the input and the corresponding output to display '20' using LET statement is given in Table 9.6.

Note: The variable num is assigned a value of 20.

Table 9.6 *Input – Output*

Input	Output
LET num = 20 PRINT num	20

For example, the input and the corresponding output to display 'David' using LET statement is given in Table 9.7.

Table 9.7 *Input – Output*

Input	Output
LET Name$ = "David" PRINT Name$	David

Note: In the above examples, num is a numeric variable whereas Name$ is a string variable.

FACT FILE

Adding two strings and storing the value in a variable is called as **concatenation**. For example, to display 'ClickStart' through concatenation, the input and the corresponding output will be as shown below.

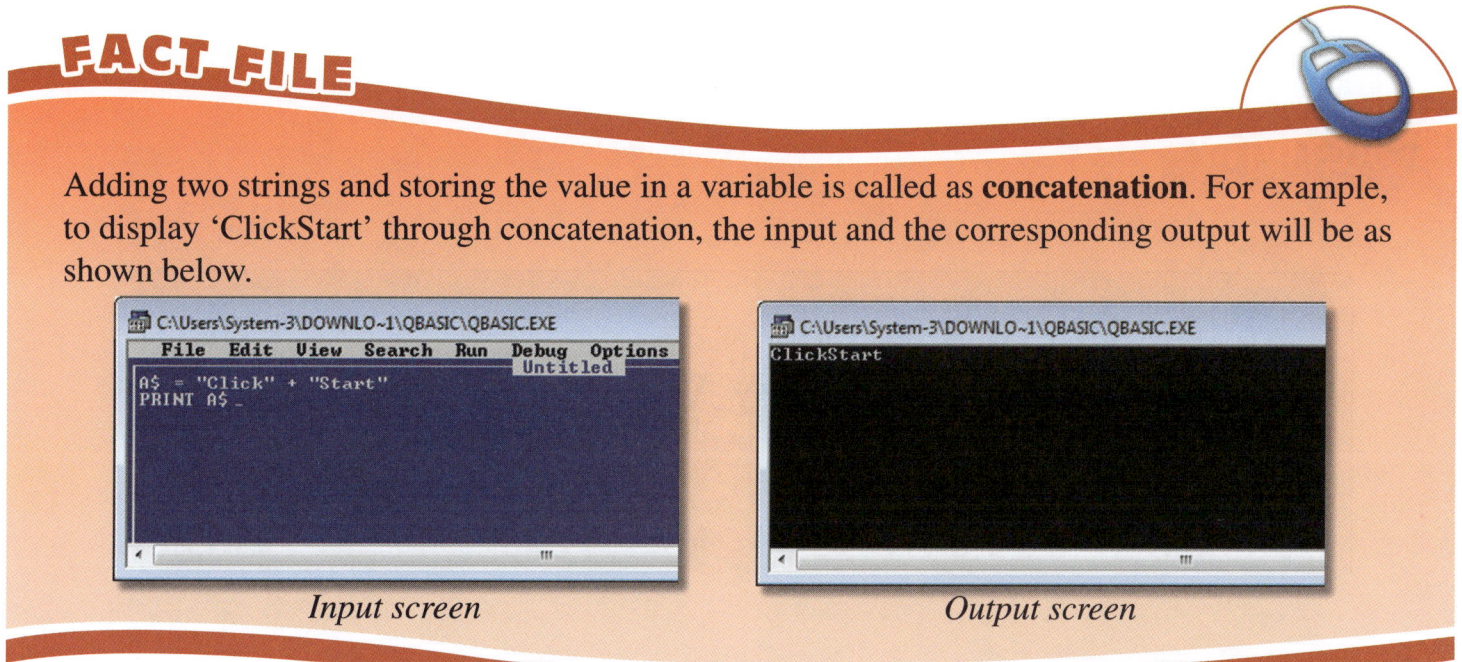

Input screen   *Output screen*

INPUT Statement

INPUT statement is used for accepting a value (text or numbers) from the user in a variable through the keyboard during run time, that is, while executing the program. The name of the variable is mentioned after the INPUT command where the accepted value will be entered.

INPUT command will print and wait for the user to enter the value and then assign this value to the variable.

Note: You can use either of the separators with INPUT command.

For example,

    INPUT, Name$

Here the program will accept a name from the user.

Now, let us consider another example and see its output in Table 9.8.

Table 9.8 *Input – Output*

Input	Output
CLS INPUT Age$ PRINT "I am"; Age$; "years old."	? 11 I am 11 years old.

Note: In the above example, the values that go into the INPUT variables are not known. To give a value, you must provide a valid input when the program is made to run and the provided window with PRINT command.

ACTIVITY

Find the output of the following program:

```
CLS
INPUT "Enter your name=", Name$
PRINT "Hello "; Name$; "! How are you today?"
```

REM Statement

REM stands for **remark**. REM adds comments in a program. Remarks are non-executable statements in a program that enhance the readability of the program code. It only appears in the programming code, and has no effect on the output of the program. In QBASIC, REM or a single quote mark (') is used to mark a statement as a comment. Whatever is written after a REM statement or a single quote mark, is ignored.

Note: Always leave a space after you write REM.

For example, comments are added in the program given below by using REM in the first case and single quote (') in the latter one.

　　PRINT "This is a trial program"
　　REM To print a statement
　　INPUT "Enter your Roll No.", roll 'To accept a value in a variable roll

Know Your Commands	
CLS	Clearscreen
PRINT	To print text numbers or a line space
LET	To assign value to a variable
INPUT	To accept value at the time of program execution
REM	To add remarks or comments

GLOSSARY

Character set: It is a set of characters and symbols based on which QBASIC commands are written.

Constant: It is a value that does not change during the execution of a program.

INPUT Statement: It is a statement used for accepting a value (text or numbers) from the user at the time of program execution.

LET Statement: It is a statement used for assigning a value to a variable within a program whose value may change during the program execution.

Numeric variable: It is a variable that stores numeric values.

PRINT Statement: It is a statement used for displaying a value, message or an output on the monitor.

REM: It stands for remark and it adds comments in a program.

String variable: It is a variable that stores strings.

String: It is an alphanumeric value that is given within double quotes (" ").

Variable: It is a named memory location that contains a value which may change during program execution.

NOW YOU KNOW

1. The character set used in QBASIC can be numeric digits, letters or special characters.
2. Constants can be numeric constants or string constants.
3. PRINT statement without anything is used to display a blank line.
4. PRINT statements with semicolon as a separator will leave a space of one tab in between.
5. PRINT statements with comma as a separator will leave a gap of one space in between.
6. A variable is a named memory location that contains a value which may change during program execution.
7. Remarks are non-executable statements in a program which enhance the readability of a program code.

EXERCISE

A Fill in the blanks.

1. ……………………… and ……………………… are the two separators used with PRINT statement.
2. ……………………… is a name of the memory location.
3. ……………………… are non-executable statements.
4. To accept a value from the user, ……………………… statement is used.
5. ……………………… sign is used with string variables.

B Write the command for the following statements. ◀HOTS▶

1. To display "Hello" message on the screen.
2. To leave a blank line.
3. To assign a value 10 to a number variable N2.
4. To assign a string value "ABC" to a string variable NAME2.
5. To give comments THIS IS A TRIAL PROGRAM.
6. To accept class teacher's name in the variable CLTEACHER.

C Give the differences between:

1. REM and PRINT
2. STRING Variable and NUMBER Variable
3. INPUT and PRINT
4. PRINT with semicolon (;) and PRINT with comma (,)

D Answer the following questions.

1. What is PRINT statement? Give two examples.
2. What is a variable? Explain two types of variables.
3. What is the use of REM statement? Give an example.
4. What is the importance of the INPUT statement? Give an example.

LAB WORK

A. Write a program for the following:

Accept the name of two friends in the variables and display a welcome message as shown here.

"Hi" <name1> "and" <name2>

"Welcome to my Party"

B. Predict the output of the following code:

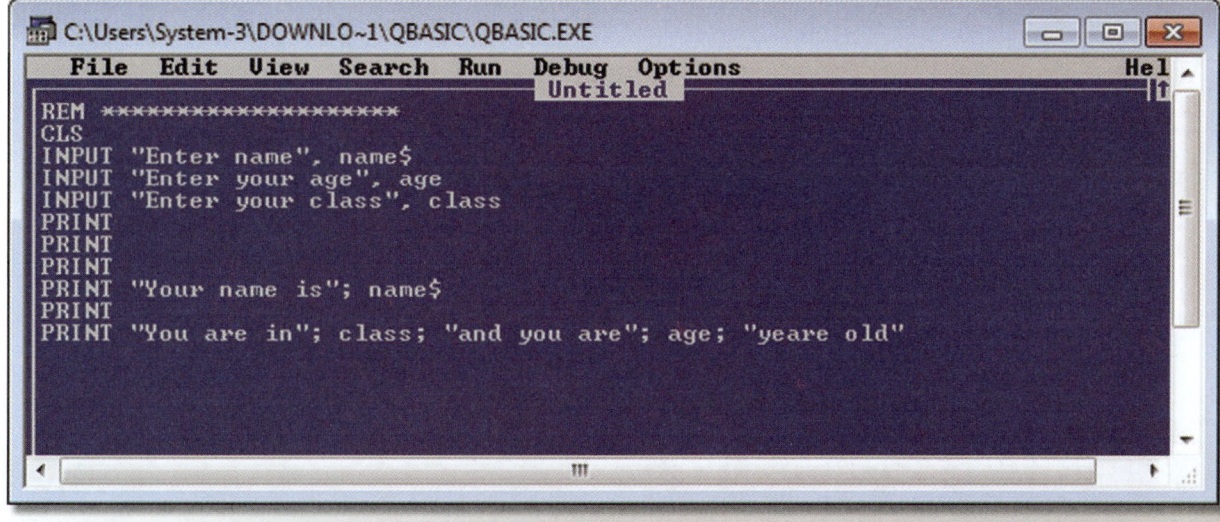

```
REM ********************
CLS
INPUT "Enter name", name$
INPUT "Enter your age", age
INPUT "Enter your class", class
PRINT
PRINT
PRINT
PRINT "Your name is"; name$
PRINT
PRINT "You are in"; class; "and you are"; age; "yeare old"
```

JOHN G. KEMENY

John G. Kemeny was born on 31 May, 1926 in Budapest, Hungary. He emigrated to the United States in 1940.

Along with Thomas E. Kurtz, Kemeny developed a completely new language, simple enough for beginners to learn quickly, yet flexible enough to handle different kinds of applications. This was the *Beginner's All-purpose Symbolic Instruction Code*, more commonly known as BASIC.

TEACHER'S NOTES

1. Ask the students to write five lines about themselves using the commands learnt in the chapter.
2. Ask the students to practice the commands learnt in the chapter by creating their own programs.

10 QBASIC – Programming Statements I

SNAP RECAP

1. The CLS command helps to clear the content on the screen.
2. The PRINT command is used for printing any text on the screen.
3. For executing a program, press Shift + F5.
4. QBASIC commands are written using some characters and symbols.
5. Remarks are non-executable statements.

LEARNING OBJECTIVES

You will learn about:
1. IF … THEN
2. IF … THEN … ELSE
3. Using ELSEIF with IF … THEN statement

Introduction

QBASIC helps us to work with several commands using various operators and looping statements. These commands help us to write programs to solve various complex problems.

The set of instructions written in a specific programming language is called as programming statements. Every programming language has three types of programming statements. They are:

1. Sequential
2. Conditional
3. Iterations or Loops

Let us learn about the sequential and conditional programming statements here.

Sequential Statements

All the programs in QBASIC that you have done so far come under sequential category. Here, the statements are executed one after the other in the sequence they are written, that is, the statements written first are executed first.

For example, for the given input (Fig. 10.1) the corresponding output is shown here (Fig. 10.2).

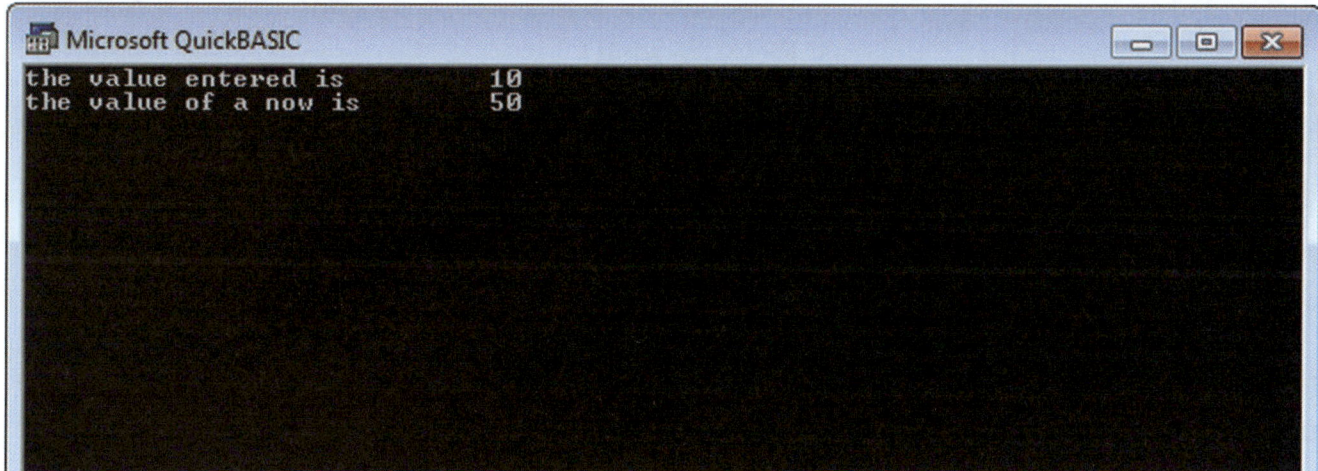

Fig. 10.1 *Input screen*

Fig. 10.2 *Output screen*

Conditional Statements

When the flow of control of the program is based on a condition then you make use of the conditional statements. For example, IF … THEN … ELSE loop.

Before you start with the conditional statements you must know the operators first.

Operators

Operators are the symbols used for evaluating an expression in a language. The following are the categories of operators used in QBASIC language.

Arithmetic operators: These are used for evaluating a mathematical expression in a programming statement (Table 10.1). These operate on the numeric constants and variables.

Table 10.1 *Arithmetic Operators*

Action	Operator	Example
Add	+	PRINT 4+5 'Displays 9
Subtract	–	PRINT 10–5 'Displays 5
Multiply	*	PRINT 2*3 'Displays 6
Divide	/	PRINT 10/2 'Displays 5 PRINT 15/2 'Displays 7.5
Exponential	^	PRINT 4^2 'Displays 16
Modulus	MOD	PRINT 15 MOD 3 'Displays the remainder by dividing 15 by 3, i.e., 0 PRINT 5 MOD 2 'Displays 1
Integer Division	\	PRINT 15\2 'Displays the integer part by dividing 15 by 2, i.e., 7 PRINT 47\7 'Displays 6

Relational operators: These set of operators are used when you want to make a comparison between any two values (Table 10.2). It displays the result as true or false depending upon the value given.

Table 10.2 *Relational Operators*

Action	Operator	Example
Less than	<	IF x < 10 THEN
Less than or equal to	=<, <=	IF marks <= 33 THEN
Greater than	>	IF age > 18 THEN
Greater than or equal to	>=, =>	IF age >= 18 THEN
Equal to	=	IF x mod 2 = 0 THEN
Not equal to	<>, ><	IF a <> 10 THEN

FACT FILE

In a statement containing both arithmetic and relational operators, arithmetic operation will be done first.

Logical operators: These are used for combining two or more conditions. These operators give a single value, which is either true or false. You generally use them to combine conditions in IF statements (Table 10.3).

Table 10.3 *Logical Operators*

Action	Operator	Example
All conditions should be true	AND	IF x > 10 AND x <= 20 THEN
Any one condition should be true	OR	IF Class = 8 OR Section$ = "A" THEN
Negates the condition	NOT	If NOT a < 10 THEN

String operator: These are also called **concatenation** operators. These are used for combining two strings together (Table 10.4).

Table 10.4 *Logical Operators*

Action	Operator	Example
Combines two strings	+	Print "Good" + "Morning" Displays GoodMorning

ACTIVITY

Find the output of the following statements:

1. X = 5 + (2 * 7)
   PRINT X

2. A = 5
   B = 2
   C = A * B
   PRINT C

3. N = 4
   M = N – 2
   If M ≥ 0
   THEN PRINT "True"

4. Y$ = "HI"
   Y$ = Y$ + " BUDDY"
   PRINT Y$

Also, make the calculations for parts 1 and 2 using a calculator and see if the answers match.

IF ... THEN ... ELSE statement

Syntax or the language rule for the IF ... THEN ... ELSE statement is:

IF *condition* THEN *statement* [ELSE *statement*]

IF command is used for executing a statement based on a condition. It implements the branching of the execution in two parts:

1. If the condition written next to IF is true then the statement part will be executed.
2. If the condition is false then the statement after the ELSE part will be executed. After the execution of the IF statement the flow of execution continues to the next line and follows the sequential method till the next control branching is encountered.

FACT FILE

Every IF statement may or may not have an ELSE part which means this statement will have only one condition.

For example,

IF score < 10 THEN PRINT "Try again!"

This is a correct statement where nothing will be displayed if score is greater than or equal to 10.

When is IF ... THEN ... ELSE command used

IF command is used when the control branching is based on one condition.

For example,

IF score < 10 THEN PRINT "Try again!" ELSE PRINT "Keep it up!"

Sample Program 1: To display text depending on the score entered.

The input and the corresponding output for Sample Program 1 is given in Table 10.5.

Table 10.5 *Input – Output*

Input	CLS INPUT "Score", score IF score < 10 THEN PRINT "Try again!" "ELSE PRINT "keep it up!"
Output	Score 9 Try again!

Sample Program 2: To accept two numbers and display the larger one. The input and the corresponding outputs for Sample Program 2 is given in Table 10.6.

Table 10.6 *Input – Output*

Input	CLS INPUT "enter the first number:", N1 INPUT "enter the second number:", N2 IF N1 > N2 THEN PRINT "N1 is bigger" ELSE PRINT "N2 is bigger" END
Output 1	enter the first number: 33 enter the second number: 45 N2 is bigger
Output 2	enter the first number: 8 enter the second number: 4 N1 is bigger

ACTIVITY

A. Find out the output of the following code:

```
CLS
INPUT "x=", x
IF x > 10 THEN PRINT "x is greater than 10"
IF x < 10 THEN PRINT "x is less than 10"
```

B. Write a program for the following:

Accept an age of a driver and if the age is more than 18 then display "Eligible for driving" else "Sorry! not eligible"

END IF statement with IF

END IF is given to end the IF statement. It is generally used when the user wants to add multiple statements to be executed. All the statements must be written within IF ... ENDIF statement.

Sample Program 3: To check whether the number is even or not.

The input and the corresponding output for Sample Program 3 is given in Table 10.7.

Table 10.7 *Input – Output*

Input	CLS LET a = 6 IF a MOD 2 = 0 THEN 'Even numbers are divisible by 2 PRINT "Even Number" END IF
Output	Even Number

In this program, the statements will be executed when the number is an even number. What will happen when the number is not even? Try to find out the answer to this question by changing the value of a = 7.

Sample Program 4: To find the greater number in a given pair of numbers.

The input and the corresponding output for Sample Program 4 is given in Table 10.8.

Table 10.8 *Input – Output*

Input	CLS
	INPUT "enter the first number:", N1
	INPUT "enter the second number:", N2
	IF N1 > N2 THEN
	PRINT N1; "is greater"
	ELSE
	PRINT N2; "is greater"
	END IF

Output	enter the first number: 56 enter the second number: 78 78 is greater

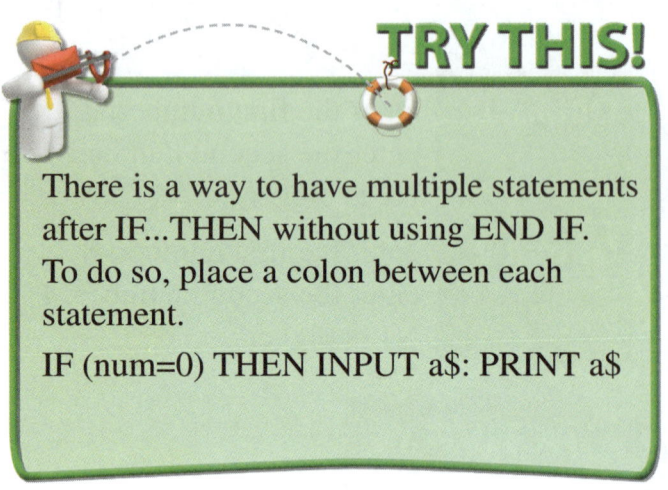

TRY THIS!

There is a way to have multiple statements after IF...THEN without using END IF. To do so, place a colon between each statement.

IF (num=0) THEN INPUT a$: PRINT a$

ELSEIF statement

The ELSEIF statement allows you to execute a set of statements if the previous condition is false. It is generally used when you have multiple conditions in a program.

Sample Program 5: To display grades according to the marks. The input and the corresponding output for Sample Program 5 is given in Table 10.9.

Table 10.9 *Input – Output*

Input	CLS
	INPUT "Enter your Marks:", Marks
	IF Marks >= 90 THEN
	PRINT "Grade A+"
	ELSEIF Marks >= 80 AND Marks < 90 THEN
	PRINT "Grade A"
	ELSEIF Marks >= 70 AND Marks < 80 THEN
	PRINT "Grade B"
	END IF

Output	Enter your Marks: 88 Grade A

Sample Program 6: To identify a letter as a vowel or a consonant.

You can have either one ELSEIF statement or even many in a program. The input and the corresponding output for Sample Program 6 is given in Table 10.10.

Table 10.10 *Input – Output*

Input	CLS
	INPUT "Enter a letter:", L$
	IF L$ = "a" THEN
	PRINT "Vowel"
	ELSELF L$ = "e" THEN
	PRINT "Vowel"
	ELSELF L$ = "i" THEN
	PRINT "Vowel"
	PRINT L$ = "o" THEN
	PRINT "Vowel"
	PRINT L$ = "u" THEN
	PRINT "Vowel"
	ELSELF L$ < > "a" OR L$ < > "e" OR L$ < > "i" OR L$ < > "o" OR L$ < > "u" THEN
	PRINT "Consonant"
	END IF
Output	Enter a letter : M
	Consonant

GLOSSARY

Arithmetic operators: It is a set of operators used to evaluate a mathematical expression.
Conditional statements: It is set of statements used when the flow of control of the program is based on a condition.
Logical operators: It is a set of operators used to combine two or more conditions.
Operator: It is a symbol used to evaluate an expression in a language.
Relational operators: It is a set of operators used to make a comparison between any two values.
Sequential statements: It is program where statements are executed in a sequence.
String operator: It is an operator which combines two strings together.

NOW YOU KNOW

1. Programming statements can be sequential, conditional and iterational.
2. You use IF…THEN… ELSE to execute a statement based on a condition.
3. END IF is given to end the IF statement. It is generally used when the user wants to add multiple statements to be executed.
4. The ELSEIF allows to execute set of statements if the previous condition is false. In other words, it is generally used when you have multiple conditions in programming.

EXERCISE

A Fill in the blanks.

1. Sequential statements are a type of ……………………… statements in QBASIC.
2. ……………………… are the symbols used for evaluating an expression in a language.
3. ……………………… and ……………………… are the logical statements.
4. String operators are used for ……………………… the strings.
5. ……………………… are also called concatenation operators.

B Give command(s) for the following:

1. To create a variable with value 5.
2. Display the addition of 2 and 4.
3. Display the division of 20 and 4.
4. Display the message "My School", "is the Best".

C Find the errors in the following codes: HOTS

1. CLS
   INPUT "ENTER NUMBER, N1
   INPUT "ENTER NUMBER, N2"
   N3 = N1 + N2
   PRINT "THE SUM IS", N3

2. INPUT "ENTER YOUR NAME", NAME
   INPUT "ENTER MARKS", M1
   PRINT "HELLO", NAME
   PRINT "YOU SCORED", M1

D Answer the following questions.

1. What are the different types of programming statements?
2. What is the use of IF… ELSE statement? Write a small code to support your answer.
3. What are operators? Give examples.
4. When do you use relational operators? Give examples.
5. Why do you use ELSEIF statement?

LAB WORK

Write a code for the following instructions:

1. Accept time in hours and display it in seconds with an appropriate message.

2. Accept a number and print an appropriate message if the number is even.

3. Accept an age and find out whether the person is eligible for voting or not in your country. Print an appropriate message.

4. Accept the percentage from the user. Display "Congratulations" if the percentage is more than 80 and "Commiseration" if it is less than 80.

TEACHER'S NOTES

1. Ask the students to summarise all the commands learnt in QBASIC so far in MS Word 2007. The different features of Word 2007 can be used to make the document attractive.
2. Use the Internet to explore the Easter Egg concept in QBASIC along with the students.

11 Introduction to Macromedia Flash

LEARNING OBJECTIVES

You will learn about:

1. starting Flash
2. Flash tools panel
3. gradient effects
4. a few important terms
5. animation in Flash
6. creating an animation
7. symbols

Introduction

Macromedia Flash is a software that enables the user to make interactive animations. It is a user-friendly software that does not require any special programming skills to work on. You can create movies and motion pictures with Flash. Flash files can also be embedded into a website to make it interactive.

Starting Flash

Flash is available in several versions such as Macromedia Flash Professional Version 8, Version 9, Version 10, etc. In this lesson, you will learn about Macromedia Flash Professional Version 8. Follow these steps to start Macromedia Flash:

1. Click on **Start** ⟹ **All Programs** ⟹ **Macromedia** ⟹ **Macromedia Flash 8**. The opening screen appears (Fig. 11.1).

FACT FILE

Macromedia flash was acquired by Adobe in 2005. The higher versions are now thus known as Adobe Flash.

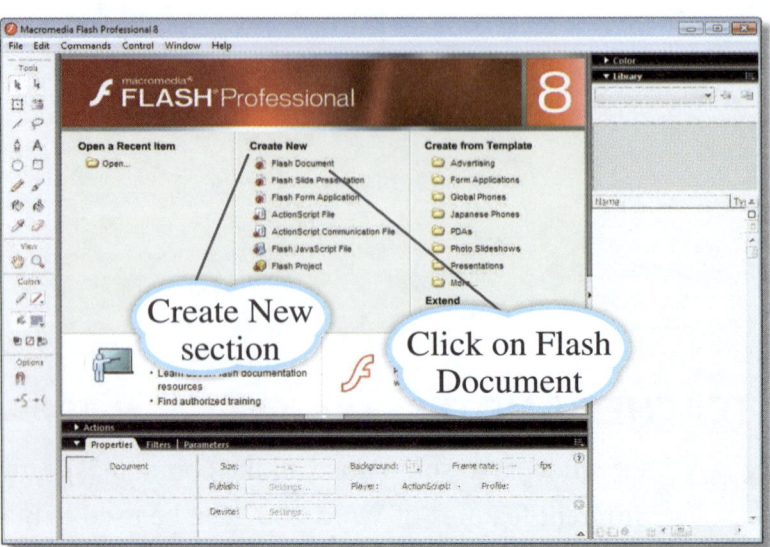

Fig. 11.1 *Macromedia Flash start window*

2. In the **Create New** section, click on the **Flash Document** option. The Flash window appears. It is named Untitled-1, by default. The main components of a Flash window are shown in Figure 11.2.

Note: Any element that is drawn or inserted in a Flash document is called an **object**.

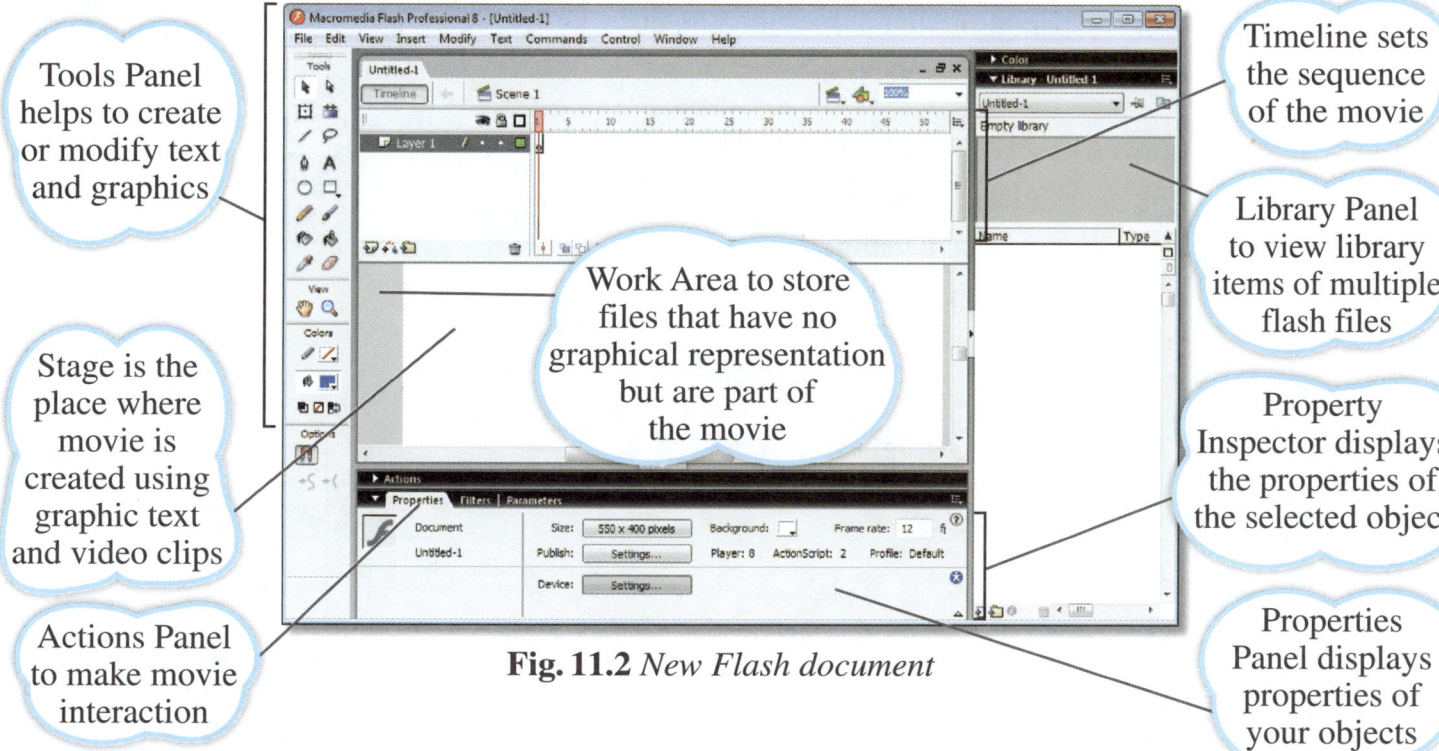

Fig. 11.2 *New Flash document*

- Tools Panel helps to create or modify text and graphics
- Stage is the place where movie is created using graphic text and video clips
- Actions Panel to make movie interaction
- Work Area to store files that have no graphical representation but are part of the movie
- Timeline sets the sequence of the movie
- Library Panel to view library items of multiple flash files
- Property Inspector displays the properties of the selected object
- Properties Panel displays properties of your objects

Flash Tools Panel

The Flash Tools panel helps to create, select paint and modify shapes for the artwork in the movies. Let us get familiar with the Flash Tools panel (Fig. 11.3). Some of the Flash tools, their icons, usage and effects are given in Table 11.1.

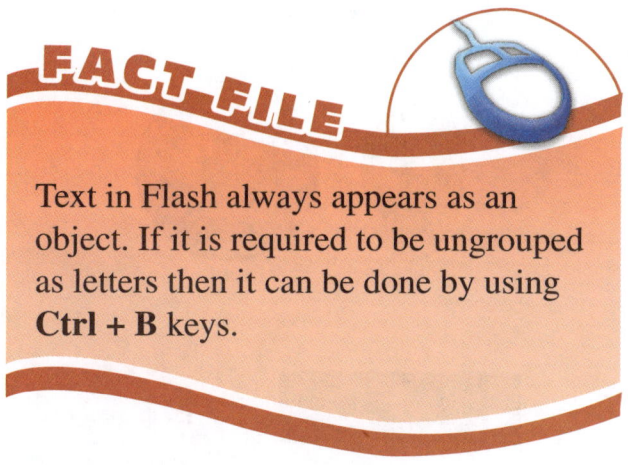

FACT FILE

Text in Flash always appears as an object. If it is required to be ungrouped as letters then it can be done by using **Ctrl + B** keys.

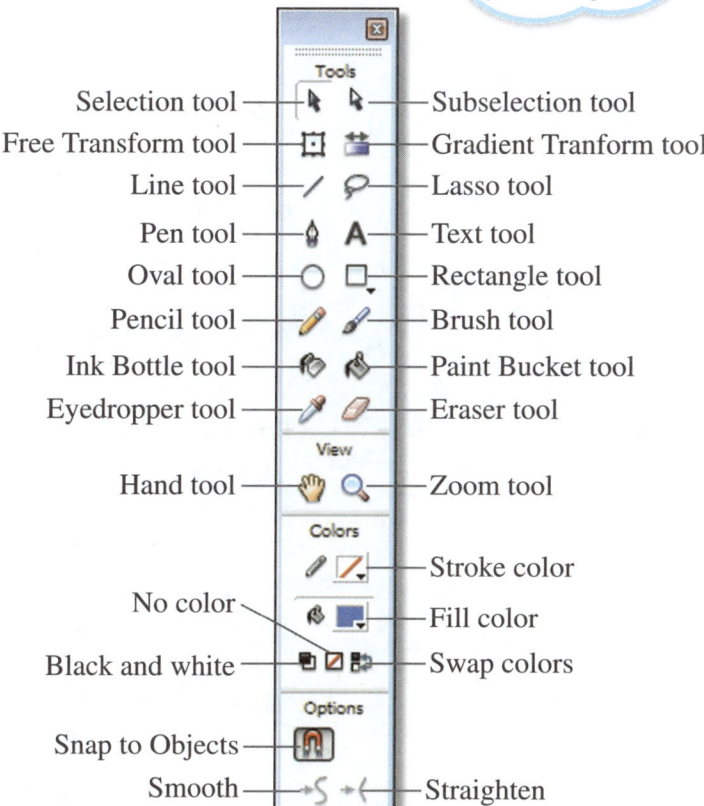

Fig. 11.3 *Flash Tools Panel*

Note: Tool modifiers are used for setting tool options.

Table 11.1 *Flash Toolbox*

Tools used	Icons	Use	Effect
Selection Tool	▶	Selects the entire object from the Stage by clicking on it or dragging to enclose the object within a selection	You can drag the entire object
Subselection Tool	▶	Selects a part of the object; it can also be stretched and thus you can mould the shape	You can drag a part of the object from these points for changing shapes
Line Tool	/	Draws straight lines	
Lasso Tool	⌒	Selects an object in a free-form	
Pen Tool	✎	Draws precise paths to make adjustments in the curves and polygons	Click and drag to create points on line segments; these can then be adjusted
Text Tool	A	Adds text to the flash document	HELLO
Oval Tool	○	Draws an oval **Note:** To draw a circle, hold the Shift key and use the Oval tool.	
Rectangle Tool	▭	Draws a rectangle **Note:** To draw a square, hold the Shift key and use the Rectangle tool.	

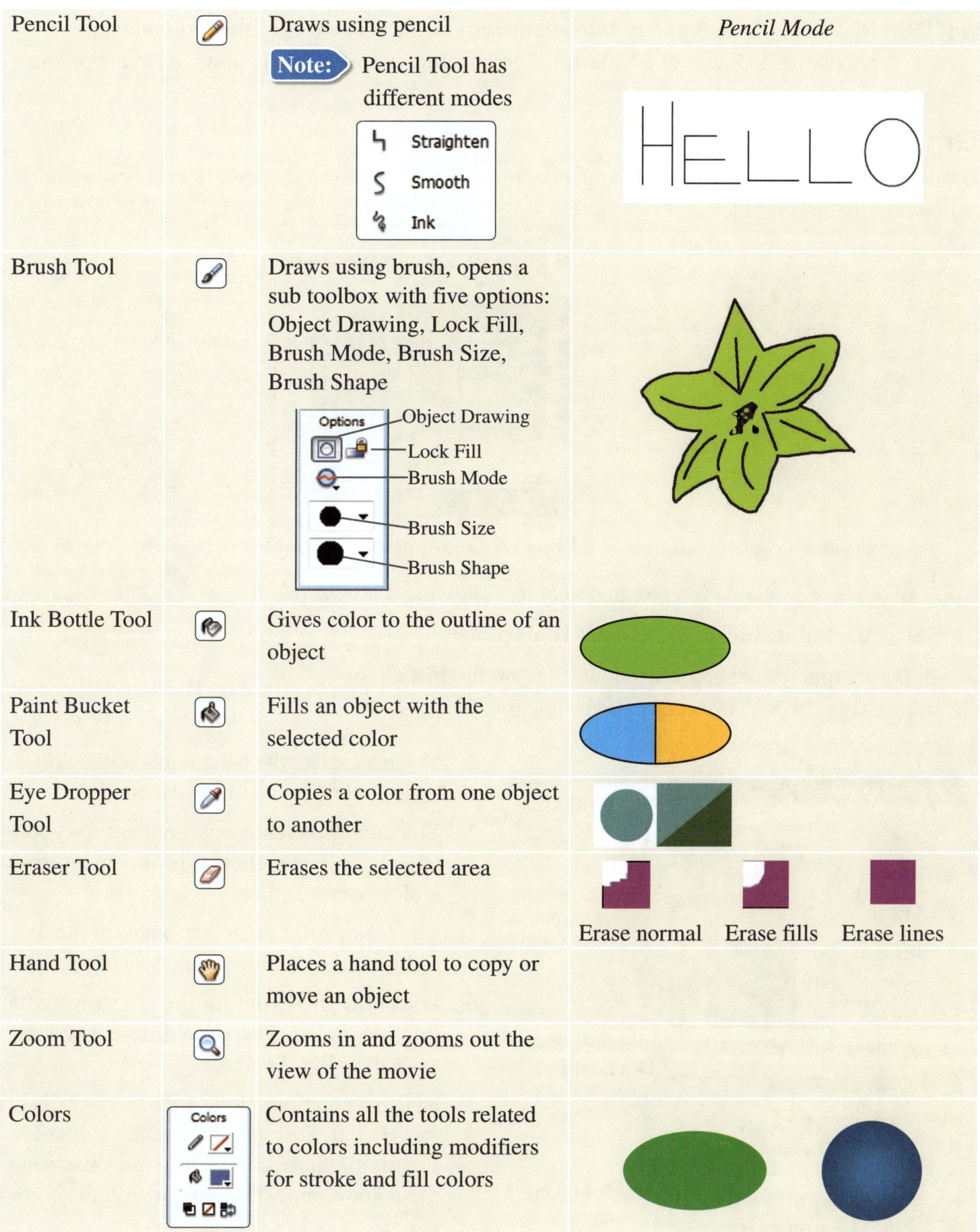

Note: Make use of the Property Inspector to adjust the properties of the tools, such as, choosing thickness of a Line Tool, or selecting colors. This displays various options for various tools.

Gradient Effects

Gradient effect is given to make the object colorful and to give it a shaded effect. Look at the following image (Fig. 11.4).

Fig. 11.4 *Gradient effect to a flower*

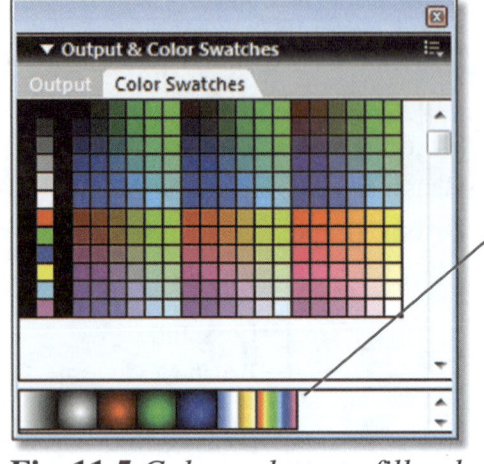

Fig. 11.5 *Color palette to fill color*

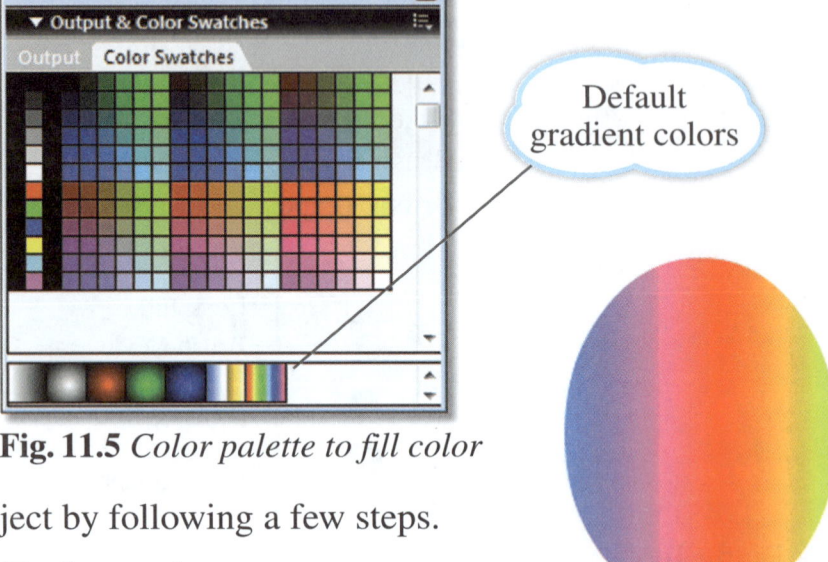

Fig. 11.6 *Default gradient colors*

You can apply a gradient effect to an object by following a few steps.

1. Select the **Paint Bucket Tool** in the **Tools panel**.
2. In the **Property Inspector** window, click on the **Fill Color** option (Fig. 11.5). The color palette appears.
3. You may select the default gradient colors given at the bottom of the palette (Fig. 11.6).
4. You can also create new gradient for your object. To do so, click **Window** menu ⇒ **Color Mixer** option.
5. The Color Mixer task bar opens at the right-hand side of the window (Fig. 11.7).
6. Select the fill **Type:** for the object from the drop-down list. There are different styles available (Fig. 11.8).
7. RGB is a combination of RED, GREEN and BLUE. Different shades are formed by mixing these colors. You may also see the color composition given with the color palette.

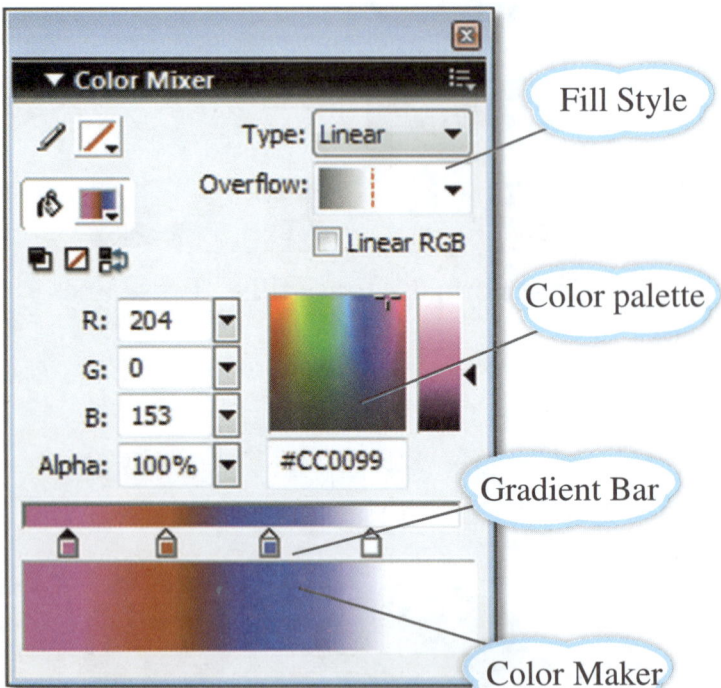

Fig. 11.7 *Color Mixer*

8. For any particular position of the object, the color markers are applied. You may click on any particular marker, and select the color from the color palette.

9. To add another color marker, click below the **Gradient Bar**. You can add several markers to give a colorful effect to the object.

Fig. 11.8 *Different gradient styles*

ACTIVITY

Draw butterflies and color them using various tools in Macromedia Flash.

FACT FILE

Flash file is saved with and extension of '.fla'. When it is executed with **Ctrl + Enter** keys, an object file is created with an extension of '.swf'.

Important Terms

To start learning the Macromedia Flash application, you must know some important related terms. These are explained here.

Movie

When you open a Flash document, the first file that opens is 'Movie1'. A movie is an animated Flash document which is saved with '.fla' extension. A Flash movie is further made of scenes.

Scene

A scene in a movie consists of the animated objects.

Let us draw an analogy in order to understand these terms and their interrelationship. A movie is like a book, the scenes are individual chapters of the book, and the layers are pages of the book that contain the actual data.

By default, every scene is named as 'Scene1'. When you save a Flash document, the movie, with its scenes and layers are all saved with the same name. You open a movie file from where you can open the individual movies and layers.

Timeline

Timeline is the area on the screen where you will be working with layers and frames to alter a movie's content and animation. A movie is a collection of frames and a Timeline is the area where you configure those frames (Fig. 11.9).

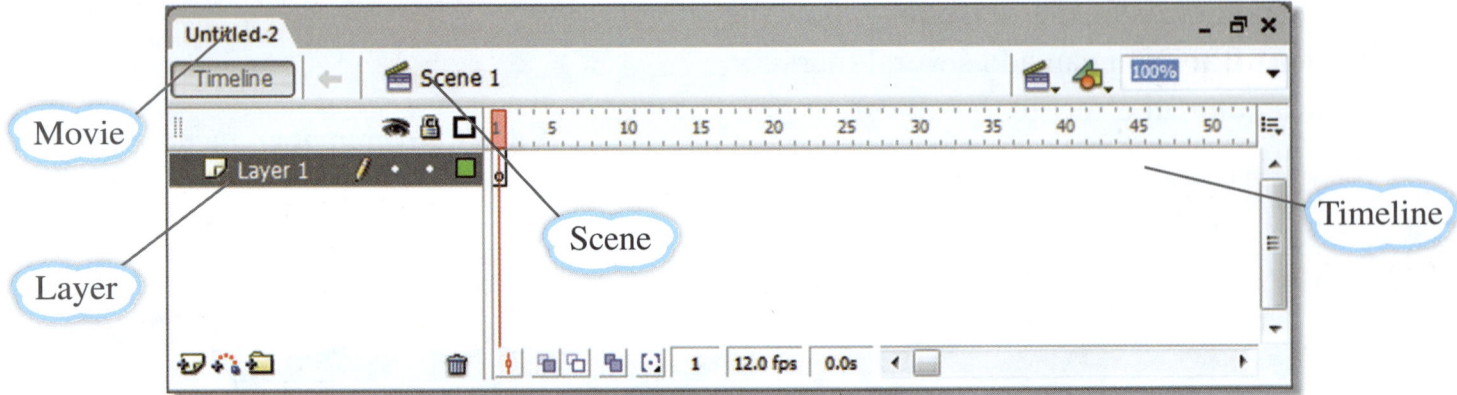

Fig. 11.9 *Macromedia Flash Timeline*

Layers

Layers in a Flash document can be explained as transparent sheets that contain various objects and can be placed on top of each other. You can see through each layer to see the layers under it, until you add colors to it. You can add layers, delete layers, and change the position of a layer. Each layer is independent of all the other layers. The layer that you work on or the working layer is called the **active layer**. You can view layer information on the Timeline (Fig. 11.10).

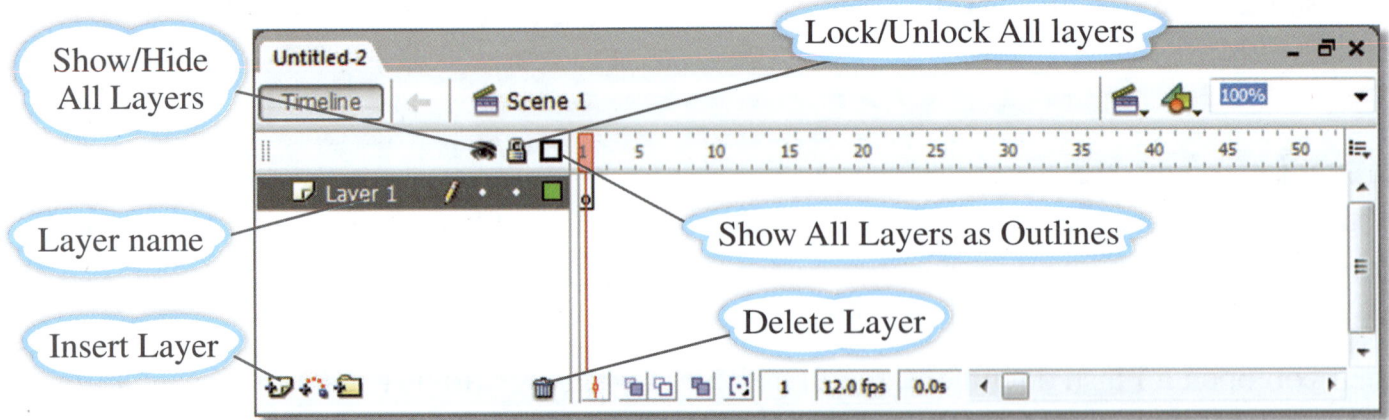

Fig. 11.10 *Default layer in Macromedia Flash*

Layers allow the users to separate the content of a movie into manageable sizes. Objects can be placed in different layers that are placed one after the other to form a sequence in a movie.

Layer name: The default name of the first layer is 'Layer1' and each layer added henceforth will be added in sequential order. For example, on adding a layer after 'Layer1', the new layer will be named Layer 2, then Layer 3, and so on.

Hiding/Showing a layer: The purpose of this button is to hide or show a layer. When the eye is highlighted, the layer will be hidden and vice versa.

Lock/Unlock All Layers: While working on several layers, user may lose track of the active layer. This is counteracted by using the Lock function.

Insert Layer: This option helps to add a new layer to the current movie. Simply click on the white box with the plus sign to add a layer. By default, a layer will be added above the current layer.

Deleting a Layer: Deleting a layer can be done in two ways: dragging the layer to the trash or clicking the trash when the unwanted layer is highlighted as the current layer.

Stage

The stage is the large white rectangle where you add every piece of content to be viewed in a movie. In other words, stage is the movie screen. There are some important points to remember about a stage:

1. Any content outside the Stage (that is in the work area) will not be visible when viewing the movie.
2. The default Stage color is white. It is the initial background color for a movie, unless changed.
3. To change color of the Stage, click on the Stage Area, then select the color from the Properties Inspector.

Frames

Each layer of a Flash movie is divided into frames. A frame represents the content of the movie at a particular moment of time. All movies and animations are made of a series of frames. So an animation is nothing more than a succession of frames. When the moving picture is displayed it is nothing but a series of individual frames appearing one after the other at a high speed so it appears to be moving.

The frame rate of a movie is measured by the number of frames per second that a movie plays. By default, the rate is set at 12 frames per second. The higher the frame rate, the better is the quality of the movie. Frame numbers appear along the top of Timeline (Fig. 11.11). You can use keyframes to specify changes in the animation.

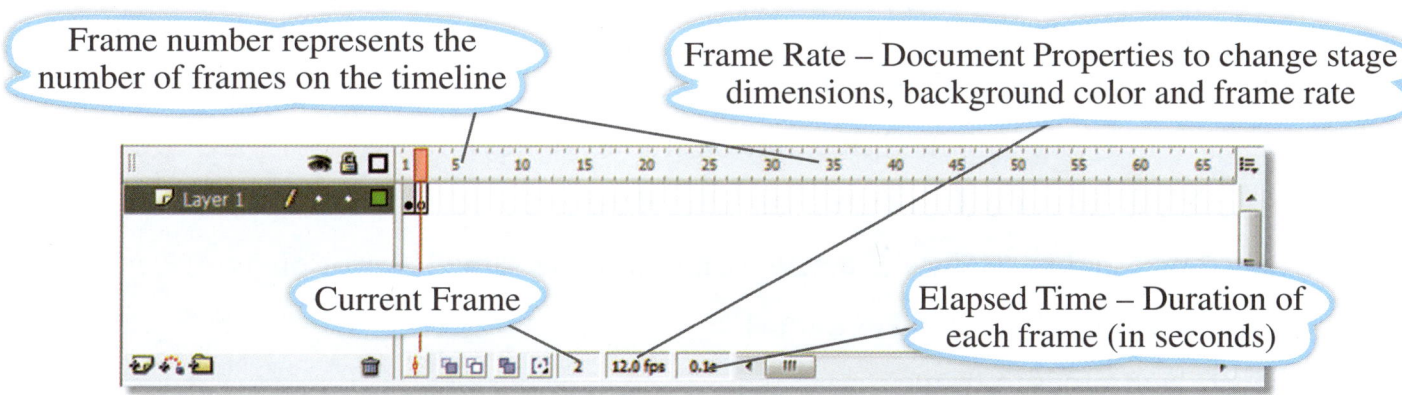

Fig. 11.11 *Frames in Macromedia Flash*

Some types of frames are given here:

Keyframe: These are the frames that are inserted into the movie and which contain the contents of the previous frame. In a keyframe, you define a change to properties of an object for animation. Since keyframes help to produce animation without drawing each individual frame, they make creating animation easier. In other words, all new objects need a keyframe. A keyframe is represented by a solid dot on Timeline (Fig. 11.12).

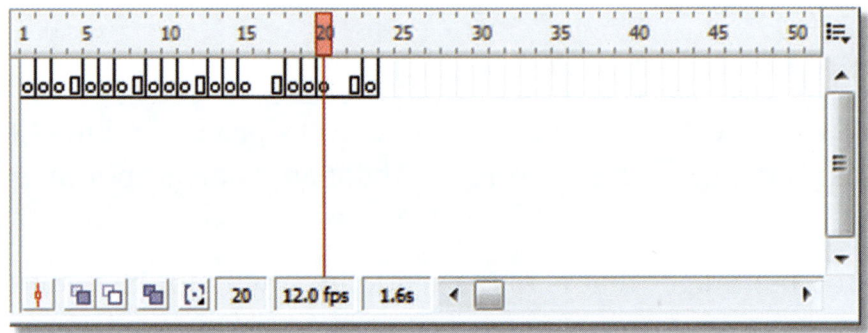

Fig. 11.12 *Keyframes on Timeline*

Blank keyframes: These are the frames with no object, and are denoted by a small circle on the Timeline (Fig. 11.13).

Figure 11.13 shows a series of **empty frames**. If you insert something in these frames, they become **keyframes.**

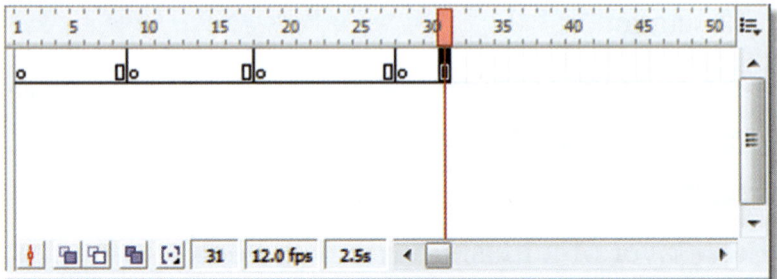

Fig. 11.13 *A blank keyframe*

Note: It is important to emphasise that Flash does not ignore these frames, and will just show a blank image. If you want a given object to appear only in frames 1 and 10, then frames 2 to 9 should be empty. In this way, the object will disappear and then reappear.

Working with frames on Timeline

The order in which frames and keyframes appear on Timeline determines the order in which they are displayed in a Flash application. You can arrange keyframes on Timeline to edit the sequence of events in an animation.

You can perform the following modifications on frames or keyframes:

- Insert, select, delete and move frames or keyframes
- Drag frames and keyframes to a new location on the same layer or on a different layer
- Copy and paste frames and keyframes
- Convert keyframes to frames
- Drag an item from the Library panel to the stage to add the item to the current keyframe

Inserting new frames on Timeline

1. To insert a new frame, click **Insert** menu ⟹ **Timeline** submenu ⟹ **Frame** option.
2. To create a new keyframe, click **Insert** menu ⟹ **Timeline** submenu ⟹ **Keyframe** option.

Right-click on the frame where you want to place a keyframe, and select **Insert Keyframe** option from the shortcut menu.

3. To create a new blank keyframe, select **Insert** menu ⟹ **Timeline** submenu ⟹ **Blank Keyframe** option.

Right-click on the frame where you want to place the keyframe, and select **Insert Blank Keyframe** from the shortcut menu.

FACT FILE

You can select all the frames simultaneously by using **Edit** menu ⟹ **Timeline** submenu ⟹ **Select All Frames** option.

Deleting frames on Timeline

1. Select the frame, keyframe, or sequence (many frames together).
2. Click on **Edit** menu ⟹ **Timeline** submenu ⟹ **Remove Frames** option.

OR

Right-click the frame, keyframe, or sequence and click **Remove Frames** from the shortcut menu.

Animation in Flash

Animation is the rapid display of a sequence of images of 2-D or 3-D artwork or model positions in order to create an illusion of movement. There are two types of animations that can be performed in flash. These are:

1. Frame-by-frame animation
2. Animation with tweening effects

Frame-by-frame animation

The basic form of animation is frame-by-frame animation. Here you create the object for each frame to produce an animation sequence. This animation employs unique drawings in each frame. Thus, it is tedious and time consuming, and the movie created occupies a lot of disk space.

Frame-by-frame animation is used when the current frame is completely different from the previous frame, or when it is required that some elements in the previous frame remain unchanged. Thus, it is ideal for complex animations that require subtle changes. For example, a man walking in a garden.

Creating an Animation of Bouncing Ball

Let us now learn to create simple actions in Macromedia Flash with an example.

1. Click on the first frame on the Timeline.
2. Select an **Oval Tool** in the **Tools panel** and make a ball at the upper-left corner of the stage.
3. Select the **Arrow Tool** to get the mouse pointer. Right click on frame 1 and select **Insert Keyframe.**
4. Right click on the 10th frame and select **Insert Frames**. You will see grey frames appearing on the Timeline.
5. Now click on frame 5. Right click and select **Insert Keyframe.** You will see a black dot appear on this frame.
6. Click on the ball and drag it to the centre bottom of the stage.
7. Now select frame 10. Right click and select **Insert Keyframe** as done earlier in frame 5.
8. Click and now drag the ball to the upper-right corner of the stage.
9. Now you have the ball at three positions as indicated by frames 1, 5 and 10.
10. Click on **Control** menu ⟹ **Play** option. The ball will appear to bounce once.
11. To repeat the bouncing, click on **Control** menu ⟹ **Loop Playback** option.
12. To stop this looping, click **Control** menu ⟹ **Stop** option.

ACTIVITY

Create an animation of apples falling from a tree.

Symbols

Symbols are objects which have been created, stored and added to the library. Once stored in the library they can be used repeatedly either in the same movie or another movie. It is like making a library of commonly used objects to save time. They can also be modified. The need to create a symbol in a movie arises when you want to reuse it. This allows your Flash animation to download quicker.

Creating a symbol

The steps to create a symbol are as follows:

1. Create an object which will be required again and again.
2. Select **Insert** menu ⟹ **New Symbol...** option.

   Press **Ctrl + F8** or **F8** key.
3. The **Create New Symbol** dialog box appears (Fig. 11.14).

Fig. 11.14 *Create New Symbol*

Give suitable names to the symbols. This will make it easier to remember them while using them in a movie.

4. Give the **Name** to the symbol you are creating. The default name is 'Symbol1'.
5. Select the desired behaviour by clicking on either of the options: **Movie clip, Button, Graphic.**
6. Click on **OK**.

Behaviour of a symbol

Select any of the following depending upon the requirement of the movie:

- *Movie clip:* The animated Flash movies that can be reused in a movie.
- *Button:* They are used for Timeline navigation and can be used for connecting a programming event.
- *Graphic:* The static images that are mainly made to create animations in a movie.

Creating instances of a symbol

A copy of the original symbol placed in your movie is an **instance** of the symbol. The size, color, shape and position can be altered without affecting the original symbol. When you create a symbol, Flash saves it to a library. Every time you use this object in a movie, it is converted into an instance.

Although a symbol and an instance seem to be the same, there is an important distinction. On modifying a symbol the instance will be updated, but the object will remain intact as it was at the moment of its creation. So you will be able to return to use it at another moment.

Follow these steps to create an instance of a symbol:

1. Click on **Window** menu ⟹ **Library** option.
2. Click on the required symbol and drag it to the current layer.
3. If certain changes in the properties of an instance are required then double-click on the instance.

   Click on **Modify** menu ⟹ **Instance** option.
4. Do the required changes and use it as many times as required.

Quick key

To create a new movie	**Ctrl + N**	To insert a new keyframe	**F6**
To open or close the Timeline window	**Ctrl + Alt + T**	To insert a blank keyframe	**F7**
To execute a Flash file	**Ctrl + Enter**	To remove a frame	**Shift + F5**
To create a symbol	**Ctrl + F8**	To clear a keyframe	**Shift + F6**
To insert a new frame	**F5**		

ACTIVITY

A. Create your school logo in flash and add it as a symbol.

B. In the falling apple activity done earlier, draw a school building and use the school logo as an instance.

GLOSSARY

Frame: It represents the content of the movie at a particular moment of time.

Instance: It is a copy of the original symbol placed in a movie.

Layer: It is a transparent sheet that contains various objects.

Movie: It is an animated Flash document.

Scene: It consists of the animated objects.

Symbols: These are objects that are created, stored and added to the library.

Timeline: It is the area on the screen to work with layers and frames.

NOW YOU KNOW

1. Macromedia Flash is a software that enables the user to make an animated movie.
2. The Flash Tools panel helps you create and modify shapes for the artwork in movies.
3. You can give gradient effects to an object to give it a colored and a shaded effect.
4. The stage is where you add every piece of content to be viewed in a movie.
5. A movie in Flash is saved with a '.fla' extension.
6. A Flash movie is made of scenes.
7. The layer that you work on or the working layer is called the active layer.
8. The frame rate of a movie is measured by the number of frames per second that a movie plays.
9. In a keyframe, you define a change to properties of an object for an animation.
10. Symbols can be movie clips, buttons or graphics.

EXERCISE

A Fill in the blanks.

1. Animated websites can be created using ....
2. .... and .... tools are used for drawing and coloring with a brush.
3. .... tool can be used to make a square.
4. .... is the default layer in a movie.
5. .... are the pages of a movie.
6. .... is the copy of a symbol used in Flash.

B Name the menu and the option to do the following tasks: HOTS

1. To create a new movie.
2. To play the existing movie.
3. To create a symbol.
4. To insert a blank keyframe.
5. To create a copy of a symbol.

C. Label the following picture.

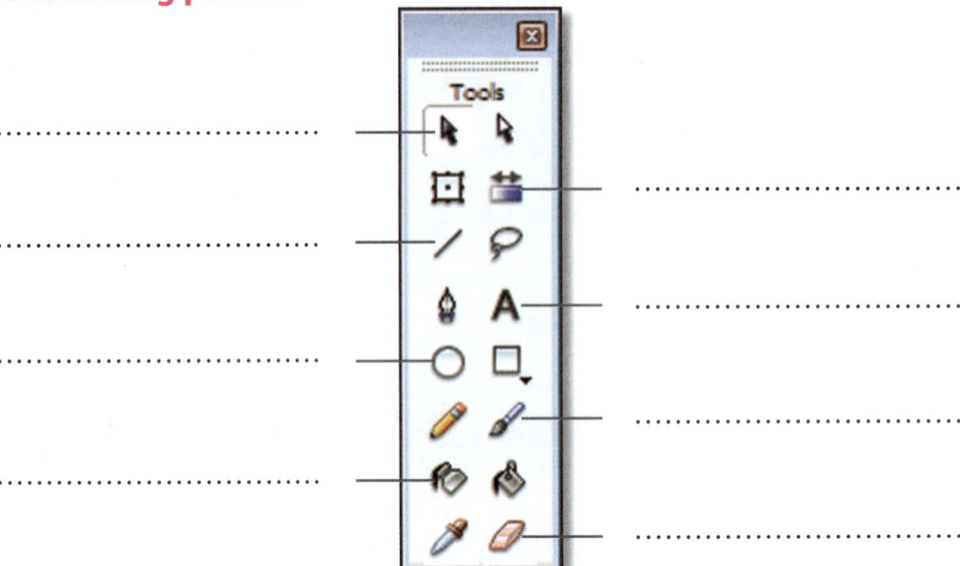

D. Answer the following questions.

1. Why do you need Macromedia Flash?
2. What is a layer? How do you add or delete a layer in a Flash document?
3. What are frames? Explain the different types of frames in short.
4. What are symbols? Give its use.
5. Define a movie and a scene.

LAB WORK

A. Draw a bouquet of colorful flowers using Flash tools.
B. Create an animation of a smiley, begin with a smiling face turning into a sad face and then finally into a face with tears (Hint: Use frames and keyframes).
C. Create an animation of a moving car.

TEACHER'S NOTES

1. Download a simple flash movie from the Internet to show the concept of working in layers to the students.
2. Show the students, movies with different frame rates to explain the quality of the movie.

12 Introduction to Email

SNAP RECAP

1. The Internet is a system of connecting computers together to enable data communication services like emails, chatting, file transfer, etc.
2. Email is an online correspondence system. Through email you can send and receive instant electronic messages which work like writing letters.

LEARNING OBJECTIVES

You will learn about:

1. Uniform Resource Locator
2. email
3. advantages of email
4. limitations of email
5. creating and opening an email account
6. compsing an email
7. signing out from an email account

Introduction

The Internet is a network that links millions of computers around the world. It contains a vast amount of information, and offers other services such as email, newsgroups and file sharing. Today, the Internet has revolutionised how people use computers. For example, one can read news stories and movie reviews, check airline and railway schedules, book tickets, shop for various items, find information on any subject, see street maps, get the weather forecast for the city, and communicate with others through the Internet.

Email is one of the most popular uses of the Internet. It is a fast and convenient way to communicate with others. You can send a message to anyone with an email address, and it will arrive almost instantly in the recipient's email inbox – even if he or she lives halfway across the world.

In this chapter, you will learn about some of the features of email. However, before you proceed further, you must first know that in order to communicate, every computer connected to the Internet has a unique address which consists of a set of characters.

Uniform Resource Locator (URL)

Uniform Resource Locator (URL) is an address that uniquely identifies a location on the Internet. Every file on the Internet has a URL. A URL is the address for a website (Fig. 12.1). For example, www.cambridgeindia.org.

Fig. 12.1 *URL*

The format of the URL is:

protocol://host/path/filename

For example, in the URL www.cambridgeindia.org:

- Protocol is http
- Host computer name is www
- Lower level domain name is cambridgeindia
- Upper level domain name is org
- Filename is default.aspx

Upper level domain name gives you the information about the organisation to which the website belongs to. For example,

- com indicates commercial enterprise
- edu indicates educational institution
- gov indicates U.S. government entity
- mil indicates U.S. military entity
- net indicates network access provider
- org indicates usually non-profit organisations.

FACT FILE

It is not necessary to type http:// while typing the web address. It shows by default.

In addition, domain names are further categorised to identify and locate files stored on the servers in different countries around the world. These are referred to as country codes, and are standardised by the International Standards Organisation (ISO). For example,

- ch indicates Switzerland
- jp indicates Japan
- in indicates India
- de indicates Germany
- uk indiates United Kingdom
- ca indicates Canada

Note: The URL is not case sensitive, that is, it can be written in lower case as well as upper case. For example, www.thesaurus.com and WWW.THesAURus.COM will direct you to the same page.

Domain Name System (DNS)

When URL is translated into a numeric address, that address becomes the Domain Name System (DNS).

The DNS is a worldwide system of servers that stores location pointers to websites. It stores the information in form of an IP address. It works as a phone book for the Internet. It converts the alphanumeric URL address into the numeric IP address. When you type the alphanumeric address in the Address Bar of the Web Browser, the DNS translates it into the IP address. It then contacts the web server and asks for a specific file located on its site.

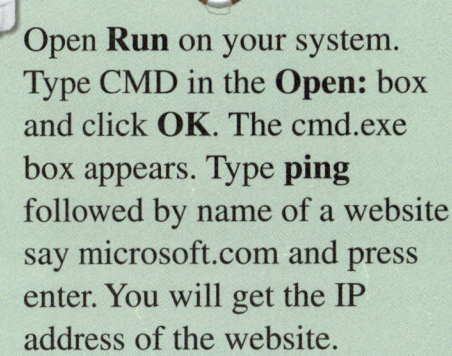

TRY THIS!

Open **Run** on your system. Type CMD in the **Open:** box and click **OK**. The cmd.exe box appears. Type **ping** followed by name of a website say microsoft.com and press enter. You will get the IP address of the website.

Email

Email stands for **Electronic Mail**. It is a fast and convenient way to communicate with others via Internet. In fact, it is the most commonly used feature of the Internet. Every day, people using the Internet send each other billions of email messages. Obviously, email has become an extremely popular medium of communication nowadays. You can send an email message to any person with an email address. You can receive messages from anyone who knows your email address, and then read and reply to those messages. When you receive an email message, you can forward it to others without retyping it. You can also send an email message to many people simultaneously.

Besides text, you can send almost any type of file in an email message, including documents, photographs and music. A file sent along with an email message is called an **attachment**. Email systems have a mail server which sends and receives a mail. A **mail server** is a computer that serves as an electronic post office for email. The mail exchanged across networks is passed between mail servers that run specially designed software and follow standardised protocols for handling mail messages and attachment files.

FACT FILE

Hotmail, one of the first free email service providers, was founded by Sabeer Bhatia.

Email address

Using an email service is just like using a letter box (Fig. 12.2). If you do not have a letter box then you will not be able to send or receive your mails.

To send and receive your emails you need to create an email account. This account can be accessed by using an email address. This address is a combination of a username and a hostname, and is written as username@hostname. For example, mymail@hotmail.com, abc@yahoo.com, xyz@gmail.com.

Username: It can be any name given by the user.
Hostname: It is the name of the email server that provides email services.

Fig. 12.2 *Sending a mail*

Advantages of Email

Some advantages of using the Email sevices are given below.

Convenient

One advantage of email over the telephone or regular mail is its convenience. You can send a message at any time of the day or at night. If the recipients are not connected to the Internet when you send the message, they will find the message waiting for them the next time they check their email.

Immediate

Your message is delivered instantly from your computer to any other computer whether it is in a nearby locality or halfway across the world (Fig. 12.3). No other method of delivery can provide such a prompt service.

Fig. 12.3 *Sending an email is convenient and fast*

Inexpensive

Compared to telephone calls, faxes, courier or postal service, email is less expensive. In fact, it is free at times. No stamp or paper cost is involved (Fig. 12.4). The cost has nothing to do with distance, and in many cases, the cost does not depend on the size of the message either.

Fig. 12.4 *Sending an email requires no paper*

Bulk data can be sent

You can send any type of data like text, video, sound, documents, pictures, etc. through email. The text goes as simple email and the rest of the files go as an attachment with the email. The person receiving the email should have the appropriate software to use those attachment files.

Environment-friendly

Email is a green and environment-friendly way of sending messages as it does not involve the use of paper in terms of writing pads, envelops, stamps, etc. For different companies also, the email is a cheaper and a faster medium to advertise. It is also greener as precious trees are not wasted.

Fig. 12.5 *Green email signature*

You can create a 'green email signature' hanging out at the bottom of your mail with the help of your teacher. It consists of a disclaimer that talks about how you can use your email to save the environment (Fig.12.5). For example, many people print their emails so that they can refer back to them. You can create a signature disclaimer that asks if they really need to print that email. You can also talk about the benefits to the environment by not printing the email because it uses paper and paper manufacturing requires to cut trees.

Emails, thus, help in saving paper and reducing the demand for paper. When the paper demand goes down, the paper factories will produce less paper. This means fewer trees will have to be cut down. Thus, you can initiate one very interesting chain reaction that will save the Earth. Remember, *every small measure taken to save the environment counts, so do your bit.*

Limitations of Email

There are some limitations of using the Email services. These are given below.

Unwanted emails

Since your email address is stored on the mail server, you may also receive some unwanted mails. These unwanted messages are known as **junk mails** or **spam mails**.

Privacy concerns

You can secure your email accounts by entering a password. However, if somebody knows your password then that person can easily access your account and may read or send messages through it. Moreover, email messages are passed through several networks. There are many possibilities for someone to intercept or read your email. Thus, email is not necessarily private.

False representation of identity

Anyone can create an email account even by giving false personal details. Some people misrepresent themselves. Without an identifiable source, the message sender's identity and claims cannot be validated.

Creating and Opening Email Account

Creating an email account is simple. The easiest way to create an email account and get the email address is to use a free online service. First, choose an email service, for example, Yahoo, Hotmail, Gmail, etc. Then, decide what email address you wish to have (Fig. 12.6).

Fig. 12.6 *Creating an email address*

Let us try creating an email account on www.gmail.com.

1. Open the web browser and type in the address *gmail.com* in the Address Bar. The following screen will appear (Fig. 12.7).

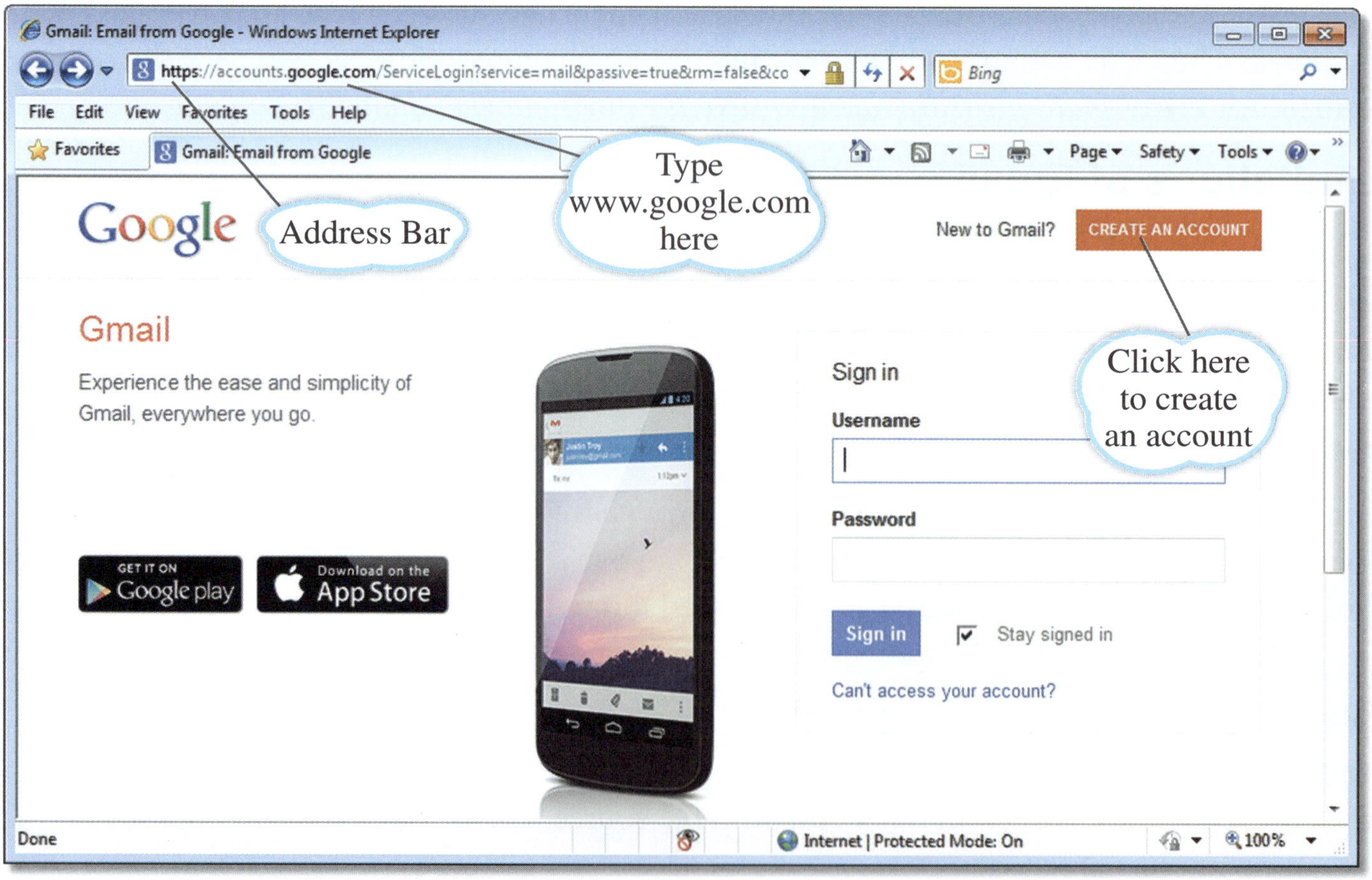

Fig. 12.7 *Opening a Gmail account*

2. If you already have an account then you may just enter your **Username, Password** and click on the **Sign in** button. But to create a new account, you need to click on **CREATE AN ACCOUNT** button on the screen, as shown in Figure 12.7. You will now see the following screen displaying an online form (Fig. 12.8).

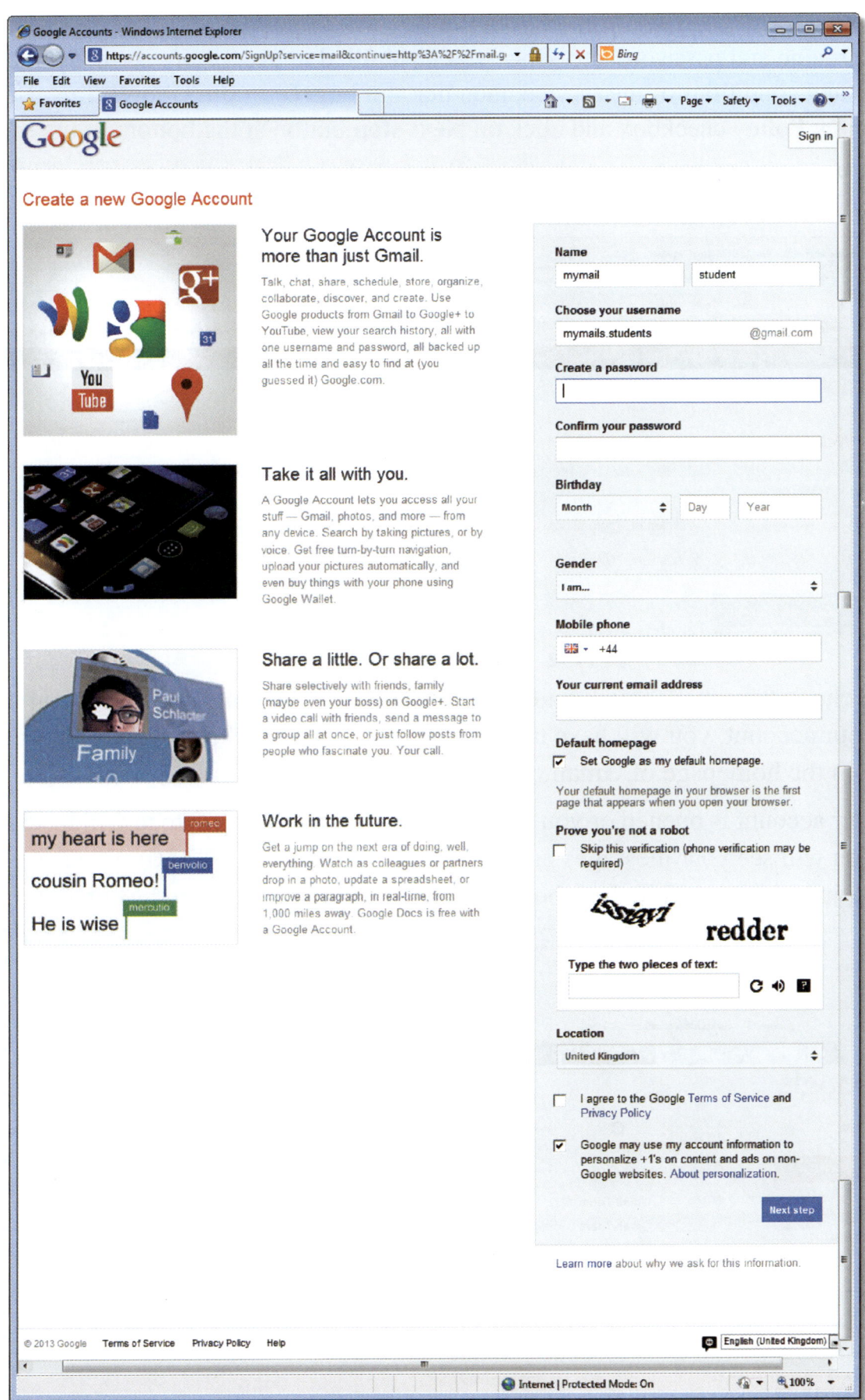

Fig. 12.8 *Online form*

3. In this online form, you have to enter your details such as your name, your location, your choice of the username and password, etc. Once you have filled in everything correctly and agreed to the terms and conditions of the service, then tick the **I agree to the Google Terms of Service and Privacy Policy** checkbox and click on **Next step** button at the bottom of the screen.

4. After the account has been created, you will get a 'Welcome!' message (Fig. 12.9). You get this message only once – the first time when you open your email account.

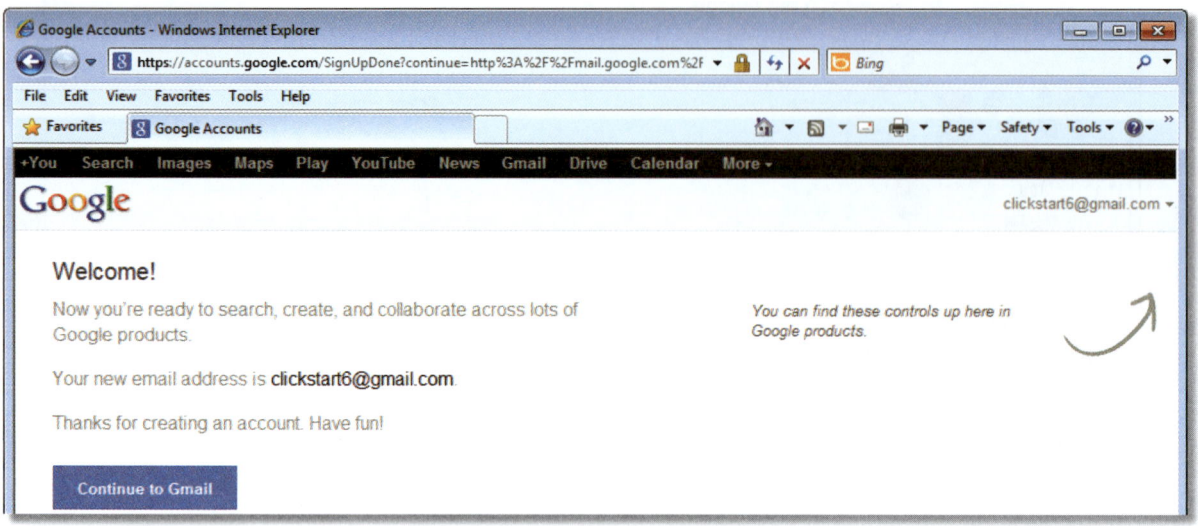

Fig. 12.9 *Welcome message*

5. Now, to check your mails, click on **Continue to Gmail** button. Every time you need to check your account, you will have to enter your username and password to open your account in the homepage of Gmail.com.

6. Once your account is opened or you are logged in, the following screen will be displayed where you will see your messages in a folder called **Inbox** (Fig. 12.10). Whenever you receive an email, it will be stored in the inbox. You can click on it, and view the contents of the email.

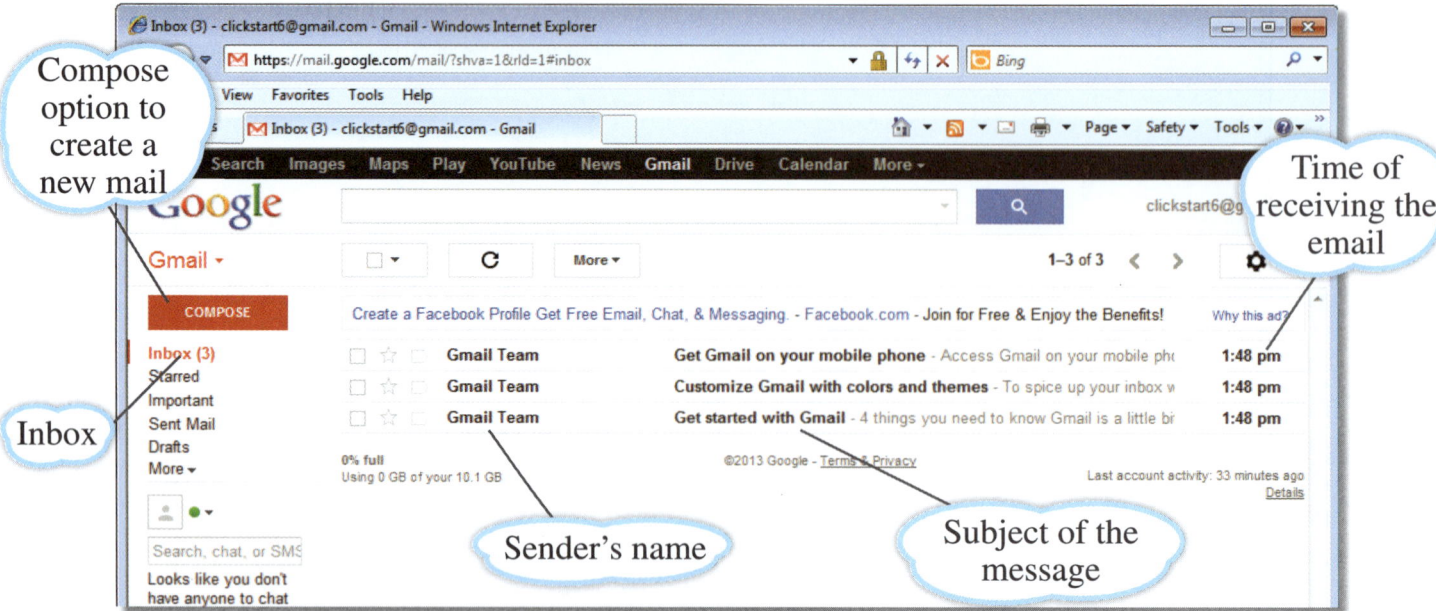

Fig. 12.10 *Inbox*

Composing an Email

Composing a mail means creating an email and then sending it to the recipient. To compose an email, you need to follow a few steps.

1. Click on **COMPOSE** option present on the left side of the window.
2. It consists of three major sections: **Header, Body** and **Footer** (Fig. 12.11).

   a. *Header:* The message header generally includes the following fields:
   - To: Here you write the email address of the person (recipient) to whom you wish to send the email.
   - Cc: It stands for **Carbon Copy**. It allows you to write email addresses of persons to whom you want to send a copy of the email at the same time.
   - Bcc: It stands for **Blind Carbon Copy**. It also contains the email addresses of persons to whom you want to send a copy of the email yet not make the address visible to the rest of the recipients addressed in **To** and **Cc** box.
   - Subject: A brief summary of the contents of the message.

   b. *Body:* The message content is written as plain text with simple formatting features in the body of the message.

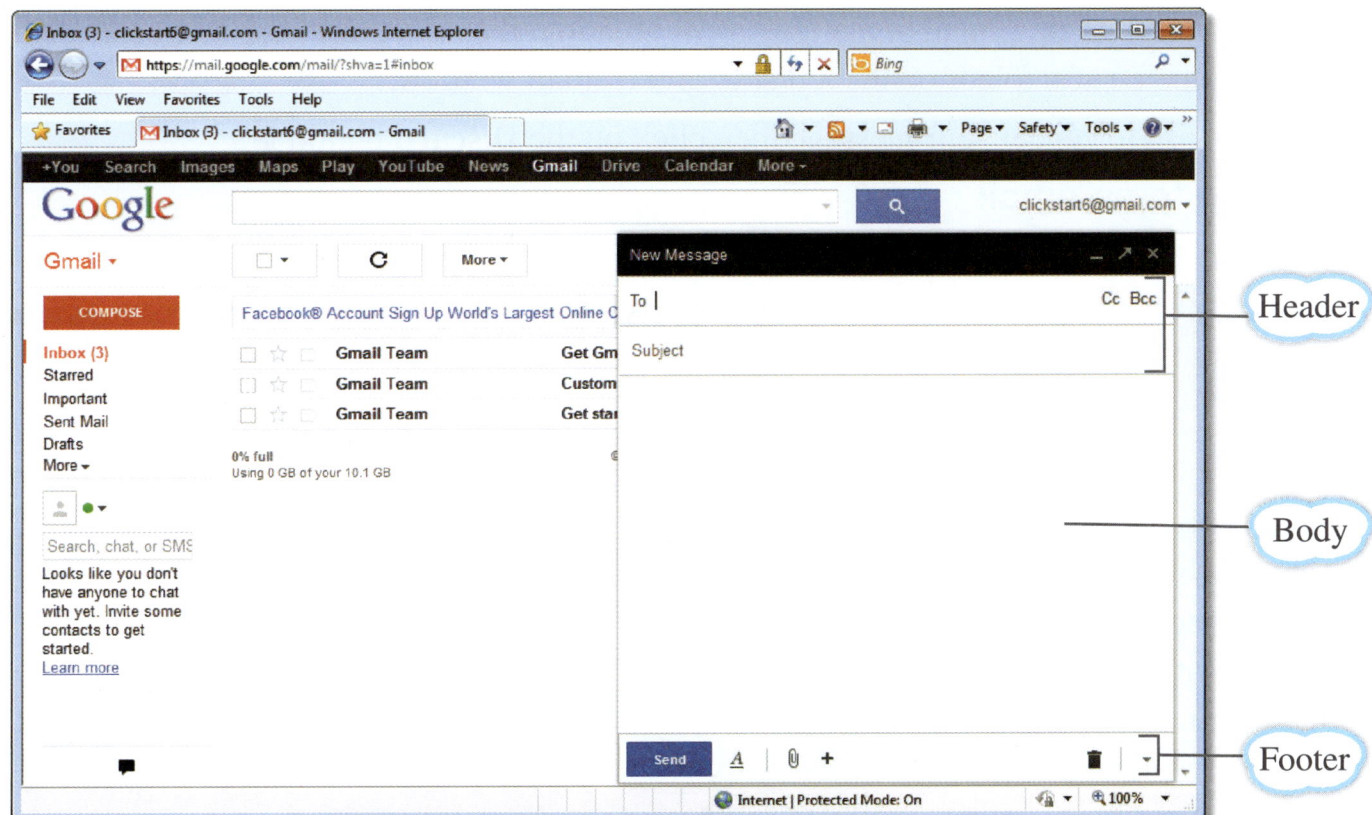

Fig. 12.11 *Header, Body and Footer*

c. *Footer:* It generally includes the following fields:
- **Send**: After adding the text, click on this button for sending the message to the specified email addresses.
- **A**: This button represents the options that can be used for formatting the text in the Body of the email. It includes the font type, font size, bold, italic, underline, bullets and numbering, text color, and other alignment features. It also consists of an option to remove the formatting done to the text in the email.
- 📎 : This button helps to attach a file to the email. The attachments can include text files, photographs, music files, movie files, etc. After attaching a file, the name and size of this file is displayed. One or more types of files can be attached with an email. The time taken to attach a file can vary depending on the size of the file and speed of the Internet connection.
- 🗂 📷 🔗 ☺ : These buttons can be used to insert files using a Drive, photos, links and emoticons (animated facial expressions) in the Body of the email.
- ▼ : A side list appears on pressing this button in the email. It gives the user the option to Print the email and also check spellings of the text written in the email.

3. After adding the text, click **Send** button for sending the message.
4. Gmail automatically saves the document you are currently working on as a draft. In case you do not send this email at the time of its creation, the saved message will be available later in the **Drafts** folder on the left side of the email window.
5. If you wish to cancel your message then click on the **Discard** button 🗑.

Replying to an email

You can reply to an email received from a contact.

For replying to an email, follow these steps:

1. Click on the email to open it.
2. Click on the reply arrow ↰ in the right corner of the email (Fig. 12.12).
3. A message box opens below the email with the address of the email sender in the 'To' section.

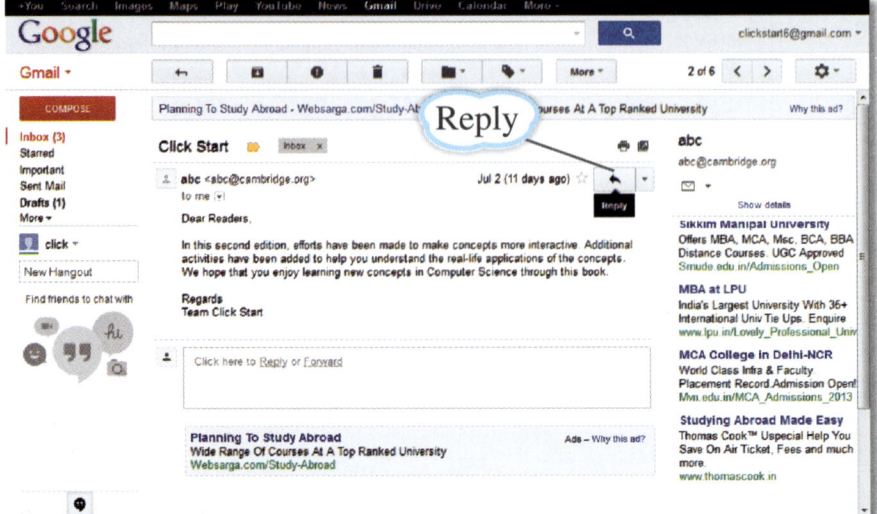

Fig. 12.12 *Clicking on the Reply button*

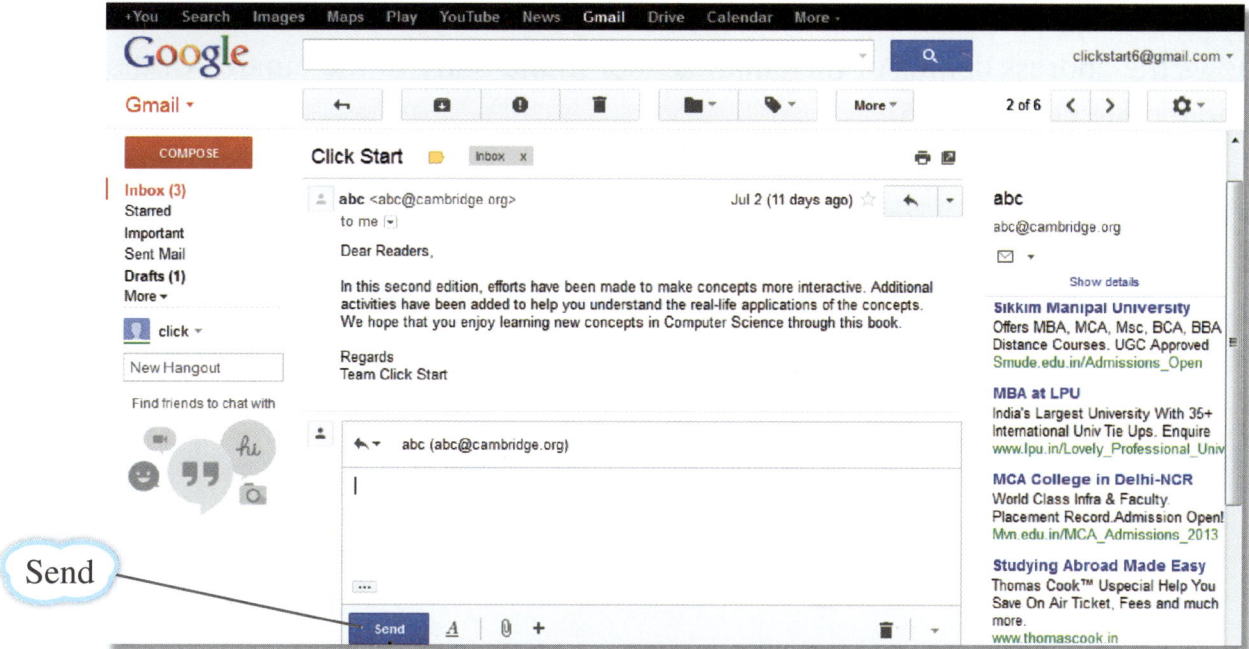

Fig. 12.13 *Replying to an email*

4. Type your reply in the same message box (Fig. 12.13).
5. Click on the **Send** button.

Note: Click on the dotted line ⋯ to see the contents of the email to which you are replying. Select the content and click **Backspace** button. Remove the attachment by deselecting it.

Forwarding an email

An email received in the Inbox can be sent to other people. This is called **forwarding** an email.

Follow these steps to forward an email to a contact:

1. Click on the email to open it.
2. Click on the arrow next to the **Reply** button and select the **Forward** option from the drop-down list (Fig. 12.14).

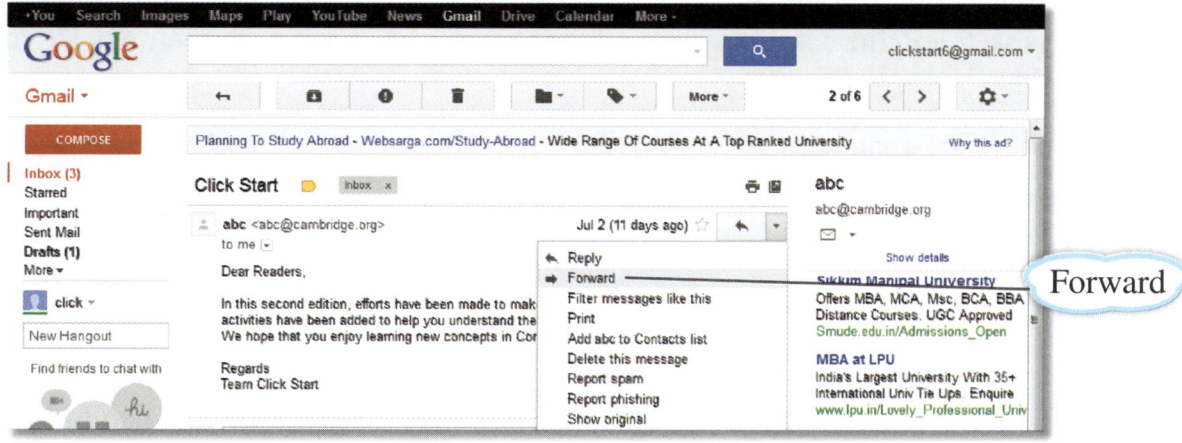

Fig. 12.14 *Selecting the forward option*

3. A message box appears below the email containing the contents of the respective email. It also shows the address details of the email sender in the body of the email. All these contents can be edited also (Fig. 12.15).

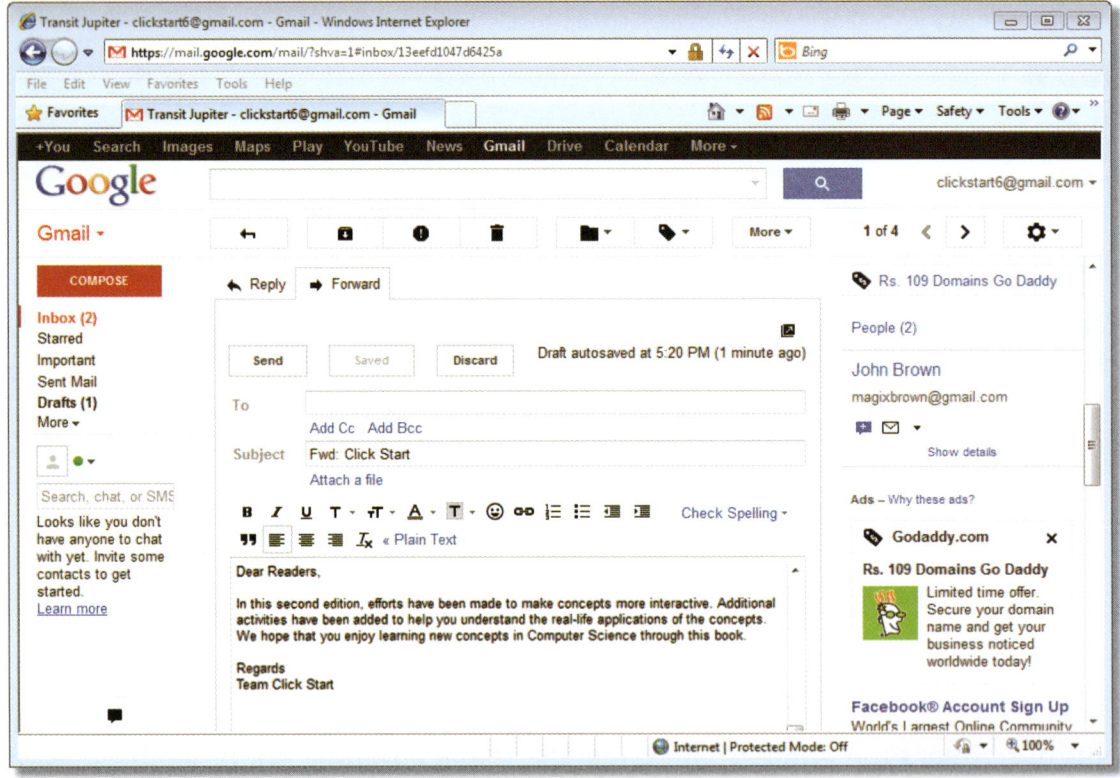

Fig. 12.15 *Forwarding an email*

4. Type the message in the Body of the email and enter the address of the contact in the 'To' section.
5. Click on the **Send** button.

FACT FILE

The drop-down list next to the **Reply** button has options for deleting and printing the email. On clicking **Print**, the **Print** window opens where the user can specify the settings for the message to be printed.

Chatting with a Contact

Most of the email services provide their users with the facility to do a live chat with their contacts.

The main advantage of using the live chat feature is that it allows the user to talk to their contacts as if sitting opposite to them.

Follow these steps to chat with a contact:

1. Look at the list of contacts in the left side of the window (Fig. 12.16).

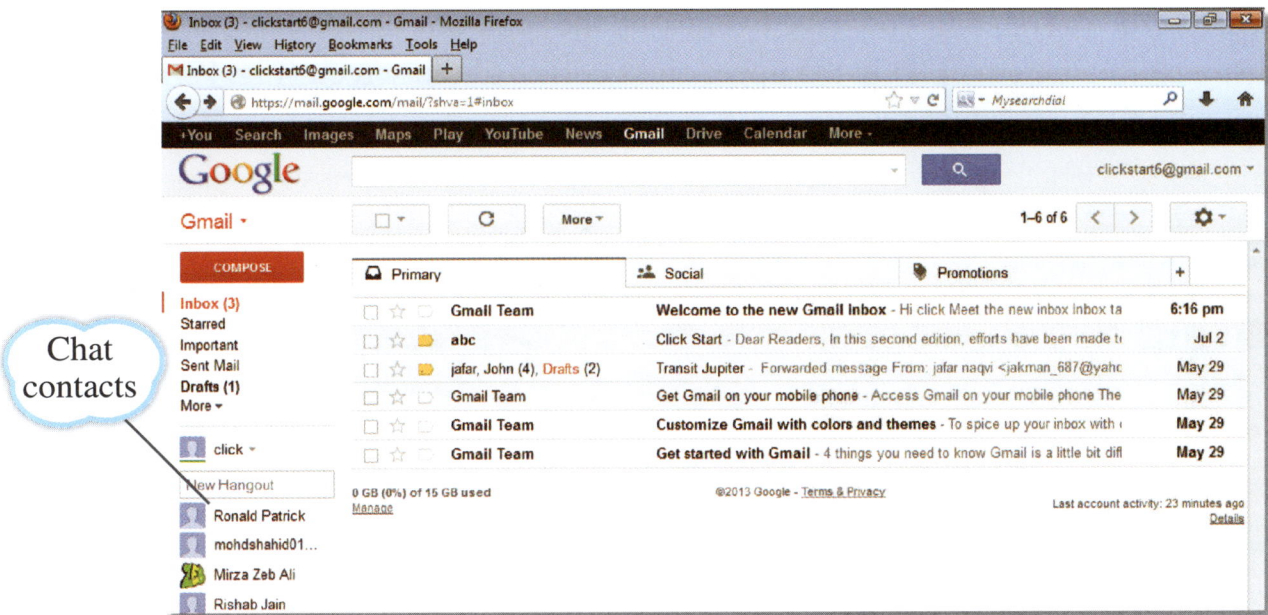

Fig. 12.16 *Selecting a contact for chatting*

2. Click on the name of the contact with whom you wish to chat with.

3. A chat window appears on the lower-right side of the window.

4. Type a message and press **Enter**. The contact will receive the message sent. They can also reply to the message and send it (Fig. 12.17).

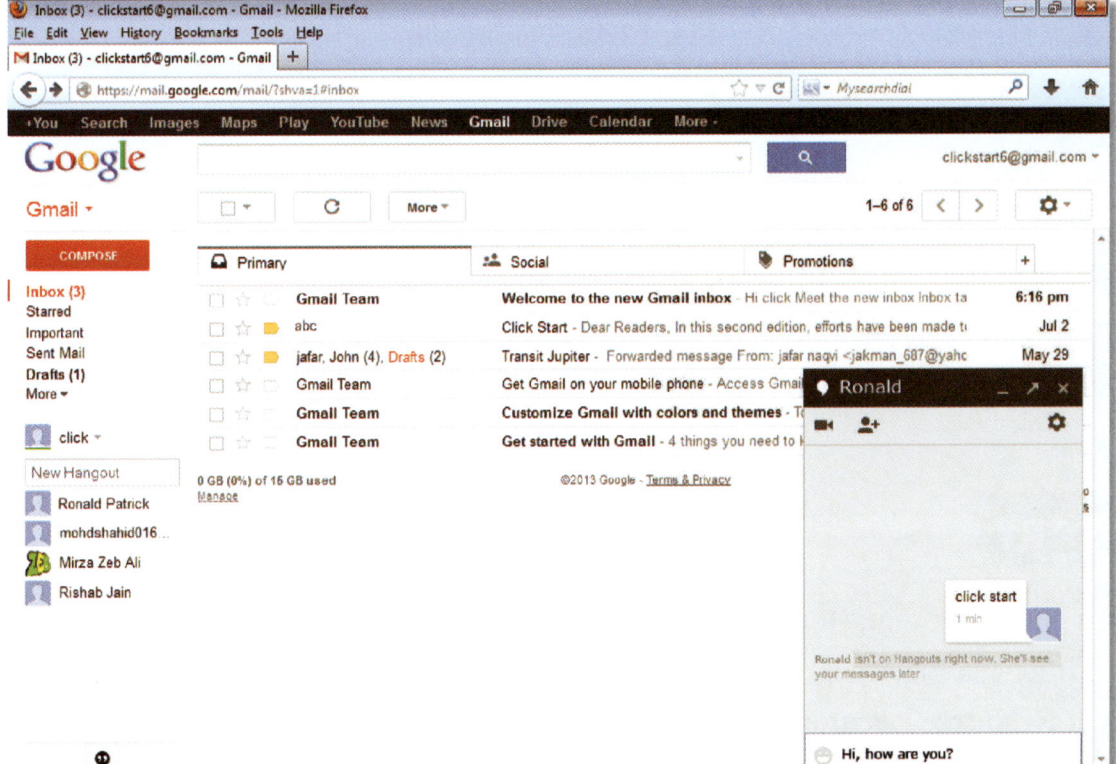

Fig. 12.17 *Chatting with the selected contact*

Signing Out from the Email Account

It is important to close your email account properly. It ensures that no one else can access it without the password. To sign out, you have to click on the **Sign out** option present in the drop-down list next to your email ID in the upper-right corner of the screen (Fig. 12.18). This will move you out of your account.

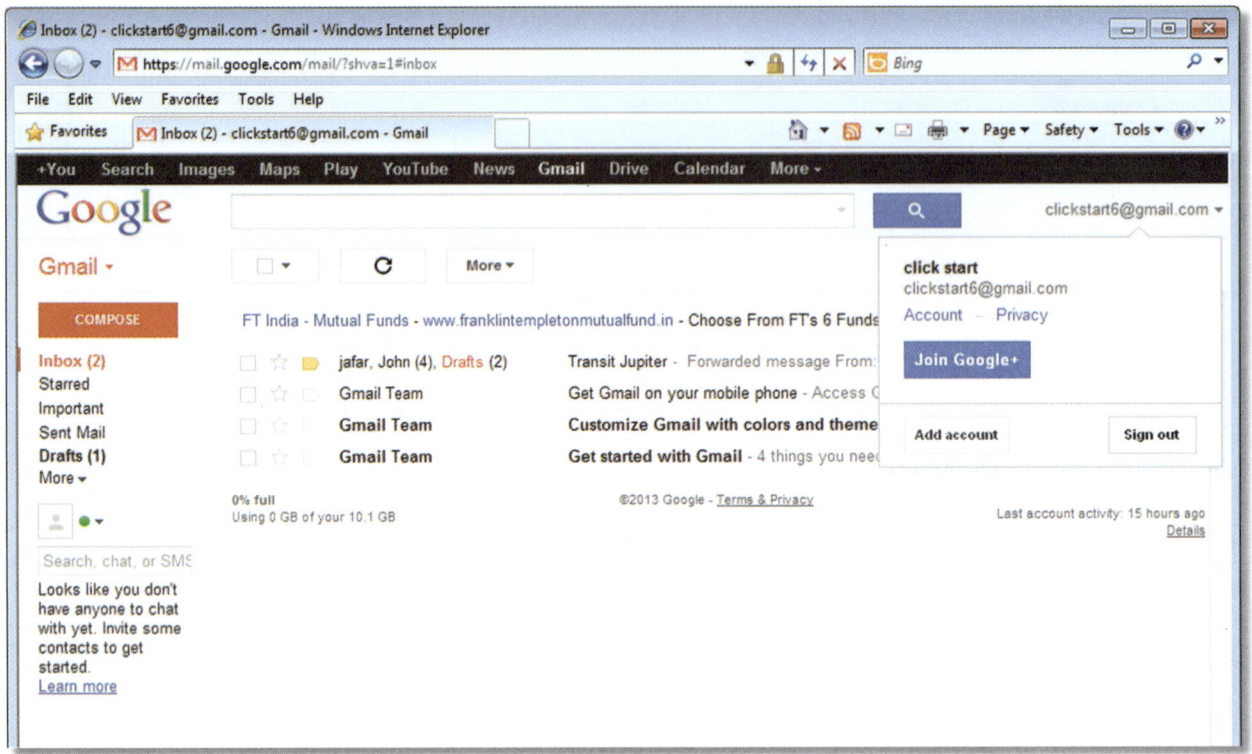

Fig. 12.18 *Signing out*

ACTIVITY

Complete the following activity based on the instructions given.

1. Create your personal email account under the supervision of your parents/teachers.
2. Compose an email and send it to your friend's email address.
3. Sign out of your account.

GLOSSARY

Domain Name System: It is the URL address translated into numeric address.
Email: It means Electronic Mail.
Uniform Resource Locator: It is the address for a website.
Emoticons: These are animated facial expressions.

NOW YOU KNOW

1. Email is a medium of sending electronic mails via Internet.
2. Email address is a combination of a username and a hostname.
3. Email is easy to use, very fast, inexpensive and data can be sent in bulks.
4. Email has some limitations like spam mails, privacy concerns, and misrepresentation of identity.
5. You can easily create an email account by following a simple procedure.
6. Composing a mail means creating an email and then sending it to the recipients.
7. It is important to close your email account properly.

EXERCISE

A Fill in the blanks.

1. ………………………………… is a network of computers.
2. ………………………………… is the full form of URL.
3. The Internet address can be either ……………………… or ……………………… .
4. ……………………………… is a medium of sending mails through the Internet.
5. A file sent in an email is called ……………………………… .

B Match the following.

1. Username   a. Blind carbon copy
2. Email   b. Worldwide system of servers
3. DNS   c. Username@hostname
4. Hostname   d. Name given by the user
5. Bcc   e. Email server name

C Expand the following words.

1. DNS _____   5. de _____
2. ISO _____   6. uk _____
3. Email _____   7. IP _____
4. edu _____   8. ch _____

D **Answer the following questions.**

1. Explain the format of the URL.
2. What is the format of an email address?
3. Give the advantages and limitations of using an email.
4. What do you mean by 'composing an email'?
5. Why is it advisable to sign out of your email account properly?

LAB WORK

Complete the following activity.

1. Open your own email account and create your own green email signature under the supervision of your parents/teachers.
2. Send a 'Hello' message to your friend.
3. Ask your friend to send one message to you. Open it and see the difference in the screen. Can you guess why it looks different?

TEACHER'S NOTES

1. Explore other features of Gmail with the students including themes, signature and other settings.
2. Ask the students to collect information about evolution of email with the help of the Internet.